W9-AOG-160

KILLING
THE
MESSENGER

KILLING THE MESSENGER

100 YEARS OF MEDIA CRITICISM

EDITED BY

TOM GOLDSTEIN

COLUMBIA UNIVERSITY PRESS   New York

COLUMBIA UNIVERSITY PRESS
New York   Guildford, Surrey
Copyright © 1989 Tom Goldstein

LIBRARY OF CONGRESS CATALOGING-IN-PUBLICATION DATA

Goldstein, Tom.
Killing the messenger : 100 years of media criticism / Tom Goldstein.
p.   cm.
Includes index.
ISBN 0-231-06602-3
1. *Press—United States—History—20th century.*
2. *Press—United States—Objectivity—History.*
3. *Press—United States—Influence—History.*
4. *Privacy, Right of—United States—History.*
5. *Reporters and reporting—United States—History.*
I. *Title. PN4867.G63   1988*
071'.3—dc19   *88-22902*
CIP

Printed in the United States of America

Casebound editions of Columbia University Press books are Smyth-sewn and are printed on permanent and durable acid-free paper

FOR

MY

PARENTS

CONTENTS

PREFACE

Enlighten me now, O Muses, tenants of Olympian homes.
For you are goddesses, inside on everything, know everything
But we mortals hear only the news, and know nothing at all.

With these elegant but depressing words from the *Iliad*, Walter
Lippmann and Charles Merz began a withering fifty-page as-
sessment of how the *New York Times* botched its coverage of
the Russian Revolution. Their article, which appeared in *The New Republic*
in 1920, was a stunning indictment of the *Times*, meticulously demonstrat-
ing how the country's greatest paper disserved the public by biased and
incomplete reporting. Like Homer, Lippmann and Merz were press bash-
ers—though they were hardly antiestablishment firebrands. (Merz eventually became editor of the *Times'* editorial page, and Lippmann, the leading
columnist of his generation, often turned down opportunities to work at
the *Times*.)

Their critique is part of a rich—and largely forgotten or ignored—body
of press criticism that has flourished at times during the last one hundred
years, especially in the first two decades of the twentieth century. Compared to other decades of this century, the 1980s have been a fallow period
for cogent press criticism. No one with the sharpness of Lippmann or the
wit and bite of A. J. Liebling, who wrote for *The New Yorker* in the 1940s
and 1950s, has focused on the press. This is unfortunate, in that tough,
knowledgeable criticism is even more essential in a period when the media
have come to so dominate our culture. And it is ironic, in that journalism
in the 1980s has been characterized by a series of upheavals crying out
for fuller scrutiny:

- Janet Cooke, a young *Washington Post* reporter, was forced to
  return the Pulitzer Prize after she admitted that she had fabri-
  cated her story about an eight-year-old heroin addict.
- The National News Council, an ambitious attempt by the press
  to regulate itself, collapsed.
- Newspapers, magazines, and the networks were struck by a
  blizzard of libel lawsuits, and while the media ordinarily prevailed
  in the legal arena, embarrassing and troubling instances of journalistic malpractice were disclosed. *Time* magazine was surely

not the ultimate victor in the lawsuit brought against it by General Ariel Sharon, the Defense Minister of Israel during the invasion of Lebanon. Nor could CBS claim it had ultimately prevailed over General William C. Westmoreland, the commander of American forces in South Vietnam.

■ In his quest for the presidency, Gary Hart forced an examination of what should be reported and what should not be, of what should legitimately be private and what needs to be public. Journalists were faced with the question: Is there anything about a public figure that should not be asked?

But these and dozens of other issues affecting the press were not new to the 1980s. They have been raised before, in different times, in different contexts, and with different emphases. I have chosen the selections in this anthology because they offer different perspectives on many of the issues that are bedeviling the press today—how the concentration of media ownership denies access to the public, how the media inadequately police themselves, how reporters could be better trained, how bias in reportage may be unavoidable, how the press sensationalizes on the one hand and censors itself on the other.

By its nature, journalism is occupied with the present or recent past— Philip Graham, who published the *Washington Post* in the 1950s and early sixties, aptly called journalism the "first rough draft of history." It is hardly surprising then that journalists have a short collective memory. Every generation seems to reinvent—or at least to rethink—the key issues of the craft. This in itself is not harmful. But in reassessing these pressing issues, journalists can benefit from the wisdom of the past. Many recent collections of essays which examine the media consist chiefly of contemporary articles. One recently published volume contains seventy-four selections, only one of which was written before 1980, and that selection was published in 1979. *Killing the Messenger* consists of fifteen essays, speeches, and book excerpts that were published during the past century. I have weighted the collection toward writings of the first part of this century, for it was then that press criticism flourished.

Over the years, an impressive amount of intellectual effort has gone into analyzing the press, and journalists and those interested in public policy and journalism need to be reminded of this. Some earlier critics, such as Upton Sinclair and George Seldes, wrote scathing books that became best-sellers. In the 1940s, Seldes published a newsletter of press criticism called *In fact* that sold more than 100,000 copies per issue—a sales feat that has not been equaled since by any other press review. Early in his

career, Louis Brandeis, with his friend and one-time law partner Samuel
Warren, wrote one of the most influential law review articles ever published. They attempted to define the boundaries of public life and privacy,
a mission as difficult today with the popularity of *People* magazine and personality journalism as it was a century ago. But their analysis is well worth
thinking about, if only to show that the problems we face in our media-
driven society are eerily similar to those of a much calmer period. Joseph
Pulitzer, the great publisher, worried about the education and training of
journalists, and his essay, published early in the 1900s, offers as cogent
an argument as ever written justifying special education for journalists.
Similarly, Theodore Roosevelt exposed the fundamental difficulties of
muckraking, the forerunner of investigative reporting, and Will Irwin's dis-
section of American newspapers is a model of thoroughness and shrewd-
ness.

The other selections in this collection offer similar insights. What I have
tried to do in this volume is collect and then link together some of the last
century's most provocative thinking about the press. I have chosen five
areas to focus on:

- reporting on private matters
- journalists and their biases
- the power and limitations of the press
- making better reporters
- the techniques journalists use to portray reality

Necessarily, this collection is incomplete—no H. L. Mencken or A. J.
Liebling appears, for instance, inasmuch as they have been widely an-
thologized elsewhere. Instead, my aim has been to bring to a wider audience some often neglected pieces of seminal thinking about the press.
Some selections come from books that have been long out of print or from
official reports. Others come from magazines or speeches. Some of the
critics have been insiders, like Lippmann and Merz. More often, as with
Brandeis, Roosevelt, or Spiro Agnew, they have not.

While some of these selections have been widely cited (Agnew's florid
attacks on the press are routinely alluded to), few are easily accessible.
As a journalist, I have been struck by how unfamiliar many of my colleagues are with the best thinking of their trade. As a teacher of journalism, I have been similarly struck by their lack of grounding in the issues
affecting them. I hope the easy availability of this original material will help
to remedy those deficiencies.

Contemporary journalists have not shown any great appetite for self-
analysis, and they pretty much hunker down when others pick on them.

Only sporadically have they trained on themselves the same skepticism they routinely bring to bear on city councilmen, police chiefs, movie directors, football coaches, and heads of state. They need to subject themselves to the same critical analysis they apply to others. And they should welcome, not recoil from, criticism of their own performance. I hope that by acquainting (or reacquainting) them with some of the most spirited criticism of the past century, this collection will encourage them to look at themselves more closely and to accept criticism by others more graciously.

I wish to thank Lonn Johnston, Christiane Badgley, Leslie Perry, and Nancy Ramsey for their invaluable help.

KILLING
THE
MESSENGER

I

REPORTING ON PUBLIC AND PRIVATE MATTERS

I n his on-again, off-again candidacy for the Presidency, Gary Hart, by
dint of his philandering, focused public attention on how far the press
should venture in reporting private lives of public officials. This fas-
cination with what public people do in their spare time is hardly new. In
the first century, Plutarch wrote: "For not only are men in public life held
responsible for their public words and actions, but people busy themselves
with all their concerns: dinner, love affairs, marriage, amusement."

If the problem of privacy is not new, the solution to reporting on private
events is still elusive. A constellation of questions is raised, questions that
cut to the bone of the newsgathering process:

What is important about people—their age, religion, their marital status? What if they were adopted? What if they are gay? Is this the public's
business?

Are candidates for president held to stricter scrutiny than candidates
for other offices? Why shouldn't important figures in the private sector be
held to similar standards?

Is there a statute of limitations for reporting on youthful indiscretions?
Or could such indiscretions be the basis for understanding an adult's character?

Are the dead entitled to privacy? In the 1950s, journalists were reluctant to report that cancer was a cause of death. It was thought to be a
stigma. Similarly, in the 1980s journalists have not clearly thought through
how to deal with AIDS.

These questions have no hard and fast answers. But these, or similar
issues, have been carefully examined in other contexts.

In this section, reprinted in its entirety is the *Harvard Law Review* article by Louis Brandeis and Samuel Warren that became the foundation for
the development of the doctrine of privacy.

I have also included a sampling of editorials by William Allen White, a
wise and witty country editor, who commented on why his newspaper de-

3

cided *not* to print information it knew. His office had a rule, for example, not to publish details of local divorce suits.

Finally, I have included a chapter from *Freedom of the Press,* written by George Seldes, probably the most durable and prolific press critic of the century. He describes how the press abused four of his contemporaries— Charles A. Lindbergh, Sr., who ran for governor of Minnesota and lost; Charles A. Lindbergh, Jr., the aviator; Robert M. La Follette, the Progressive Party politician; and Upton Sinclair, the novelist and critic who wrote *The Brass Check.*

THE RIGHT TO PRIVACY

LOUIS BRANDEIS AND SAMUEL WARREN

Harvard Law Review
December 15, 1890

———
———
———

In 1886, in *The Bostonians* Henry James created the character of
Matthias Pardon, the indelicate journalist who held that everything
and everyone was everyone's business: "All things, with him, referred themselves to print, and print meant simply infinite reporting,
a promptitude of announcement, abusive when necessary, or even
when not about his fellow citizens. He poured contumely on their
private life, on their personal appearance, with the best conscience
in the world." Two years later, in *The Reverberator,* James created
another intrusive and insensitive reporter, this one named George
P. Flack, who went "for the inside view, the choice bits, the chro-
nique intime."

It was within this milieu—in which proper Bostonians regarded
as a disgrace the appearance of their names in print—that Louis
Brandeis, a law professor and practitioner who later would become
a distinguished Supreme Court Justice, and Samuel Warren, a social
and business figure in Boston, set forth the first important exposition
of the right to be left alone. (Years later, as a member of the high
court, Brandeis eloquently restated the "right to be left alone" in a
vigorous dissent in *Olmstead v. U.S.,* in which he protested the government's use of wiretaps.)

Brandeis and Warren had been classmates at Harvard Law School
and had for a time been law partners. Warren, the son of a wealthy
paper manufacturer, was a member of the well-established social elite
in Boston. Legal historians long thought their article had been inspired by Warren's indignant reaction to a gossip column reporting
on his daughter's wedding breakfast. But this would have been utterly impossible: she was only six or seven when the article was
written. Instead, the genesis of the article most likely lay more generally in Warren's deep-seated abhorrence of the invasions of social
privacy.

Their influential article, doubtless more cited in legal writings than actually read, has left a permanent imprint on jurisprudence. Alarmed by what they viewed as the increasing depravity of the daily press, Brandeis and Warren took the view that the individual could be protected against unwarranted intrusions and publicity without fashioning new rules of law.

Footnotes have been omitted, and original spellings have been retained.

THE RIGHT TO PRIVACY

It could be done only on principles of private justice, moral fitness, and public convenience, which, when applied to a new subject, make common law without a precedent; much more when received and approved by usage.

—J. WILLES, in Millar v. Taylor

That the individual shall have full protection in person and in property is a principle as old as the common law; but it has been found necessary from time to time to define anew the exact nature and extent of such protection. Political, social, and economic changes entail the recognition of new rights, and the common law, in its eternal youth, grows to meet the demands of society. Thus, in very early times, the law gave a remedy only for physical interference with life and property, for trespasses *vi et armis*. Then the "right to life" served only to protect the subject from battery in its various forms; liberty meant freedom from actual restraint; and the right to property secured to the individual his lands and his cattle. Later, there came a recognition of man's spiritual nature, of his feelings and his intellect. Gradually the scope of these legal rights broadened; and now the right to life has come to mean the right to enjoy life,— the right to be let alone; the right to liberty secures the exercise of extensive civil privileges; and the term "property" has grown to comprise every form of possession— intangible, as well as tangible.

Thus, with the recognition of the legal value of sensations, the protection against actual bodily injury was extended to prohibit mere attempts to do such injury; that is, the putting another in fear of such injury. From the action of battery grew that of assault. Much later there came a qualified protection of the individual against offensive noises and odors, against dust and smoke, and excessive vibration. The law of nuisance was developed. So regard for human emotions soon extended the scope of personal immunity beyond the body of the individual. His reputation, the standing among his fellow-men, was considered, and the law of slander and libel arose. Man's family relations became a part of the legal conception of his life, and the alienation of a wife's affections was held remediable. Occasionally the law halted,—as in its refusal to recognize the intrusion by seduction upon the honor of the family. But even here the demands of society were met.

A mean fiction, the action *per quod servitium amisit,* was resorted to, and by allowing damages for injury to the parents' feelings, an adequate remedy was ordinarily afforded. Similar to the expansion of the right to life was the growth of the legal conception of property. From corporeal property arose the incorporeal rights issuing out of it; and then there opened the wide realm of intangible property, in the products and processes of the mind, as works of literature and art, goodwill, trade secrets, and trademarks.

This development of the law was inevitable. The intense intellectual and emotional life, and the heightening of sensations which came with the advance of civilization, made it clear to men that only a part of the pain, pleasure, and profit of life lay in physical things. Thoughts, emotions, and sensations demanded legal recognition, and the beautiful capacity for growth which characterizes the common law enabled the judges to afford the requisite protection, without the interposition of the legislature.

Recent inventions and business methods call attention to the next step which must be taken for the protection of the person, and for securing to the individual what Judge Cooley calls the right "to be let alone." Instantaneous photographs and newspaper enterprise have invaded the sacred precincts of private and domestic life; and numerous mechanical devices threaten to make good the prediction that "what is whispered in the closet shall be proclaimed from the housetops." For years there has been a feeling that the law must afford some remedy for the unauthorized circulation of portraits of private persons; and the evil of the invasion of privacy by the newspapers, long keenly felt, has been but recently discussed by an able writer. The alleged facts of a somewhat notorious case brought before an inferior tribunal in New York a few months ago, directly involved the consideration of the right of circulating portraits; and the question whether our law will recognize and protect the right to privacy in this and in other respects must soon come before our courts for consideration.

Of the desirability—indeed of the necessity—of some such protection, there can, it is believed, be no doubt. The press is overstepping in every direction the obvious bounds of propriety and of decency. Gossip is no longer the resource of the idle and of the vicious, but has become a trade, which is pursued with industry as well as effrontery. To satisfy a prurient taste the details of sexual relations are spread broadcast in the columns of the daily papers. To occupy the indolent, column upon column is filled with idle gossip, which can only be procured by intrusion upon the domestic circle. The intensity and complexity of life, attendant upon advancing civilization, have rendered necessary some retreat from the world, and man, under the refining influence of culture, has become more sensitive to publicity, so that solitude and privacy have become more essential to the individual; but modern enterprise and invention have, through invasions upon his privacy, subjected him to mental pain and distress, far greater than could be inflicted by mere bodily injury. Nor is the harm wrought by such invasions confined to the suffering of those who may be made the subjects of journalistic or other enterprise. In this, as in other branches of commerce, the supply creates the demand. Each crop of unseemly gossip, thus harvested, becomes the seed of more, and, in direct proportion to its circulation, results in a lowering of social standards and of morality. Even gossip apparently harmless, when widely and persistently circulated, is potent for evil. It both belittles and perverts. It belittles by inverting the relative importance of things, thus dwarfing the thoughts and aspirations of a people. When personal gossip attains the dignity of print, and crowds the space available for matters of real interest to the community, what wonder that the ignorant and thoughtless mistake its relative importance. Easy of comprehension, appealing to that weak side of human nature which is never wholly cast down by the misfortunes and frailties of our neighbors, no one can be surprised that it usurps the place of interest in brains capable of other things. Triviality destroys at once robustness of thought and delicacy of feeling. No enthusiasm can flourish, no generous impulse can survive under its blighting influence.

It is our purpose to consider whether the existing law affords a principle which can properly be invoked to protect the privacy of the individual; and, if it does, what the nature and extent of such protection is.

Owing to the nature of the instruments by which privacy is invaded, the injury inflicted bears a superficial resemblance to the wrongs dealt with by the law of slander and of libel, while a legal remedy for such injury seems to involve the treatment of mere wounded feelings, as a substantive cause of action. The principle on which the law of defamation rests, covers, however, a radically different class of effects from those for which attention is now asked. It deals only with damage to reputation, with the injury done to the individual in his external relations to the community, by lowering him in the estimation of his fellows. The matter published of him, however widely circulated, and however unsuited to publicity, must, in order to be actionable, have a direct tendency to injure him in his intercourse with others, and even if in writing or in print, must subject him to the hatred, ridicule, or contempt of his fellowmen, — the effect of the publication upon his estimate of himself and upon his own feelings not forming an essential element in the cause of action. In short, the wrongs and correlative rights recognized by the law of slander and libel are in their nature material rather than spiritual. That branch of the law simply extends the protection surrounding physical property to certain of the conditions necessary or helpful to worldly prosperity. On the other hand, our law recognizes no principle upon which compensation can be granted for mere injury to the feelings. However painful the mental effects upon another of an act, though purely wanton or even malicious, yet if the act itself is otherwise lawful, the suffering inflicted is *damnum absque injuria.* Injury of feelings may indeed be taken account of in ascertaining the amount of damages when attending what is recognized as a legal injury; but our system, unlike the Roman law, does not afford a remedy even for mental suffering which results from mere contumely and insult, from an intentional and unwarranted violation of the "honor" of another.

It is not however necessary, in order to sustain the view that the common law recognizes and upholds a principle applicable to cases of invasion of privacy, to invoke the analogy, which is but superficial, to injuries sustained, either by an attack upon reputation or by what the civilians called a violation of honor; for the legal doctrines relating to infractions of what is ordinarily termed the common-law right to intellectual and artistic property are, it is believed, but instances and applications of a general right to privacy, which properly understood afford a remedy for the evils under consideration.

The common law secures to each individual the right of determining, ordinarily, to what extent his thoughts, sentiments, and emotions shall be communicated to others. Under our system of government, he can never be compelled to express them (except when upon the witness-stand); and even if he has chosen to give them expression, he generally retains the power to fix the limits of the publicity which shall be given them. The existence of this right does not depend upon the particular method of expression adopted. It is immaterial whether it be by word or by signs, in painting, by sculpture, or in music. Neither does the existence of the right depend upon the nature or value of the thought or emotion, nor upon the excellence of the means of expression. The same protection is accorded to a casual letter or an entry in a diary and to the most valuable poem or essay, to a botch or daub and to a masterpiece. In every such case the individual is entitled to decide whether that which is his shall be given to the public. No other has the right to publish his productions in any form, without his consent. This right is wholly independent of the material on which, or the means by which, the thought, sentiment, or emotion is expressed. It may exist independently of any corporeal being, as in words spoken, a song sung, a drama acted. Or if expressed on any material, as a poem in writing, the author may have parted with the paper, without forfeiting any proprietary right in the composition itself. The right is lost

only when the author himself communicates his production to the public, —
in other words, publishes it. It is entirely independent of the copyright
laws, and their extension into the domain of art. The aim of those statutes
is to secure to the author, composer, or artist the entire profits arising
from publication; but the common-law protection enables him to control
absolutely the act of publication, and in the exercise of his own discretion,
to decide whether there shall be any publication at all. The statutory right
is of no value, *unless* there is a publication; the common-law right is lost
as soon as there is a publication.

What is the nature, the basis, of this right to prevent the publication of
manuscripts or works of art? It is stated to be the enforcement of a right
of property; and no difficulty arises in accepting this view, so long as we
have only to deal with the reproduction of literary and artistic compositions.
They certainly possess many of the attributes of ordinary property: they
are transferable; they have a value; and publication or reproduction is a
use by which that value is realized. But where the value of the production
is found not in the right to take the profits arising from publication, but in
the peace of mind or the relief afforded by the ability to prevent any publication at all, it is difficult to regard the right as one of property, in the
common acceptation of that term. A man records in a letter to his son, or
in his diary, that he did not dine with his wife on a certain day. No one
into whose hands those papers fall could publish them to the world, even
if possession of the documents had been obtained rightfully; and the prohibition would not be confined to the publication of a copy of the letter
itself, or of the diary entry; the restraint extends also to a publication of
the contents. What is the thing which is protected? Surely, not the intellectual act of recording the fact that the husband did not dine with his wife,
but that fact itself. It is not the intellectual product, but the domestic occurrence. Man writes a dozen letters to different people. No person would
be permitted to publish a list of the letters written. If the letters or the
contents of the diary were protected as literary compositions, the scope
of the protection afforded should be the same secured to a published writing under the copyright law. But the copyright law would not prevent an
enumeration of the letters, or the publication of some of the facts contained
therein. The copyright of a series of paintings or etchings would prevent
a reproduction of the paintings as pictures; but it would not prevent a publication of a list or even a description of them. Yet in the famous case of
Prince Albert v. Strange, the court held that the common-law rule prohib-
ited not merely the reproduction of the etchings which the plaintiff and
Queen Victoria had made for their own pleasure, but also "the publishing
(at least by printing or writing), though not by copy or resemblance, a

description of them, whether more or less limited or summary, whether in the form of a catalogue or otherwise." Likewise, an unpublished collection of news possessing no element of a literary nature is protected from piracy.

That this protection cannot rest upon the right to literary or artistic property in any exact sense, appears the more clearly when the subject-matter for which protection is invoked is not even in the form of intellectual property, but has the attributes of ordinary tangible property. Suppose a man has a collection of gems or curiosities which he keeps private: it would hardly be contended that any person could publish a catalogue of them, and yet the articles enumerated are certainly not intellectual property in the legal sense, any more than a collection of stoves or of chairs.

The belief that the idea of property in its narrow sense was the basis of the protection of unpublished manuscripts led an able court to refuse, in several cases, injunctions against the publication of private letters, on the ground that "letters not possessing the attributes of literary compositions are not property entitled to protection;" and that it was "evident the plaintiff could not have considered the letters as of any value whatever as literary productions, for a letter cannot be considered of value to the author which he never would consent to have published." But these decisions have not been followed, and it may now be considered settled that the protection afforded by the common law to the author of any writing is entirely independent of its pecuniary value, its intrinsic merits, or of any intention to publish the same, and, of course, also, wholly independent of the material, if any, upon which, or the mode in which, the thought or sentiment was expressed.

Although the courts have asserted that they rested their decisions on the narrow grounds of protection to property, yet there are recognitions of a more liberal doctrine. Thus in the case of Prince Albert v. Strange, already referred to, the opinions both of the Vice-Chancellor and of the Lord Chancellor, on appeal, show a more or less clearly defined perception of a principle broader than those which were mainly discussed, and on which they both placed their chief reliance. Vice-Chancellor Knight Bruce referred to publishing of a man that he had "written to particular persons or on particular subjects" as an instance of possibly injurious disclosures as to private matters, that the courts would in a proper case prevent; yet it is difficult to perceive how, in such a case, any right of property, in the narrow sense, would be drawn in question, or why, if such a publication would be restrained when it threatened to expose the victim not merely to sarcasm, but to ruin, it should not equally be enjoined, if it threatened to embitter his life. To deprive a man of the potential profits to be realized by publishing a catalogue of his gems cannot *per se* be a wrong to him. The possibility of future profits is not a right of property which the law ordinarily recognizes; it must, therefore, be an infraction of other rights which constitutes the wrongful act, and that infraction is equally wrongful, whether its results are to forestall the profits that the individual himself might secure by giving the matter a publicity obnoxious to him, or to gain an advantage at the expense of his mental pain and suffering. If the fiction of property in a narrow sense must be preserved, it is still true that the end accomplished by the gossip-monger is attained by the use of that which is another's, the facts relating to his private life, which he has seen fit to keep private. Lord Cottenham stated that a man "is entitled to be protected in the exclusive use and enjoyment of that which is exclusively his," and cited with approval the opinion of Lord Eldon, as reported in a manuscript note of the case of Wyatt v. Wilson, in 1820, respecting an engraving of George the Third during his illness, to the effect that "if one of the late king's physicians had kept a diary of what he heard and saw, the court would not, in the king's lifetime, have permitted him to print and publish it;" and Lord Cottenham declared, in respect to the acts of the defendants in the case before him, that "privacy is the right invaded." But if privacy is once recognized as a right entitled to legal protection, the interposition of the courts cannot depend on the particular nature of the injuries resulting.

These considerations lead to the conclusion that the protection afforded to thoughts, sentiments, and emotions, expressed through the medium of writing or of the arts, so far as it consists in preventing publication, is merely an instance of the enforcement of the more general right of the individual to be let alone. It is like the right not to be assaulted or beaten, the right not to be imprisoned, the right not to be maliciously prosecuted, the right not to be defamed. In each of these rights, as indeed in all other rights recognized by the law, there inheres the quality of being owned or possessed—and (as that is the distinguishing attribute of property) there may be some propriety in speaking of those rights of property. But, obviously, they bear little resemblance to what is ordinarily comprehended under that term. The principle which protects personal writings and all other personal productions, not against theft and physical appropriation, but against publication in any form, is in reality not the principle of private property, but that of inviolate personality.

If we are correct in this conclusion, the existing law affords a principle which may be invoked to protect the privacy of the individual from invasion either by the too enterprising press, the photographer, or the possessor of any other modern device for recording or reproducing scenes or sounds.

For the protection afforded is not confined by the authorities to those cases where any particular medium or form of expression has been adopted, nor to products of the intellect. The same protection is afforded to emotions and sensations expressed in a musical composition or other work of art as to a literary composition; and words spoken, a pantomime acted, a sonata performed, is no less entitled to protection than if each had been reduced to writing. The circumstance that a thought or emotion has been recorded in a permanent form renders its identification easier, and hence may be important from the point of view of evidence, but it has no significance as a matter of substantive right. If, then, the decisions indicate a general right to privacy for thoughts, emotions, and sensations, these should receive the same protection, whether expressed in writing, or in conduct, in conversation, in attitudes, or in facial expression.

It may be urged that a distinction should be taken between the deliberate expression of thoughts and emotions in literary or artistic compositions and the casual and often involuntary expression given to them in the ordinary conduct of life. In other words, it may be contended that the protection afforded is granted to the conscious products of labor, perhaps as an encouragement to effort. This contention, however plausible, has, in fact, little to recommend it. If the amount of labor involved be adopted as the test, we might well find that the effort to conduct one's self properly in business and in domestic relations had been far greater than that involved in painting a picture or writing a book; one would find that it was far easier to express lofty sentiments in a diary than in the conduct of a noble life. If the test of deliberateness of the act be adopted, much casual correspondence which is now accorded full protection would be excluded from the beneficent operation of existing rules. After the decisions denying the distinction attempted to be made between those literary productions which it was intended to publish and those which it was not, all considerations of the amount of labor involved, the degree of deliberation, the value of the product, and the intention of publishing must be abandoned, and no basis is discerned upon which the right to restrain publication and reproduction of such so-called literary and artistic works can be rested, except the right to privacy, as a part of the more general right to the immunity of the person,—the right to one's personality.

It should be stated that, in some instances where protection has been afforded against wrongful publication, the jurisdiction has been asserted, not on the ground of property, or at least not wholly on that ground, but upon the ground of an alleged breach of an implied contract or of a trust or confidence.

Thus, in Abernethy v. Hutchinson (1825), where the plaintiff, a distin-

guished surgeon, sought to restrain the publication in the "Lancet" of unpublished lectures which he had delivered at St. Bartholomew's Hospital
in London, Lord Eldon doubted whether there could be property in lectures which had not been reduced to writing, but granted the injunction on
the ground of breach of confidence, holding "that when persons were admitted as pupils or otherwise, to hear these lectures, although they were
orally delivered, and although the parties might go to the extent, if they
were able to do so, of putting down the whole by means of shorthand, yet
they could do that only for the purposes of their own information, and could
not publish, for profit, that which they had not obtained the right of selling."

In Prince Albert v. Strange (1849), Lord Cottenham, on appeal, while
recognizing a right of property in the etchings which of itself would justify
the issuance of the injunction, stated, after discussing the evidence, that
he was bound to assume that the possession of the etchings by the defendant had "its foundation in a breach of trust, confidence, or contract,"
and that upon such ground also the plaintiff's title to the injunction was fully
sustained.

In Tuck v. Priester (1887), the plaintiffs were owners of a picture, and
employed the defendant to make a certain number of copies. He did so,
and made also a number of other copies for himself, and offered them for
sale in England at a lower price. Subsequently, the plaintiffs registered
their copyright in the picture, and then brought suit for an injunction and
damages. The Lords Justices differed as to the application of the copyright
acts to the case, but held unanimously that independently of those acts,
the plaintiffs were entitled to an injunction and damages for breach of contract.

In Pollard v. Photographic Co. (1888), a photographer who had taken
a lady's photograph under the ordinary circumstances was restrained from
exhibiting it, and also from selling copies of it, on the ground that it was
a breach of an implied term in the contract, and also that it was a breach
of confidence. Mr. Justice North interjected in the argument of the plaintiff's counsel the inquiry: "Do you dispute that if the negative likeness were
taken on the sly, the person who took it might exhibit copies?" and counsel
for the plaintiff answered: "In that case there would be no trust or consideration to support a contract." Later, the defendant's counsel argued
that "a person has no property in his own features; short of doing what is
libellous or otherwise illegal, there is no restriction on the photographer's
using his negative." But the court, while expressly finding a breach of contract and of trust sufficient to justify its interposition, still seems to have
felt the necessity of resting the decision also upon a right of property, in

order to bring it within the line of those cases which were relied upon as precedents.

This process of implying a term in a contract, or of implying a trust (particularly where the contract is written, and where there is no established usage of custom), is nothing more nor less than a judicial declaration that public morality, private justice, and general convenience demand the recognition of such a rule, and that the publication under similar circumstances would be considered an intolerable abuse. So long as these circumstances happen to present a contract upon which such a term can be engrafted by the judicial mind, or to supply relations upon which a trust or confidence can be erected, there may be no objection to working out the desired protection through the doctrines of contract or of trust. But the court can hardly stop there. The narrower doctrine may have satisfied the demands of society at a time when the abuse to be guarded against could rarely have arisen without violating a contract or a special confidence; but now that modern devices afford abundant opportunities for the perpetration of such wrongs without any participation by the injured party, the protection granted by the law must be placed upon a broader foundation. While, for instance, the state of the photographic art was such that one's picture could seldom be taken without his consciously "sitting" for the purpose, the law of contract or of trust might afford the prudent man sufficient safeguards against the improper circulation of his portrait; but since the latest advances in photographic art have rendered it possible to take pictures surreptitiously, the doctrines of contract and of trust are inadequate to support the required protection, and the law of tort must be resorted to. The right of property in its widest sense, including all possession, including all rights and privileges, and hence embracing the right to an inviolate personality, affords alone that broad basis upon which the protection which the individual demands can be rested.

Thus, the courts, in searching for some principle upon which the publication of private letters could be enjoined, naturally came upon the ideas of a breach of confidence, and of an implied contract; but it required little consideration to discern that this doctrine could not afford all the protection required, since it would not support the court in granting a remedy against a stranger; and so the theory of property in the contents of letters was adopted. Indeed, it is difficult to conceive on what theory of the law the casual recipient of a letter, who proceeds to publish it, is guilty of a breach of contract, express or implied, or of any breach of trust, in the ordinary acceptation of that term. Suppose a letter has been addressed to him without his solicitation. He opens it, and reads. Surely, he has not made any contract; he has not accepted any trust. He cannot, by opening and reading the letter, have come under any obligation save what the law declares; and, however expressed, that obligation is simply to observe the legal right of the sender, whatever it may be, and whether it be called his right of property in the contents of the letter, or his right to privacy.

A similar groping for the principle upon which a wrongful publication can be enjoined is found in the law of trade secrets. There, injunctions have generally been granted on the theory of a breach of contract, or of an abuse of confidence. It would, of course, rarely happen that any one would be in the possession of a secret unless confidence had been reposed in him. But can it be supposed that the court would hesitate to grant relief against one who had obtained his knowledge by an ordinary trespass,—for instance, by wrongfully looking into a book in which the secret was recorded, or by eavesdropping? Indeed, in Yovtt v. Winyard, where an injunction was granted against making any use of or communicating certain recipes for veterinary medicine, it appeared that the defendant, while in the plaintiff's employ, had surreptitiously got access to his book of recipes, and copied them. Lord Eldon "granted the injunction, upon the ground of there having been a breach of trust and confidence;" but it would seem to be difficult to draw any sound legal distinction between such a case and one where a mere stranger wrongfully obtained access to the book.

We must therefore conclude that the rights, so protected, whatever their exact nature, are not rights arising from contract or from special trust, but are rights as against the world; and, as above stated, the principle which has been applied to protect these rights is in reality not the principle of private property, unless that word be used in an extended and unusual sense. The principle which protects personal writings and any other productions of the intellect or of the emotions, is the right to privacy, and the law has no new principle to formulate when it extends this protection to the personal appearance, saying, acts, and to personal relations, domestic or otherwise.

If the invasion of privacy constitutes a legal *injuria,* the elements for demanding redress exist, since already the value of mental suffering, caused by an act wrongful in itself, is recognized as a basis for compensation.

The right of one who has remained a private individual, to prevent his public portraiture, presents the simplest case for such extension; the right to protect one's self from pen portraiture, from a discussion by the press of one's private affairs, would be a more important and far-reaching one. If casual and unimportant statements in a letter, if handiwork, however inartistic and valueless, if possessions of all sorts are protected not only against reproduction, but against description and enumeration, how much more should the acts and sayings of a man in his social and domestic relations be guarded from ruthless publicity. If you may not reproduce a woman's face photographically without her consent, how much less should be tolerated the reproduction of her face, her form, and her actions, by graphic descriptions colored to suit a gross and depraved imagination.

The right to privacy, limited as such right must necessarily be, has found expression in the law of France.

It remains to consider what are the limitations of this right to privacy, and what remedies may be granted for the enforcement of the right. To determine in advance of experience the exact line at which the dignity and convenience of the individual must yield to the demands of the public welfare or of private justice would be a difficult task; but the more general rules are furnished by the legal analogies already developed in the law of slander and libel, and in the law of literary and artistic property.

1. The right to privacy does not prohibit any publication of matter which is of public or general interest.

In determining the scope of this rule, aid would be afforded by the analogy, in the law of libel and slander, of cases which deal with the qualified privilege of comment and criticism on matters of public and general interest. There are of course difficulties in applying such a rule, but they are inherent in the subject matter, and are certainly no greater than those which exist in many other branches of the law, — for instance, in that large class of cases in which the reasonableness or unreasonableness of an act is made the test of liabilty. The design of the law must be to protect those persons with whose affairs the community has no legitimate concern, from being dragged into an undesirable and undesired publicity and to protect all persons, whatsoever; their position or station, from having matters which they may properly prefer to keep private, made public against their will. It is the unwarranted invasion of individual privacy which is reprehended, and to be, so far as possible, prevented. The distinction, however, noted in the above statement is obvious and fundamental. There are persons who may reasonably claim as a right, protection from the notoriety entailed by being made the victims of journalistic enterprisè. There are others who, in varying degrees, have renounced the right to live their lives screened from public observation. Matters which men of the first class may justly contend, concern themselves alone, may in those of the second be the subject of legitimate interest to their fellow-citizens. Peculiarities of manner and person, which in the ordinary individual should be free from comment, may acquire a public importance, if found in a candidate for political office. Some further discrimination is necessary, therefore, than to class facts or deeds as public or private according to a standard to be applied to the fact or deed *per se*. To publish of a modest and retiring individual that he suffers from an impediment in his speech or that he cannot spell correctly, is an unwarranted, if not an unexampled, infringement of his rights, while to state and comment on the same characteristics found in a would-be congressman could not be regarded as beyond the pale of propriety.

The general object in view is to protect the privacy of private life, and to whatever degree and in whatever connection a man's life has ceased to be private, before the publication under consideration has been made, to that extent the protection is to be withdrawn. Since, then, the propriety of publishing the very same facts may depend wholly upon the person concerning whom they are published, no fixed formula can be used to prohibit obnoxious publications. Any rule of liability adopted must have in it an elasticity which shall take account of the varying circumstances of each case, — a necessity which unfortunately renders such a doctrine not only more difficult of application, but also to a certain extent uncertain in its operation and easily rendered abortive. Besides, it is only the more flagrant breaches of decency and propriety that could in practice be reached, and it is not perhaps desirable even to attempt to repress everything which the nicest taste and keenest sense of the respect due to private life would condemn.

In general, then, the matters of which the publication should be repressed may be described as those which concern the private life, habits, acts, and relations of an individual, and have no legitimate connection with his fitness for a public office which he seeks or for which he is suggested, or for any public or quasi public capacity. The foregoing is not designed as a wholly accurate or exhaustive definition, since that which must ultimately in a vast number of cases become a question of individual judgment and opinion is incapable of such definition; but it is an attempt to indicate broadly the class of matters referred to. Some things all men alike are entitled to keep from popular curiosity, whether in public life or not, while others are only private because the persons concerned have not assumed a position which makes their doings legitimate matters of public investigation.

2. The right to privacy does not prohibit the communication of any matter, though in its nature private, when the publication is made under circumstances which would render it a privileged communication according to the law of slander and libel.

Under this rule, the right to privacy is not invaded by any publication made in a court of justice, in legislative bodies, or the committees of those bodies; in municipal assemblies, or the committees of such assemblies, or practically by any communication made in any other public body, municipal or parochial, or in any body quasi public, like the large voluntary associations formed for almost every purpose of benevolence, business, or other general interest; and (at least in many jurisdictions) reports of any such proceedings would in some measure be accorded a like privilege. Nor would the rule prohibit any publication made by one in the discharge of some public or private duty, whether legal or moral, or in conduct of one's own affairs, in matters where his own interest is concerned.

3. The law would probably not grant any redress for the invasion of privacy by oral publication in the absence of special damage.

The same reasons exist for distinguishing between oral and written publications of private matters, as is afforded in the law of defamation by the restricted liability for slander as compared with the liability for libel. The injury resulting from such oral communications would ordinarily be so trifling that the law might well, in the interest of free speech, disregard it altogether.

4. The right to privacy ceases upon the publication of the facts by the individual, or with his consent.

This is but another application of the rule which has become familiar in the law of literary and artistic property. The cases there decided establish also what should be deemed a publication, — the important principle in this connection being that a private communication of circulation for a restricted purpose is not a publication within the meaning of the law.

5. The truth of the matter published does not afford a defence. Obviously this branch of the law should have no concern with the truth or falsehood of the matters published. It is not for injury to the individual's character that redress or prevention is sought, but for injury to the right of privacy. For the former, the law of slander and libel provides perhaps a sufficient safeguard. The latter implies the right not merely to prevent inaccurate portrayal of private life, but to prevent its being depicted at all.

6. The absence of "malice" in the publisher does not afford a defence.

Personal ill-will is not an ingredient of the offence, any more than in an ordinary case of trespass to person or to property. Such malice is never necessary to be shown in an action for libel or slander at common law, except in rebuttal of some defence, e.g., that the occasion rendered the communication privileged, or, under the statutes in this State and elsewhere, that the statement complained of was true. The invasion of the privacy that is to be protected is equally complete and equally injurious, whether the motives by which the speaker or writer was actuated are, taken by themselves, culpable or not; just as the damage to character, and to some extent the tendency to provoke a breach of the peace, is equally the result of defamation without regard to the motives leading to its publication. Viewed as a wrong to the individual, this rule is the same pervading the whole law of torts, by which one is held responsible for his intentional acts, even though they are committed with no sinister intent; and viewed as a wrong to society, it is the same principle adopted in a large category of statutory offences.

The remedies for an invasion of the right of privacy are also suggested by those administered in the law of defamation, and in the law of literary and artistic property, namely: —

1. An action of tort for damages in all cases. Even in the absence of special damages, substantial compensation could be allowed for injury to feelings as in the action of slander and libel.

2. An injunction, in perhaps a very limited class of cases.

It would doubtless be desirable that the privacy of the individual should receive the added protection of the criminal law, but for this, legislation would be required. Perhaps it would be deemed proper to bring the criminal liability for such publication within narrower limits; but that the community has an interest in preventing such invasions of privacy, sufficiently strong to justify the introduction of such a remedy, cannot be doubted. Still, the protection of society must come mainly through a recognition of the rights of the individual. Each man is responsible for his own acts and omissions only. If he condones what he reprobates, with a weapon at hand equal to his defence, he is responsible for the results. If he resists, public opinion will rally to his support. Has he then such a weapon? It is believed that the common law provides him with one, forged in the slow fire of the centuries, and to-day fitly tempered to his hand. The common law has always recognized a man's house as his castle, impregnable, often, even to its own officers engaged in the execution of its commands. Shall the courts thus close the front entrance to constituted authority, and open wide the back door to idle or prurient curiosity?

EDITORIALS

WILLIAM ALLEN WHITE

The Emporia Gazette, 1901–1921

———

———

———

One of the best-known journalists of his generation, William Allen White epitomized small-town America. He was born in Emporia, Kansas, in 1868, and he died there in 1944. Shortly after he purchased the *Emporia Gazette* in 1895, when he was only twenty-seven years old, he wrote in his first editorial:

> The new editor of the *Gazette* desires to make a clean, honest local paper. He is a Republican and will support Republican nominees first, last and all the time. . . . In this paper, while the politics will be straight, it will not be obtrusive. It will be confined to the editorial page—where gentle reader may venture at his peril. The main thing is to have this paper represent the average thought of the best people of Emporia.

A friend of muckrakers, White moved easily in the world of press and politics beyond Kansas. But little of his exposure to the faster pace and toughness of the muckrakers rubbed off on his local coverage. He was a booster of his home town and a censor of bad news and came to be known as the Sage of Emporia. His papers became identified with upstanding personal journalism and with centrist values.

Over the years, in speeches, articles for national magazines, but mostly on his editorial page, he expressed his views about the appropriate role of journalism and those who practiced it. In his autobiography, published in 1946—more than half a century after he became a country editor—he reminisced: "People choose their paper not because of its politics but because of its integrity, its enterprise, and its intelligence. They want an honest paper, well written, where they can find all the news to which they are entitled."

Entitled! White let the readers know what he thought they should know. That did not mean he was a mere conveyor belt, letting them in on *everything* he knew. By his example, he demonstrated that journalists could show restraint. In these editorials, he sets forth his philosophy of what is printable and what is not.

EDITORIALS FROM THE
EMPORIA GAZETTE

HONESTY PAYS

JULY 1, 1901.

The valedictory of Editor Johnson of the *Peabody News* contains this statement:

> After a man has spent a score of years in a country printing office, trying to please the people, humoring their peccadillos, praising their good qualities and charitably concealing their bad ones, what has he left? Does he hold a life tenure on their good will? Do they appreciate him for the good he has done? No.

Well why should they appreciate such a man? Doubtless Editor Johnson is a better man than he paints himself, but too many editors are like the one he describes. Why should a man who "has spent a score of years trying to please the people, humoring their peccadillos, praising their good qualities, charitably concealing their bad ones," expect anything? He has been a panderer. He has done the people no good. He has not helped the world. He has not added one bit to the world's store of wisdom, to the world's store of moral courage, to the world's store of capacity for work. If a man has been brave, if he has lambasted the people for their folly, if he has told them their bad points as well as their good ones, and thereby made them mend their ways, if he has put an occasional thinking cap on the people, if he has worked for their enlightenment in spite of their ignorant ests—then he should expect reward and be disappointed when he fails of it. But an editor who believes in the infallibility of the people and knuckles to them never succeeds, and he should not. A glance over the newspapers in Kansas and elsewhere in the world will prove that the editor who says what he thinks and scorns consequences is the editor who makes money. The people never respect a man who grovels to them, and they never put their money and their contempt into the same hand.

If an editor would make money he must go on the Vanderbiltian theory. It's a fine thing to love the people—but it's a poor policy to humor them. In other words, honesty is the best policy in the newspaper business as it is in the grocery and dry goods or real estate business, and an editor is not honest and does not run an honest paper, who "tries to please the people, to humor their peccadillos, to praise their good qualities and charitably conceal their bad ones." Such an editor may not know he is dishonest—but he is, and his business doesn't prosper—which is a proof of his moral poverty.

THE SICKENING DETAILS

JUNE 2, 1911.

> The Illinois legislature has passed a bill prohibiting newspapers from publishing gruesome details. The fault is not in the newspapers, it is in the people. If the newspapers of Illinois should be prohibited from publishing such things outside newspapers would swamp the state. Newspapers are blamed for giving the people what they want. There is not a gruesome case in any town but the newspapers are besieged for information and unless they give it the public is rebellious.—*Lawrence Journal.*

All of which is not true. The *Gazette* has printed some sickening details—as, for instance, the Thaw case—and was thoroughly ashamed of itself for so doing, and lost much more than it made. Perhaps it learned a lesson. Perhaps it did not. A famous local scandal once came upon the local court. The *Gazette* spent $25 printing a verbatim report of the evidence and didn't sell $10 worth of papers, but made both sides mad and lost money. There is an office rule not to print details of local divorce suits, statutory assaults, and other local stories in court and out involving the sex question. Excepting the big local lawsuit above mentioned, the rule has never been violated. Recently there was the nastiest kind of divorce suit in the district court. It got three lines in the *Gazette*. No one asked why we didn't insert more of it. The writer of this has been in the newspaper business steadily for twenty-six years. He has got one thing in his head: The news is what the newspapers play up. Moreover, the newspapers should be regulated. Some day the people will appoint or elect or hire town managers and their duty, among other things, will be to go after the newspapers.

Details of murders, hangings, suicides, sex crimes, highway robberies, burglaries, and crimes of violence generally should be suppressed under the police power of the state. They are bad for public morals, and a newspaper that prints such things inveterately should be declared a nuisance.

The *Gazette* is a sinner with the rest of the craft. But it makes no claim that it is forced into it. Whenever it has fallen it has been through carelessness or natural meanness.

Newspapers could quit if they would. The community should make them quit, and some day the good sense of the people will organize and go after the newspapers just as it has gone after offenders in other walks of life. The day is coming when sickening details will be as disgusting to good people as the crimes of high finance. (*But until editors and reporters are licensed as lawyers and doctors are, this public malpractice will continue.— W.A.W.)

SCANDAL

JUNE 22, 1913.

A few months ago the town buzzed with a sad story. It did not appear in the *Gazette*. It will not appear in the *Gazette*. The sad stories of life, unless they are forced into publicity by court record, or by some crisis of a public event, are not, as a rule, good reading. Lives of men and women are not always pleasant. The good Lord, looking down on us, sees much that must make him smile and sigh at the perversity of his handiwork. For the ways of a serpent on a rock and an eagle in the air are not the only queer things in this queer world. But queer things are not important. The important things of life are its kindnesses, its nobility, its self-denials, its great renunciations.

BUMS AND SCANDALS

MAY 23, 1921.

To the Editor of the Gazette.

Sir: Why have you let two big divorce suits go by without a line in the Gazette? Are you shielding them because they are big bugs? Does the fact that a man has money keep his name out of the paper when he runs around with other women and when a poor devil gets drunk you slap his name in the paper— A Reader.

That is a fair question; the answer is this: For 26 years the *Gazette* has made an invariable rule to keep divorce scandals out of the local news. Also we have had an invariable rule to print the actual news of divorces;

the names of the parties, the causes briefly stated, and the disposition of
the children, if any. The community has a right to this news. But the har-
rowing details that mark the wreck of any home are not news; they are
often salacious, sometimes debasing, and always abnormal. We have felt
that the wreck of a home is bad enough; to pry among the wreckage is
ghoulish. So readers of the *Gazette* who want Emporia divorce scandals
elaborated should subscribe for some other paper.

Now about the drunk. The man who fills up with whisky and goes about
making a fool of himself becomes a public nuisance. If permitted to continue
it, he becomes a public charge. The public has an interest in him. Publicity
is one of the things that keeps him straight. His first offense is not recorded in the *Gazette* when he is arrested, but on his second offense and
no matter how high or how low he is, his name goes in. We have printed
this warning time and again; so when the drunks come around asking us
to think of their wives and children, or their sick mothers or poor fathers,
we always tell them to remember that they had fair warning, and if their
fathers and mothers and wives and children are nothing to them before
taking they are nothing to us after taking.

The bum and the divorce are treated always from the standpoint of the
community interest.

THE PRESS AND
THE INDIVIDUAL

GEORGE SELDES

Freedom of the Press, 1935

———
———
———

George Seldes began his career as a journalist as a teenager at the
turn of the century. He wrote his first best-selling book in 1929. As
he neared his one hundredth year, in 1987, he wrote another best-
seller, *Witness to a Century*, a leisurely, curmudgeonly autobiography.

Beginning in the late 1920s, when he was past forty and with a
career as an investigative reporter and foreign correspondent behind
him, Seldes dedicated himself to correcting what he felt were mistaken impressions of the press. "People never get the whole story,"
Seldes said in a 1980 interview, "and the critic can help keep the
press honest." He published nearly twenty books, and, in 1940, he
started a journalism review, *In fact*, with its distinctive and defiant
lower case "f." It lasted for ten years, finally becoming a casualty of
the Cold War that Seldes denounced so vehemently. The newsletter
had a circulation of more than 100,000—it reached 176,000 in 1947,
a feat which no journalism review equaled before or since. After 1950,
Seldes remained prolific, but he reached a much smaller audience
until he published his autobiography.

In the 1930s, two of his books, *Freedom of the Press* (1935) and
Lords of the Press (1938), sold well and helped shape his reputation
as a media critic. "Newspapers, like kings, pretend they can do no
wrong," he wrote in *Freedom of the Press*. Its first subtitle was *For
the Millions Who Want a Free Press*. It was changed to *An Antidote
for Falsehood in the Daily Press*. In this book, he poked into the inner
workings of the press and underscored that the threats to press freedom came not only from government but from the corrupting influences of business as well. In the following chapter from his book, he
describes how the press invaded the privacy of public figures and

28

how reporters violated notions of fair play and decency in covering controversial figures in the early part of the century.

Seldes is the link that connects most of the press critics of the past century. In his autobiography, he acknowledged his debt to Will Irwin, the muckraker, and to Upton Sinclair, the novelist and social reformer. As he was influenced by some of the early press critics, so too has he influenced those who are now the elder statesmen of the current generation of critics. Glowing blurbs to his latest book were provided by two of the sturdiest contemporary press critics, I. F. Stone and Studs Terkel. Nat Hentoff, another shrewd press analyst, once called Seldes "the father of some of us all."

THE PRESS AND
THE INDIVIDUAL

*There is nothing covered, that shall not be revealed, and hid,
that shall not be known.*

The laws of most countries provide the redress when a citizen or subject
is injured by the newspapers. In almost every suit, freedom of the press,
its rights and privileges, are argued before judge and jury. Almost always
the newspaper wins. Almost always freedom of the press is recognized,
and this is as it should be, and no better fight can be waged than that for
its maintenance since all other liberties depend upon it.

But freedom of the press is one thing and the invasion of the home and
the privacy of the citizen is quite another, as the elder Bennett discovered
(when he engaged in the so-called new journalism) and the recently departed *Graphic*—which Ring Lardner immediately called the porno-*Graphic*—
later attested. The best proof of the matter is the appearance in all journalistic codes of ethics of planks respecting personal liberty and private
rights.

The question is well put by a leading American journalist, William Allen
White. Newspaper men, he says, are expressing deep concern nowadays
over the invasion of the privacy of individuals by the press. "Is there no
self-respect in our profession?" he asks. "Are we all quacks? . . . Have
we purified our columns by refusing to accept the bribe direct only to take
the bribe indirect in seeking circulation through the salacious and the pornographic? Is journalism a whited sepulchre proudly calcimined outside by
our probity in the matter of control by coarse and direct influence of advertisers while inside we are a charnal house of corruption through the
circulation department? Isn't it as bad to sell a family's privacy, a man's
individual rights to self respect in order to gain circulation and so acquire
higher advertising rates, isn't it as bad, I repeat, to do this as to take
money directly from interested parties for perverting the news?"

In a more bitter mood Sinclair Lewis declares that recent newspaper
publicity has gone mad; its "sunset wonders," he believes, are worse than
honest paid advertising: "Lindbergh cannot become engaged without
110,000,000 people leeringly looking on; . . . that not unromantic figure
Queen Marie was turned into a clown; . . . the judicial murder of our
murderers holds daily the front page. . . . For this is perhaps our great-

est achievement over Europe; not our electric irons nor our concrete sky-scraper constructions, but our changing of the ancient right of privacy so that the most secret and perhaps agonized thoughts of any human being are the property now of any swine who cares to read them."

Another aspect of the matter, newspaper trial of accused persons, brings similar pessimism from Clarence Darrow. "Trial by jury," he believes,

> is being rapidly destroyed in America by the manner in which the newspapers handle sensational cases. Of course it could not happen in England, as far as I know, or in other European countries. It is a species of mob law more insidious and dangerous than the ordinary mob law. I don't know what should be done about it. The truth is the courts and the lawyers don't like to proceed against newspapers. They are too powerful. As the law stands today, there is no important tribunal case where the newspapers are not guilty of contempt of court day after day. All lawyers know it, all judges know it, and all newspapers know it. But nothing is done about it. . . . No new laws are necessary. The court has full jurisdiction to see that no one influences a verdict or a decision. But everyone is afraid to act!

The journalistic holiday which is being made nowadays out of a personal fortune or misfortune is thoroughly discussed by Silas Bent in *Ballyhoo*, which is required reading for those who are interested in the press generally. Louis Weitzenkorn has dramatized the tragedy of a family whose home a newspaper of the *Graphic* type has invaded. Here, as in many other instances, it is a matter not of freedom but of license of the press. In the four instances which follow in some will be told the history of men of more or less fame, who, becoming national figures, naturally had to endure a certain amount of legitimate invasion of their privacy; but at least three of these men were antagonists of the American press, and the fourth hated a large part of it, and all have suffered abuses from it.

The four examples are Lindbergh the Bolshevik, Lindbergh the Hero, La Follette, Sr., and Upton Sinclair, the Don Quixote of our journalism. In the case of Lindbergh, Jr., and Sinclair, privacy was invaded; in all four cases the journalistic canons—Accuracy, Impartiality, Fair Play, and Decency—were violated many times.

When Charles A. Lindbergh, Sr., in 1918 was defeated for governor of Minnesota, Eva Lindbergh said: "Father had no adequate means of combating a hysterically lying press."

The newspapers of America had reason to hate Lindbergh. He was a great enemy of the bankers, he believed in the public ownership of the power companies as well as the public ownership of natural resources. He was an enemy of the Montana copper magnates and the Montana copper members of Congress, he fought the flour millers, he believed in the farmers' cooperatives, and in December 1915, he warned President Wilson that "speculations and loans in foreign fields are likely to bring us into war. . . . The war-for-profit group has counterfeited patriotism."

There was also a private and financial reason for national journalistic opposition. In 1911, when the packers and millers and steel and wool and other interests had got or were getting what they wanted from a businessmen's Congress, the newspapers joined in the game. The question of reciprocity with Canada had come up and suddenly the national press began a campaign to make this measure popular. It contained two important points: it freed from duty type-casting and type-setting machinery, and pulpwood and newsprint paper.

These were native industries which would be hurt, of course, and these succeeded in having the Senate Committee on Finances look into the matter. One of the disclosures was the following telegram:

New York
February 17, 1911

By request: private to editors:

It is of vital importance to newspapers that their Washington correspondents be instructed to treat favorably the Canadian reciprocity agreement, because print paper and wood pulp are made free of duty by this agreement.

HERMAN RIDDER
President,
American Newspaper Publishers' Association

The plan was for all papers to cooperate in putting through the reciprocity bill so they could get newsprint free of duty. Ridder's telegram was addressed to Democrats and Republicans, high tariff and anti-tariff advocates. In other words, at least half of the American press, which was Republican and pledged to tariff, was to run a campaign for free trade in those things which concerned their own pocketbooks.

Lindbergh opposed and voted against the bill the editors of America favored.

Practically the entire press of Minnesota opposed Lindbergh's bill to tax iron tonnage. St. Paul, Minneapolis, and Duluth newspapers were almost solid against him. In 1918 he ran for governor on the Nonpartisan or farmer's ticket. On one occasion he was arrested and jailed.

Lindbergh's platform (as given by Walter Quigley in a post-bellum introduction to *Your Country at War*) included conscription of wealth in time of war, elimination of the profiteers, price-fixing for farm produce. The campaign was vicious. Quigley arrived one day when Lindbergh was about to address ten thousand persons gathered in a grove. A sheriff and thirty sworn deputies tried to break up the meeting and the crowd wanted to fight, but Lindbergh protested it would do the party no good if blood were shed. "I suggest we adjourn a few miles south into the state of Iowa which still seems to be part of the United States," said Lindbergh. Later he was charged with conspiring to obstruct the war, but was not prosecuted. Lynn and Dora Haines, his biographers, write:

> The defeat of Lindbergh again became a national affair. He was the one who must go down and every possible weapon was used against him. Never had such a campaign been waged in the state; never one more unfair. As one editor said, "this campaign is in no sense a local Minnesota affair; beneath the furious battle special privilege is waging in this state lies all the combined power of entrenched politics and wealth from Wall Street to San Francisco."

A choice sample of the journalistic campaign against Lindbergh is this editorial from a St. Cloud newspaper: "A vote for Burnquist will cheer our soldiers in France. A vote for his opponent [Lindbergh] will be sad news to them and will bring a smile to the Kaiser."

The press ruined Lindbergh. In a speech in Congress in 1916 he had said:

> The public gets no information from the press about it [the money system, his favorite object of attack] for anyone who dares uncover the system and expose the schemes for deceiving the public finds that a certain part of the press will attack him and call him a radical and obstructionist, and excoriate him in every way possible. If to tell the truth about things makes him a radical, then radicals ought to be at a premium. But they have not been so far politically.

After his defeat Lindbergh wrote *Your Country at War*. Government agents raided the printing shop and destroyed the plates, also the plates of *Banking and Currency*, which attacked the big banks and the Federal Reserve Law. Lindbergh was by now known as a dangerous citizen, a Bolshevik to the Red-baiting press. The reason is obvious. Here are some of the opinions, mostly about the newspapers, he dared express from 1916 to 1918:

It is impossible according to the big press to be a true American unless you are pro-British. If you are really for America first, last and all the time, and solely for America and for the masses primarily, then you are classed as pro-German by the big press which is supported by the speculators. . . .

"Big Business," washing the hands of their captains: In all issues of their big press and other publications, you can read about what noble patriots we have in the men who profit by the war, while it is the plain, toiling people who are really supporting the entire system, including the payment of the profits to the big fellows. . . .

It has indeed been humiliating to the American people to see how the wealth grabbers, owners of the "big press," really attempt by scurrilous editorials and specially prepared articles to drive the people as if we were a lot of cattle, to buy bonds, subscribe to the Red Cross, to register for conscription and all the other things. The people will do their duty without being hectored in advance by the "big interest" press. What right, anyway, has the "big press" to heckle the people as if we really belonged to the wealth grabbers and were their chattel property? . . .

The attempt has been made by the press to make the farmers believe that the officers of the Nonpartisan League were selfish and later that they were not loyal Americans, also that they were Socialists, as if Socialists were criminals. Not many of those who criticize Socialists know the first principles of Socialism. Socialism and Socialists are libeled and slandered by the false and by the ignorant only, for no one who has studied Socialism can for a single moment question that it has a program whereby, if it could be followed out and put into execution, this world would be cleared of much of its misery and degradation.

Quoting parts of this book in May 1918, the *New York Times* said: "Such is the gospel which Duluth refused to hear. Such is the platform of this candidate of the Non-partisan league. More fortunate than many of the managers and orators of that concern, Mr. Lindbergh, so far as we know, is not under indictment for sedition."

In the *Chicago Tribune* a staff writer, Arthur M. Evans, in June 1918, wrote, "The reader looks instinctively to see if it bears the German copyright. It doesn't, but it contains many choice morsels of thought that might be gobbled with relish in Potsdam." The *Tribune* Washington correspondent, according to Margaret Ernst, telegraphed a report that in the House, Representative Miller said that "because of the attacks he had made upon the American Government" Lindbergh should be called "a friend of the Kaiser."

In 1923 when Lindbergh went campaigning again, his son, "Slim," took him from place to place in an airplane. They were almost killed one day when an unidentified enemy cut a cable on the machine. The elder Lindbergh was still known as a "red-hot Bolshevik."

Lindbergh was one of the many victims of an unfair press. The Nonpartisan League, headed by A. C. Townley, had only its weekly magazine to answer the attacks of its political and economic enemies. When the Lindbergh campaign began the members of the League were called "everything under the sun,—anarchists, I.W.W.'s, pro-Germans, disloyal. They [the opposition] used the press, the power of their money and position— every force they could muster to fight the farmers' league."

Although Lindbergh lost, North Dakota went Nonpartisan. Said the official League journal:

> The part the big daily press of Minnesota played in the political campaign in North Dakota was contemptible. For weeks before the vote, which resulted in the complete and sweeping victory for the Nonpartisan league, the *Pioneer Press* and *Dispatch* of St. Paul and the *Journal* and *Tribune* of Minneapolis were full of poisoned news and perverted editorial comment to the effect that if North Dakota votes returned Governor Frazier and the League to power it would be a "German victory." Every day these papers carried great headlines and editorials declaring that a victory for the farmers' administration would be a victory for disloyalty. They said that the only way North Dakota could "purge itself of disloyalty" would be to restore the old political gang of North Dakota to power and turn out the farmers' administration.
>
> This version of the North Dakota campaign was spread all over the United States through the activities of the poison press of Minnesota.

One of the typical stories during the campaign was that in the *St. Paul Dispatch* "to the effect that Mrs. Townley had told a woman in Detroit, Minnesota, that she had deposited $60,000 at a Detroit bank, money that Mr. Townley had stolen from the farmers." (I am quoting the words of the *Nonpartisan Leader*.) The Associated Press sent this by wire to all the country. It was printed in thousands of papers. Other papers copied verbatim the *Dispatch* story, which took up nearly a page.

> No deposition of this kind was ever introduced in court. No women of the name given ever existed. . . . It was just a hoax. . . . The story if true could have been verified in an hour by the Associated Press and the *Dispatch* lie nailed. . . . [The hoax was exposed by the Detroit banks.] So far as the *Leader* knows, no paper in American that published the original lie has yet retracted it.

During the Lindbergh campaign the organ of the League further charged that "practically every weekly and daily newspaper in Montana which is fighting the League is either a debtor to the copper trust or is owned outright by them." And again, "The newspapers do not attack the National Nonpartisan League because of any principles or convictions of their own, for they have none. They are merely the tools of those higher up, of the big business interests who are their masters. Think of the fight the organized farmers are making against war profiteering and you will see one reason for the frantic, lying articles in the poison press."

The campaign against Lindbergh, Townley, La Follette, was largely a press campaign. Wherever the progressives got a hearing they were fairly certain of making converts, but with the entire press of that section of the country against them they were terribly handicapped. As it was so much a journalistic war, the Nonpartisan League was fortunate in the midst of this campaign in gaining as a convert Walter W. Liggett who came out of the editorial office of the *St. Paul Dispatch*. He had been discharged for "disloyalty," it being alleged that he had attended a Nonpartisan League meeting and applauded. For the League Liggett wrote:

> A newspaper is a double-barreled weapon. It can suppress news entirely or distort it under misleading headlines in its news columns. If this fails to have the required result it often will continue publishing unfair attacks in its editorial columns. The editorial columns of the *St. Paul Dispatch* and *Pioneer Press* are even more unfair than their alleged news columns.
>
> The *St. Paul Dispatch* and *Pioneer Press* are notorious for their subservience to the great special interests—the railroads, the steel trust, the packers, the millers, the bankers, and the Twin City Rapid Transit company. They have served these interests for years and done their bidding on every occasion. The *Dispatch* and *Pioneer Press* can not deny that they have fought

for the corporations and fought against the people every time
there was a real fundamental issue involved.

Lindbergh, Sr., made no distinction between the newspapers which were
fair to him and those which were unfair. He lived and died believing that
the entire press was contemptible. Lindbergh, Jr.—the aviator—has always tried to distinguish between the newspapers which treated him well
and those he thinks treated him badly. Moreover, on more than one occasion he issued statements in which he absolved the actions of reporters,
saying they were only doing the work assigned them by the newspapers.
In other words it is the so-called rules of the so-called newspaper game
which Lindbergh was challenging as much as the things done to him.

When he married privately, the tabloid press felt itself insulted. When
he tried to take his honeymoon without benefit of publicity, the sensational
press hounded him. One tabloid called him a "Grade A celebrity," therefore
a public commodity, like gas or electric light.

The case of Lindbergh the Hero involves canon 6 of the code adopted
by the American Society of Newspaper Editors: "A newspaper should not
invade private rights or feelings without sure warrant of public right as
distinguished from public curiosity." To Marlen Pew, Lindbergh said that
several New York newspapers, five of which he named, do not respect
this rule. In July 1930, Pew and Lindbergh discussed the press and privacy,
and here is Pew's story of the famous interview:

> Lindbergh draws the line strictly between the right of the
> press to report his activities as they relate to the scientific de-
> velopment of air travel and what he calls personal curiosity. He
> said in sincere terms that he valued and deeply appreciated the
> "remarkable liberality" of the press in support of what he terms
> his "work." "The constructive press has been both kind and
> generous to me ever since I have been flying," he said, and he
> mentioned newspaper men who have been helpful, intelligently
> critical, fair in their reports and considerate of his private rights.

> Col. Lindbergh, without the slightest hesitation, but with no
> show of anger, also mentioned five New York newspapers which
> he said Mrs. Lindbergh and he had decided they could not "co-
> operate with and maintain our self-respect." These newspa-
> pers, he said, represent an idea of journalism to which he can-
> not subscribe. He called their practices "contemptible" and
> thought them to be "a social drag," "non-constructive," and "a
> waste of time." He minced no words in condemning newspa-
> pers which, in his view, cater to morbid curiosity and are con-

cerned with private gossip to the exclusion of matters in the realm of "things, ideas, and ideals."

. . . Reporting their courtship, marriage, honeymoon, and recently the expectancy and arrival of their infant son. Col. Lindbergh admitted these activities had been the bane of his life, that they had been "disgusting" and "humiliating," but contended that his feeling was not against individual reporters, though he thought they might be engaged in "some more decent business." His expressed resentment was against editors and publishers who "force reporters to do these unjust and intolerable things." He said he had become fairly used to indignities from a section of the New York newspaper press and was past personal feelings in relation to them, "only I wish they would given me time to do my work," but he felt as a citizen he had to "protest against such journalism in behalf of other persons who are similarly plagued and cannot defend themselves." He thought it weak merely to grin and bear injustice. Col. Lindbergh asserted he was "through trying to deal with them," meaning the five New York newspapers he had mentioned.

. . . He did not want to blame specific newspapermen. He did admit he felt outraged when some reporters followed him and Mrs. Lindbergh on their honeymoon and "for eight straight hours circled about out boat, at anchor in a New England harbor, in a noisy motorboat and occasionally called across the water to us that if we would pose for one picture they would go away." He thought that particularly mean and unworthy. He considered it absurd that he should have been forced to keep a guard constantly at duty at the gate of his wife's home, and told of an incident wherein a reporter had attempted to bribe a servant with $2,000 to "betray the secrets of the household." He also mentioned, with resentment, the publication of Mrs. Lindbergh's expectation last Spring. On no ground, in his view, could this be justified. He spoke of other disagreeable matters.

Lindbergh had forced every reporter and photographer to sign a pledge that he would use the baby's photograph only in his own paper or his own service, making sure that the following newspapers did not receive a copy: *Graphic, News, Mirror, American,* and *Journal.* When the photograph appeared in the *Daily News,* Lindbergh ascertained that it was from the copy furnished the Associated Press. *Time* reported (July 21, 1930) that several days later when an airplane belonging to a company of which Lindbergh was a technical adviser ran into a crowd, the *Daily News* headline read:

LINDBERGH LINER KILLS 2

At the next regular meeting of the board of directors formal protests against the Asssociated Press action in accepting a picture for distribution to clients on condition that it would not be released to certain ones were made by the editor of the *News* and the general manager of the Hearst newspapers.

On the other hand, the liberal weeklies called upon the society of editors to explain "what justification it has for existing when in the face of this monstrous persecution of Col. and Mrs. Lindbergh no voice has yet been raised by it or any of its members in any of its sessions against this degrading of their profession." Colonel Lindbergh's constitutional right to liberty and the pursuit of happiness were held infringed.

When the Lindbergh baby was kidnapped the press descended upon him again. Mitchell Dawson, Chicago lawyer, speaks of "an army of enthusiastic ghouls . . . prying, spying and trespassing in a ruthless stampede for news," but Pew believes this report false. We do know, however, that all Colonel Lindbergh said was, "Please go away." The Lindbergh case has been summed up by Silas Bent as follows:

> Charles A. Lindbergh has suffered more, probably, than any other citizen at the hands of newspapermen. They capitalized for revenue only (their revenue) a stunt flight to France, they built up about his personality a myth which he has never been quite free to dissipate, they outrageously invaded the privacy of his honeymoon, and now they have made more difficult the return by kidnappers of his son. Colonel Lindbergh has an ugly score against the daily press.

In April 1932, Colonel Lindbergh was forced to issue a statement that "the continued following of our representatives by members of the press is making it extremely difficult, if not impossible, for us to establish contact with whoever is in possession of our son . . . our attempts are still greatly hampered or made impossible by press activity . . ." And in August, upon the birth of another son, Colonel Lindbergh issued the following statement which can leave no doubt in anyone's mind that he feels bitterly about the press:

> Mrs. Lindbergh and I have made our home in New Jersey, and it is naturally our wish to continue to live there near our friends and interests. Obviously, however, it is impossible for us to subject the life of our second son to the publicity we feel was in a large measure responsible for the death of our first child.

> We feel that our children have the right to grow up normally
> with other children. Continued publicity makes this impossible.
> I am appealing to the press to permit our children to lead lives
> of normal Americans.

Robert M. La Follette fought "invisible government." He attacked all
the business interests which were supporting the Republican and Democratic parties. His financial support came largely from the Pinchots, Gifford
and Amos; Charles R. Crane, William Kent, Alfred L. Baker. He had a
naive belief that the Progressive Party was different from the two major
parties, that it had no financial roots in the same invisible government, and
he even asked Theodore Roosevelt to endorse him for the presidency in
December 1911.

The Progressives, however, had decided on Roosevelt. Medill
McCormick, one of the heirs of the *Chicago Tribune*, the Pinchots, and
others, asked La Follette on January 19, 1912, to quit in Roosevelt's favor,
but La Follette refused. He began his campaign for nomination. Twelve
years later Colonel Dickinson, retired from the State Department, wrote
in the *World* that Roosevelt's campaign had been underwritten "just as
they would underwrite building a railroad from here to San Francisco." The
underwriters were given as James Stillman, then head of the National City
Bank (father of the James Stillman of divorce notoriety); E. H. Gary,
E. H. Harriman; Daniel G. Reid, railroad manupulator, founder of American Can; Charles F. Brooker, vice president of the New Haven; George
W. Perkins and Robert L. Bacon, Morgan partners. To fighting these very
men and interests La Follette had dedicated his platform and career.

On the second of February La Follette delivered an address to the Periodical Publishers' Association, banqueting in Philadelphia. He made his
usual attack on Wall Street, Morgan, the Rockefellers, the trusts, big business in general, and said that the money trust

> controls the newspaper press . . . newspapers of course are
> still patronized for news. But wherever news items bear in any
> way upon control of government by business, the news is col-
> ored, so confidence in the newspaper as a newspaper is being
> undermined. . . . The control [of the press] comes through
> that community of interests, that interdependence of invest-
> ments and credits which ties the publicity up to the banks, the
> advertisers, and the special interests. We may expect this same
> kind of control sooner or later to reach out for the magazines.
> But more than this. I warned you of a subtle new peril, the
> centralization of advertising that will in time seek to gag you.

La Follette was on the verge of a nervous breakdown. According to the *New York Sun* he "would recover a page, divert to explain a page discarded a half hour ago," etc. He himself said later, "I talked too long without realizing it. I went home, really ill from exhaustion." There is no doubt that he acted in a muddled manner, that his speech became a tirade, but there is absolute proof that this confirmed buttermilk drinker was not maudlin, that he had not touched a drop of alcohol, as was alleged for years afterward.

A few days later the *New York Herald* reported that La Follette "is being hustled ruthlessly inside the hearse, although he still insists that he is strong enough to occupy a seat alongside the driver." A few great papers were lenient if not impartial in their attacks upon him, but generally speaking the press of the nation smashed his career. Whether or not the publishers in Philadelphia got together and decided upon united action is not so important as the fact that the press never forgave his attack, and either by innuendo, charges of drunkenness, or by silence, for several years made it impossible for him to have a fair hearing from the reading public.

Naturally enough La Follette fought back. If he could not make himself heard in the nation, he could at least let himself go in the Senate, and he did. When the press asked for an appropriation of five million dollars to advertise the Liberty Loan in 1917, La Follette struck at the publishers' pocketbooks. He called theirs "a business that is already subsidized by the United States government to the extent of ninety million dollars a year," meaning of course the loss the post office incurs annually in carrying second class mail. On that subject and the loan advertising he said:

> While engaged daily in impugning and questioning the loyalty and patriotism of others, the newspapers went to Congress and asked to be paid for being patriotic.
>
> The debates on the recent revenue bill throw some interesting light on the "patriotism" of newspapers,—particularly when the kind of patriotism applied affects the cash register of business offices.
>
> For years and years it has been known fact in Washington that the government has been carrying second class mail,—newspapers and magazines, at a huge deficit. Because of the tremendous influence wielded by newspapers among politicians, nothing has ever come of any efforts to reduce the deficit and place the charges on a business basis. Government estimates show that it costs 8 cents a pound for the government to carry second class mail. The remuneration received is 1 cent a pound from the newspapers.

When members of Congress began scanning about for sources of revenue to meet the huge war appropriations the second class postage was hit upon. Members argued that at a time such as the present no business should be subsidized. It developed that the government is paying $100,000,000 for carrying second class postage and they were receiving in return from the newspapers about $11,000,000—a subsidy of $89,000,000. . . .

The "patriotism plus profit" policy of the newspapers is most sordidly illustrated by the history of the attempt to get a $5,000,000 slice of the government money for advertising the Liberty Loan.

The Senator, however, pointed out that when the question of raising rates on second-class matter was before Congress, and when the big New York newspaper publishers adopted a resolution against any change in rates, two leading papers, the *New York Tribune* and the *Brooklyn Daily Eagle* refused to subscribe to such a move, the first named editorially calling the government loss of millions "a clear subsidy to the publishers."

Shortly after this attack on the press, Senator La Follette made a speech at St. Paul in which he favored high increases in the taxes on the war profiteers. The story which follows was compiled by Senator La Follette from the *Congressional Record* and published by him shortly before his death in 1925:

The body of Senator La Follette's address, as submitted by the official stenographer to the Committee on Privileges and Elections of the United States Sentate, was a discussion of progressive policies and the necessity of organization by the farmers. In the midst of the delivery of the speech, Senator La Follette was interrupted by questions from the audience concerning the war. In response to these questions, Senator La Follette declared at one point in his speech:

"For my own part I was not in favor of beginning the war. I don't mean to say that we hadn't suffered grievances; we had— at the hands of Germany. Serious grievances!"

In reporting this speech to more than 1,200 newspapers in as many cities throughout the country, the Associated Press quoted Senator La Follette as follows:

"I wasn't in favor of beginning the war. We had *No* grievances!"

It was this false report which appeared in the *Chicago Trib-*

une, the *New York Times*, the *Washington Post*, and more than 1,200 other newspapers in their issues of September 21, 1917. It was reproduced by publications in every part of the country. . . .

This speech, as reported by the Associated Press, was the immediate cause for the introduction in the Senate of a resolution to expel Senator La Follette from the body as a disloyalist.

The storm broke on Senator La Follette after the publication of the report of his St. Paul speech, quoting him as saying "We had no grievance" against Germany.

As early as October 11, 1917, Senator La Follette in an open letter to the Chairman of the Senate Committee which was investigating his right to his seat, branded the Associated Press report of his speech as "wholly false."

It was not until May 23, 1918, however—eight months after the delivery of the speech—that the Associated Press took any action on the matter. On that date, Frederick Roy Martin, Assistant General Manager of the Associated Press, wrote a letter to the Senate Committee, apologizing for the misquotation and specifically retracting the erroneous report.

Admitting that the Associated Press had "distributed accurately one important phrase" of the St. Paul speech, Mr. Martin concluded his letter:

"The error was regrettable and the Associated Press seizes the first opportunity to do justice to Senator La Follette."

Thus, eight months after the delivery of the speech, the Associated Press repudiated as false and untrue the statement credited to Senator La Follette and played upon the headlines of newspapers in more than 1,200 cities throughout the United States. . . .

Why was it that Robert M. La Follette was singled out for the most savage and relentless abuse ever directed against a public man in the history of the United States? [he himself asks, and replies]: The answer is clear to every fair minded person who will examine the official records.

Senator La Follette was pilloried and persecuted because for twenty years in Wisconsin and in the Senate he had been fighting to protect the American people from the unjust exactions of powerful corporate interests; because he had organized and led the Progressive movement; because in the midst of war he

fought to lay upon organized wealth and war profiteers a fair
proportion of the enormous cost of paying for the war. . . .

"The record shows that the resolution to expel La Follette
from the Senate was based on the distorted reports of the St.
Paul speech, and that after an investigation of more than fourteen months, the United States Senate voted overwhelmingly
to dismiss all the charges against La Follette." . . .

La Follette's St. Paul speech was falsely reported to the
people, and immediately made the basis of an organized demand
from Chambers of Commerce, Dollar-A-Year Men, Bankers'
Associations, State Councils of Defense, and other bodies, that
La Follette be driven from the Senate, under the blot of treason
to his country.

La Follette for years alleged that there was a conspiracy of silence against
him in the press. As the official record shows, he did not obtain a retraction
for eight months. That the *New York Evening Post* was ignorant of the
fact that the Senator had challenged the Associated Press immediately after it made its error and that he had requested the newspapers of the
country to correct it, corroborates La Follette's charge. Said the *Post*:

The Associated Press has handsomely and promptly admitted its grievous fault in misreporting Senator La
Follette . . . but the fact remains that irreparable injury was
done to the Senator, and that a large part of the outcry against
him was due to this misstatement in the one thousand newspapers which are served by the Associated Press. Senator La
Follette declared at the time that the press had misquoted him,
but the matter was never brought to the attention of the Associated Press until Mr. Gilbert E. Roe, his attorney, stated
the fact before the Senate Committee on Inquiry on Tuesday.
Why the Senator delayed so long is a mystery; but the serious
wrong done by this error needs no expatiating. No amount of
apology can undo it.

No, replied Senator La Follette, he did not neglect or delay,

But the newspapers neglected to make any correction but on
the contrary continued for months afterward to use the false
report as a text upon which to base arguments concerning the
Senator and creating public sentiment against him. The Senator
had no adequate opportunity to give to the public the truth of
the matter. The press was not open to him. As the *Post* says,

"the thought that unintentionally so extreme an injustice may be done a public man is one to sober all responsible journalism." The injustice done the public is far more serious. If public men fighting in the interest of the public may be ruined and discredited while the fight is on, the public may lose its fight and its servants become intimidated and afraid to make any real fight in its behalf.

In the 1922 campaign Senator La Follette said that the press of Wisconsin with two exceptions was opposed to him, and that inasmuch as the press of his state usually opposed him his election was an interesting proof that the press had lost political influence and that readers mistrusted their newspapers.

In 1924, however, all commentators agreed that while the smaller papers suppressed the news of the La Follette campaign, the larger city papers, notably the *New York Times*, covered it completely and objectively.

The case of Upton Sinclair has been brilliantly illuminated by President Theodore Roosevelt who said to him: "Mr. Sinclair, I have been in public life longer than you and I will give you this bit of advice: if you pay any attention to what the newspapers say about you, you will have an unhappy time."

Upton Sinclair has had an unhappy time.

The latest episode of which was his candidacy for governor of California in 1934. Then, as ever, Sinclair got a raw deal from so many newspapers that there is hardly an exaggeration in saying he got a raw deal from the press.

A newspaper man should not attempt to sit in judgment on the case of Sinclair vs. the *New York Times*. The complainant has stated his side in a pamphlet he calls *The Crimes of the Times*, and the defendant usually has chosen the role of silence.

Relations between the two began most favorably following the publication of *The Jungle*. A stockyards investigation was ordered by Theodore Roosevelt. Sinclair, who knew the contents of the report, offered a story which the Associated Press refused. It probably did not believe in its authenticity. Sinclair says that "throughout the campaign against the Beef Trust they [the A. P.] never sent out a single line injurious to the interests of the packers." But Managing Editor Van Anda, of the *Times*, not only trusted Sinclair but received him with joy and made a three-day sensation of the story. It certainly was news.

During the Colorado bloodshed Sinclair, with the cunning of an Ivy Lee, conceived the idea of breaking the silence of the newspapers by putting on a stunt in front of the Rockefeller offices in New York. It was known as "the mourning pickets." The eastern press saw it as a human-interest story and published news which counteracted the tainted stories or the silence from Colorado. Several of the reporters, says Sinclair,

> were men of conscience. One, Isaac Russell of the *Times*, became our friend and day after day he would tell of his struggles in the *Times* office, and how nearly every word favorable to myself or to the strikers was blue-pencilled from his story. So during the Broadway demonstration . . . we lived, as it were, on the inside of the *Times* office, and watched the process of strangling the news.

But now the case becomes more complicated. The mourning pickets were a news item. Sinclair, however, believes that the fact that he wrote a letter to Vincent Astor chiding him about his million-dollar recreation building, is equally news. And every newspaperman knows that such a letter is not news. The *Times, Herald, Press, Tribune* did not print his letter, Sinclair complains, but it is not a fair complaint, journalism being what it is and was.

On the other hand, Sinclair charges the *Times* with failure to review his *Brass Check* and with refusing money for an advertisement for that same book. Here again it seems to me he has no case. But later when James Melvin Lee of the New York University school of journalism denounced the book the *Times* published two columns of vitriol and refused to give Sinclair the equal opportunity of rebuttal. In this point I believe Sinclair is right.

He has a much better case against the Associated Press although here also it is his failure to understand the American principle of what constitutes news that leads him into error. We know that the news out of Colorado was perverted. We know that Sinclair accused the A. P. of poisoning the news there and that after a fanfare from the A. P. the cases against the *Masses* were dropped. But when Sinclair bases a test of the news on the fact that the Associated Press refused to send as news a telegram which he himself sent to President Wilson, newspapermen know that the A. P. was right, because no telegram which an individual sends is necessarily news. On the other hand, that telegram contained a serious charge of corruption which the A. P. may or may not have investigated. It certainly should have done so and published the result.

In the mourning pickets story Sinclair says, "The United Press, which is a liberal organization, sent out a perfectly truthful account of what had happened. The Associated Press, which is a reactionary organization, sent out a false account."

He enlisted the aid of John P. Gavit, managing editor of the *Post*, who wrote to Melville Stone, saying that the matter "on its face . . . certainly created a prima facie case of suppression of important facts regarding the situation in Denver," and Stone replied he would investigate. Nothing ever happened, so far as I can find out. The A. P. still, apparently owes Sinclair an apology.

One Chicago newspaper reviewer said of *The Jungle* that it showed Sinclair knew more about the inside of brothels than the stockyards. I do not think any large paper in America would employ a book reviewer today who reviewed in that manner.

Bennett, of the *New York Herald*, ordered a story from Sinclair, *Packingtown a Year Later*, but neither paid for it nor used it. Incidentally the *Herald* did pay him twenty-five hundred dollars for personal libel.

That Sinclair was hounded by the press and frequently libeled is an indisputable fact. He had become a public figure when he founded Helicon Home Colony which the newspapers used as a butt for jokes, just as they always use Utopian, idealistic, socialistic, "brain trust," and reform theories. The papers which cater most to the masses delight in ridiculing any action by an individual which is outside conventional mass life. It is the snobbery of the vulgar. The yellow press in its time and the tabloid press today not only cater to the *polloi* but the publishers instead of being leaders of public opinion are merely leaders of herd prejudices. A reporter from the *Sun* told Sinclair he liked Helicon Hall, its people and its idea, and "I feel like a cur to have to write as I do, but you know what the *Sun* is." The *Sun* was then still the newspaperman's newspaper. The reporter asked for an amusing story and Sinclair said his collie dog had disappeared. The *Sun* story said that even a dog refused to stay at the Sinclair Utopia.

In Los Angeles one day Sinclair unwisely remarked he could not find a barber shop because the city was so beflagged. The *Los Angeles Times* thereupon called his speech "prattlings of an anarchist."

The 1934 campaign certainly has furnished Sinclair with a grand concluding chapter to a new edition of *The Brass Check*.

No sooner had he received the nomination for governor on the Democratic ticket than the Democratic newspapers deserted him. And this is a significant fact. It brings up the whole question as to why certain newspapers are Democratic and certain newspapers are Republican, and who gets paid for being what it is, and what are the benefits, financial or otherwise, for representing a party.

Although a Democratic party candidate, Sinclair also had a program which big busines disapproved. When big business disapproves anything party lines disappear. It was so with La Follette in Wisconsin and it was so in Washington when Ridder told the Republican and Democratic press alike to support the bill making newsprint exempt from Republican tariff. "To my knowledge no daily newspaper in the state is supporting me. I believe this situation is unique in political history," sighed Sinclair.

Immediately afterward he found that "masses of falsehood" were poured over his campaign "by newspapers and radio and pamphlets." Heywood Broun's "magnificant articles exposing the California reactionaries were appearing in the *New York World-Telegram*, but were not wanted in California." There is no law requiring subscribers to Broun's column to print them, but there is an agreement that the column must not be cut or distorted and Broun himself has complained against certain papers for doing so.

Sinclair had another unhappy experience with the *San Francisco News*. He claims that he told one of the editors a story in confidence and that that confidence, which journalists respect fanatically throughout the world, was broken when the story appeared in the paper under the signature of another staff member.

Summing up the reports in the eastern press regarding his campaign, Sinclair says:

> The great newspapers of the country also reported the battle, mostly according to their prejudices. The *New York Times* gets its California stories from George P. West of the *San Francisco News* and Chapin Hall of the *Los Angeles Times*.
>
> West, who used to be a civil liberties man, has become a tired liberal, and talked to me sadly about his lack of faith, and the inevitability of Fascism in America. In his writings he did his best to equal the *Los Angeles Times* in depreciation of our movement; but Chapin Hall ran clean away from him in the last couple of weeks when he sent to the *New York Times* a story about the Communists supporting us in California. What do you think was his sole bit of evidence? That fake Communist circular which had been got out by Creel headquarters two months back, and was now reproduced on the front page of "Ham" Cotton's newspaper! Not merely had this wretched piece of trickery been exposed in the EPIC News, but a facsimile of it had been reproduced in *Today* of October 6, with a statement of its fraudulent nature. "All the News That's Fit to Print," says the majestic *New York Times*.

It is not necessary to go the liberal weeklies for proof that Sinclair got a raw deal. After the *Nation* called it "one of the nastiest campaigns on record" and the *New Republic* said that the press lied about Sinclair, the

New York Daily News reported the tricks of the Hollywood movie producers; Broun in the *World-Telegram* mentioned the "dirty tactics" and "wilful fraud"; the Scripps-Howard papers printed the statement from Los Angeles that

> local newspapers have struck a new low in political reporting. The big dailies make little pretense of printing both sides of the conflict and most of them have passed the sentence of silence on the big Sinclair meetings. The *Los Angeles Times* displays daily a box quoting from Mr. Sinclair's earlier writings on marriage, the church, the Legion, other American establishments. The series has proved damaging to Mr. Sinclair.

Early in the campaign the *New York Times* had reported that a west coast newspaper had headlined it, "This is not politics. This is war." When the battle was over Sinclair had polled more than eight hundred and seventy-five thousand votes, which every fair-minded man admitted was a remarkable showing when the money the Republicans had spent and their control of the press is considered. Many eastern newspapers thought it quite a victory for Sinclair. But the *New York Times* began its editorial the next morning with these remarkable words: "The total failure of the Sinclair campaign" and concluded with "the people of California . . . attacked the entire Sinclair plan and repudiated it emphatically." Several days later the *Times* reported in its news columns that the governor-elect was using Sinclair platform planks.

The hysterical Red baiting *Los Angeles Times* naturally enough called Merriam's victory a "retreat from Moscow." It said that the state had "served notice on the world yesterday that she has not gone crazy. There was nothing uncertain or equivocal about her answer to Upton Sinclair's invitation to forsake her proven paths for the red route of radicalism. . . . It has given the nation-wide radical movement a set-back from which it will not soon recover. The retreat from Moscow has started."

But the unfairest document, in my estimation, was the front-page interview of the *New York Times* of September 2, 1934, in which William Randolph Hearst denounced Sinclair, communism, Socialism, and Bolshevism. The cable contained the statement that the *Times* "invited" Mr. Hearst to interrupt his vacation in Bad Nauheim to comment on developments at home. It seems to me that the *Times* has gone very far afield when it chooses, of all men in the world, the rival publisher Hearst as a stick with which to beat Sinclair. This is a continuation of the feud with an amazing weapon. It is reminiscent of the James Melvin Lee attack on *The Brass Check*. The *Times*, refusing to review the book, published Lee, then refused Sinclair space to reply. Now it called upon the man the *Times* regards as holding the lowest place in American journalism to join in a common attack upon the enemy. It parallels the interview other papers had with Al Capone in which the gangster denounced Bolshevik methods.

And yet "Fair Play" stands high in the code of the American Society of Newspaper Editors.

2

JOURNALISTS AND THEIR BIASES

A familiar argument against the press is that America's leading journalists view the world in a way directly opposite to prevailing values. Journalists are more than cantankerous, the argument goes. They are biased, and they slant their news to the left. At the core of this critique is the notion that journalists are unhelpful, that their adversarial posture becomes destructive, perhaps unpatriotic. They are too preoccupied with the negative aspects of life.

This view of journalists was articulated by Theodore Roosevelt, who had been thought to be a friend of the press. He applied the term "muckraker" to journalists who had been aggressively exposing the wealthy and powerful, in and out of government. He intended the term to be taken as a negative, although his targets confounded him and took it as a compliment. After Roosevelt, relations between public officials and those reporters who covered them veered from cordial to hostile. Perhaps the public official who was most contemptuous of the press was Spiro Agnew, who served as Richard Nixon's Vice President until he resigned in disgrace shortly before his boss had to. Agnew was a master of the memorable phrase—he called journalists "nattering nabobs of negativism," a phrase actually coined by William Safire, then a White House speechwriter.

Such press bashing flourishes today. But many critics fall into the same trap Agnew did. They treat the media as a monolith, thereby ignoring fundamental distinctions and shadings. If there is one accurate generalization about the press, it is this: it is unsafe to generalize. There is the politically and ideologically committed press—on the right is the *National Review,* on the left is the *Nation.* Then there is the vast middle, the mainstream, which consists of the networks; the newsweeklies; the large daily newspapers, including the *New York Times,* the *Chicago Tribune,* the *Washington Post,* and the *Los Angeles Times;* and the important chains, such as Knight Ridder, which owns papers in Detroit, Philadelphia, and Miami, and Gannett, the owner of *USA Today* and nearly one hundred other papers. The country's major wire service, the Associated Press, is owned cooperatively by newspapers, and is dedicated to serving up the news in stripped down objective doses.

Of course, there are individual differences among all these organizations. And, of course, they compete for stories, readers, and advertising dollars (although outside the very largest cities, there is little head-to-head competition among newspapers because most markets are now monopolies).

The basic formula of newsgathering in the mainstream media is to report what government officials and business executives say. Fairness means only that an accusation must be balanced by a response, not by independent examination. Rarely does reporting go deeper than this, especially reporting emanating from Washington. After enjoying a brief vogue following Watergate, investigative reporting (the modern-day version of muckraking) is not practiced widely in the mainstream press. Thousands of reporters work out of Washington, but it took what President Reagan called a Lebanese "rag" to uncover the Iran-contra diversion.

These large news operations share a broad common perception of the common interest: they do not wish to be out in front, to attack the establishment, to criticize major institutions too harshly, or to be accused of endangering national security.

When matters of national interest and security are at stake, the press is usually more complaisant than cantankerous. Evidence of bias melts away. This phenomenon was starkly reported by Walter Lippmann and Charles Merz in their reconstruction of how the *New York Times* covered the Russian Revolution. Nearly half a century later, Clifton Daniel, a *New York Times* editor, in a rare act of self-examination, explained how the *Times* caved in to government pressure in its coverage of the Bay of Pigs.

THE MAN WITH THE MUCKRAKE

THEODORE ROOSEVELT

Speech on Laying of the Cornerstone of the New House of Representatives Office Building, April 14, 1906

———
———
———

In the early years of the twentieth century, President Theodore Roosevelt lavished praise on a group of journalists, among them Lincoln Steffens, who had been aggressively exposing abuses in government and business in such publications as *McClure's* and *Everybody's*. Then he turned on his journalistic allies, attacking those very writers who had helped elevate him to hero status. He compared "these reckless journalists" to the Man with the Muckrake in John Bunyan's *Pilgrim's Progress.*

The President borrowed the phrase from an editorial that appeared in 1906 in the *New York Post* which had accused the editor of *Town Topics,* a local scandal sheet, of "muckrakism." (The crusade against *Town Topics* had apparently been set in motion by an item that imputed improper behavior to Roosevelt's daughter Alice.) Roosevelt used the phrase first in March 1906 at the Gridiron Dinner in Washington (which in spite of—or perhaps because of—the presence of so many journalists and politicians was a strictly off-the-record affair until a very few years ago). In that speech, he charged that writers who engaged in exposing corruption were "muckrakers." Weeks later, at the dedication of the cornerstone of the new House of Representatives office building, he gave a similar speech. In one breath he praised journalists. In the next, he condemned their indiscriminate assaults on public officials. This was on the record and was the lead story in the *New York Times* the following day.

In *Pilgrim's Progress,* Bunyan had warned against a single-minded pursuit of worldly goods and rewards by describing "the man who could look no way but downward, with a muckrake in his hands; who was offered a celestial crown for his muckrake, but who would neither look up nor regard the crown he was offered, but continued to rake to himself the filth on the floor."

Roosevelt read the allegory to suggest that the excesses of the contemporary press, with its preoccupation with the negative aspects of American life, was contrary to the public interest. But in his speech, he failed to identify a single story or reporter in support of his point. Although the pejorative connotation of "muckraker" has lingered, the journalists came to embrace the designation as a badge of distinction.

THE MAN WITH THE MUCKRAKE

Over a century ago Washington laid the cornerstone of the Capitol in what was then little more than a tract of wooded wilderness here beside the Potomac. We now find it necessary to provide by great additional buildings for the business of the government. This growth in the need for the housing of the government is but proof and example of the way in which the nation has grown and the sphere of action of the national government has grown. We now administer the affairs of a nation in which the extraordinary growth of population has been outstripped by the growth of wealth and the growth in complex interests. The material problems that face us today are not such as they were in Washington's time, but the underlying facts of human nature are the same now as they were then. Under altered external form we war with the same tendencies toward evil that were evident in Washington's time, and are helped by the same tendencies for good. It is about some of these that I wish to say a word today.

In Bunyan's *Pilgrim's Progress* you may recall the description of the Man with the Muckrake, the man who could look no way but downward, with a muckrake in his hands; who was offered a celestial crown for his muckrake, but who would neither look up nor regard the crown he was offered, but continued to rake to himself the filth of the floor.

In *Pilgrim's Progress* the Man with the Muckrake is set forth as the example of him whose vision is fixed on carnal instead of on spiritual things. Yet he also typifies the man who in this life consistently refuses to see aught that is lofty, and fixes his eyes with solemn intentness only on that which is vile and debasing. Now, it is very necessary that we should not flinch from seeing what is vile and debasing. There is filth on the floor, and it must be scraped up with the muckrake; and there are times and places where this service is the most needed of all the services that can be performed. But the man who never does anything else, who never thinks or speaks or writes save of his feats with the muckrake, speedily becomes, not a help to society, not an incitement to good, but one of the most potent forces of evil.

There are in the body politic, economic and social, many and grave evils, and there is urgent necessity for the sternest war upon them. There should be relentless exposure of and attack upon every evil man, whether politician or businessman, every evil practice, whether in politics, in business, or in social life. I hail as a benefactor every writer or speaker, every man who, on the platform or in book, magazine, or newspaper, with merciless severity makes such attack, provided always that he in his turn remembers that the attack is of use only if it is absolutely truthful. The liar is no whit better than the thief, and if his mendacity takes the form of slander he may be worse than most thieves. It puts a premium upon knavery untruthfully to attack an honest man, or even with hysterical exaggeration to assail a bad man with untruth. An epidemic of indiscriminate assault upon character does not good but very great harm. The soul of every scoundrel is gladdened whenever an honest man is assailed, or even when a scoundrel is untruthfully assailed.

Now, it is easy to twist out of shape what I have just said, easy to affect to misunderstand it, and, if it is slurred over in repetition, not difficult really to misunderstand it. Some persons are sincerely incapable of understanding that to denounce mudslinging does not mean the indorsement of whitewashing; and both the interested individuals who need whitewashing and those others who practice mudslinging like to encourage such confusion of ideas. One of the chief counts against those who make indiscriminate assault upon men in business or men in public life is that they invite a reaction which is sure to tell powerfully in favor of the unscrupulous scoundrel who really ought to be attacked, who ought to be exposed, who ought, if possible, to be put in the penitentiary. If Aristides is praised overmuch as just, people get tired of hearing it; and over-censure of the unjust finally and from similar reasons results in their favor.

Any excess is almost sure to invite a reaction; and, unfortunately, the reaction, instead of taking the form of punishment of those guilty of the excess, is very apt to take the form either of punishment of the unoffending or of giving immunity, and even strength, to offenders. The effort to make financial or political profit out of the destruction of character can only result in public calamity. Gross and reckless assaults on character—whether on the stump or in newspaper, magazine, or book—create a morbid and vicious public sentiment, and at the same time act as a profound deterrent to able men of normal sensitiveness and tend to prevent them from entering the public service at any price. As an instance in point, I may mention that one serious difficulty encountered in getting the right type of men to dig the Panama Canal is the certainty that they will be exposed, both without, and, I am sorry to say, sometimes within, Congress, to utterly reckless assaults on their character and capacity.

At the risk of repetition let me say again that my plea is, not for immunity to, but for the most unsparing exposure of, the politician who betrays his trust, of the big businessman who makes or spends his fortune in illegitimate or corrupt ways. There should be a resolute effort to hunt every such man out of the position he has disgraced. Expose the crime and hunt down the criminal; but remember that even in the case of crime, if it is attacked in sensational, lurid, and untruthful fashion, the attack may do more damage to the public mind than the crime itself. It is because I feel that there should be no rest in the endless war against the forces of evil that I ask that the war be conducted with sanity as well as with resolution. The men with the muckrakes are often indispensable to the well-being of society, but only if they know when to stop raking the muck, and to look upward to the celestial crown above them, to the crown of worthy endeavor. There are beautiful things above and round about them; and if they gradually grow to feel that the whole world is nothing but muck their power of usefulness is gone. If the whole picture is painted black there remains no hue whereby to single out the rascals for distinction from their fellows. Such painting finally induces a kind of moral color blindness; and people affected by it come to the conclusion that no man is really black and no man really white, but they are all gray. In other words, they neither believe in the truth of the attack nor in the honesty of the man who is attacked; they grow as suspicious of the accusation as of the offense; it becomes well-nigh hopeless to stir them either to wrath against wrong-doing or to enthusiasm for what is right; and such a mental attitude in the public gives hope to every knave, and is the despair of honest men.

To assail the great and admitted evils of our political and industrial life with such crude and sweeping generalizations as to include decent men in the general condemnation means the searing of the public conscience. There results a general attitude either of cynical belief in and indifference to public corruption or else of a distrustful inability to discriminate between the good and the bad. Either attitude is fraught with untold damage to the country as a whole. The fool who has not sense to discriminate between what is good and what is bad is well-nigh as dangerous as the man who does discriminate and yet chooses the bad. There is nothing more distressing to every good patriot, to every good American, than the hard, scoffing spirit which treats the allegation of dishonesty in a public man as a cause for laughter. Such laughter is worse than the crackling of thorns under a pot, for it denotes not merely the vacant mind, but the heart in which high emotions have been choked before they could grow to fruition.

There is any amount of good in the world, and there never was a time when loftier and more disinterested work for the betterment of mankind was being done than now. The forces that tend for evil are great and terrible, but the forces of truth and love and courage and honesty and generosity and sympathy are also stronger than ever before. It is foolish and timid no less than a wicked thing to blink the fact that the forces of evil are strong, but it is even worse to fail to take into account the strength of the forces that tell for good. Hysterical sensationalism is the very poorest weapon wherewith to fight for lasting righteousness. The men who with stern sobriety and truth assail the many evils of our time, whether in the public press, or in magazines, or in books, are the leaders and allies of all engaged in the work for social and political betterment. But if they give good reason for distrust of what they say, if they chill the ardor of those who demand truth as a primary virtue, they thereby betray the good cause and play into the hands of the very men against whom they are nominally at war.

In his *Ecclesiastical Polity* that fine old Elizabethan divine, Bishop Hooker, wrote:

> He that goeth about to persuade a multitude that they are not so well governed as they ought to be, shall never want attentive and favorable hearers; because they know the manifold defects whereunto every kind of regimen is subject, but the secret lets and difficulties, which in public proceedings are innumerable and inevitable, they have not ordinarily the judgment to consider.

This truth should be kept constantly in mind by every free people desiring to preserve the sanity and poise indispensable to the permanent success of self-government. Yet, on the other hand, it is vital not to permit this spirit of sanity and self-command to degenerate into mere mental stagnation. Bad though a state of hysterical excitement is, and evil though the results are which come from the violent oscillations such excitement invariably produces, yet a sodden acquiescence in evil is even worse. At this moment we are passing through a period of great unrest—social, political, and industrial unrest. It is of the utmost importance for our future that this should prove to be not the unrest of mere rebelliousness against life, of mere dissatisfaction with the inevitable inequality of conditions, but the unrest of a resolute and eager ambition to secure the betterment of the individual and the nation. So far as this movement of agitation throughout the country takes the form of a fierce discontent with evil, of a determination to punish the authors of evil, whether in industry or politics, the feeling is to be heartily welcomed as a sign of healthy life.

If, on the other hand, it turns into a mere crusade of appetite against appetite, of a contest between the brutal greed of the "have-nots" and the brutal greed of the "haves," then it has no significance for good, but only for evil. If it seeks to establish a line of cleavage, not along the line which divides good men from bad, but along that other line, running at right angles thereto, which divides those who are well off from those who are less well off, then it will be fraught with immeasurable harm to the body politic.

We can no more and no less afford to condone evil in the man of capital than evil in the man of no capital. The wealthy man who exults because there is a failure of justice in the effort to bring some trust magnate to an account for his misdeeds is as bad as, and no worse than, the so-called labor leader who clamorously strives to excite a foul class feeling on behalf of some other labor leader who is implicated in murder. One attitude is as bad as the other, and no worse; in each case the accused is entitled to exact justice; and in neither case is there need of action by others which can be construed into an expression of sympathy for crime.

It is a prime necessity that if the present unrest is to result in permanent good the emotion shall be translated into action, and that the action shall be marked by honesty, sanity, and self-restraint. There is mighty little good in a mere spasm of reform. The reform that counts is that which comes through steady, continuous growth; violent emotionalism leads to exhaustion.

It is important to this people to grapple with the problems connected with the massing of enormous fortunes, and the use of those fortunes, both corporate and individual, in business. We should discriminate in the sharpest way between fortunes well won and fortunes ill won; between those gained as an incident to performing great services to the community as whole, and those gained in evil fashion by keeping just within the limits of mere law-honesty. Of course no amount of charity in spending such fortunes in any way compensates for misconduct in making them. As a matter of personal conviction, and without pretending to discuss the details or formulate the system, I feel that we shall ultimately have to consider the adoption of some such scheme as that of a progressive tax on all fortunes, beyond a certain amount, either given in life or devised or bequeathed upon death to any individual—a tax so framed as to put it out of the power of the owner of one of these enormous fortunes to hand on more than a certain amount to any individual; the tax, of course, to be imposed by the national and not the state government. Such taxation should, of course, be aimed merely at the inheritance or transmission in their entirety of those fortunes swollen beyond all healthy limits.

Again, the national government must in some form exercise supervision over corporations engaged in interstate business—and all large corporations are engaged in interstate business—whether by license or otherwise, so as to permit us to deal with the far-reaching evils of over-capitalization. This year we are making a beginning in the direction of serious effort to settle some of these economic problems by the railway rate legislation. Such legislation, if so framed, as I am sure it will be, as to secure definite and tangible results, will amount to something of itself; and it will amount to a great deal more in so far as it is taken as a first step in the direction of a policy of superintendence and control over corporate wealth engaged in interstate commerce, this superintendence and control not to be exercised in a spirit of malevolence toward the men who have created the wealth, but with the firm purpose both to do justice to them and to see that they in their turn do justice to the public at large.

The first requisite in the public servants who are to deal in this shape with corporations, whether as legislators or as executives, is honesty. This honesty can be no respecter of persons. There can be no such thing as unilateral honesty. The danger is not really from corrupt corporations; it springs from the corruption itself, whether exercised for or against corporations.

The eighth commandment reads, "Thou shalt not steal." It does not read, "Thou shalt not steal from the rich man." It does not read, "Thou shalt not steal from the poor man." It reads simply and plainly, "Thou shalt not steal." No good whatever will come from that warped and mock morality which denounces the misdeeds of men of wealth and forgets the misdeeds practiced at their expense; which denounces bribery, but blinds itself to blackmail; which foams with rage if a corporation secures favors by improper methods, but merely leers with hideous mirth if the corporation is itself wronged. The only public servant who can be trusted honestly to protect the rights of the public against the misdeed of a corporation is that public man who will just as surely protect the corporation itself from wrongful aggression. If a public man is willing to yield to popular clamor and do wrong to the men of wealth or to rich corporations, it may be set down as certain that if the opportunity comes he will secretly and furtively do wrong to the public in the interest of a corporation.

But, in addition to honesty, we need sanity. No honesty will make a public man useful if that man is timid or foolish, if he is a hotheaded zealot or an impracticable visionary. As we strive for reform we find that it is not at all merely the case of a long uphill pull. On the contrary, there is almost as much of breeching work as of collar work; to depend only on traces means that there will soon be a runaway and an upset. The men of wealth who today are trying to prevent the regulation and control of their business in the interest of the public by the proper government authorities will not succeed, in my judgment, in checking the progress of the movement. But if they did succeed they would find that they had sown the wind and would surely reap the whirlwind, for they ultimately provoke the violent excesses which accompany a reform coming by convulsion instead of by steady and natural growth.

On the other hand, the wild preachers of unrest and discontent, the wild agitators against the entire existing order, the men who act crookedly, whether because of sinister design or mere puzzleheadedness, the men who preach destruction without proposing any substitute for what they intend to destroy, or who propose a substitute which would be far worse than the existing evils—all these men are the most dangerous opponents of real reform. If they get their way they will lead the people into a deeper pit than any into which they would fall under the present system. If they fail to get their way they will still do incalculable harm by provoking the kind of reaction which in its revolt against the senseless evil of their teaching would enthrone more securely than ever the very evils which their misguided followers believe they are attacking.

More important than aught is the development of the broadest sympathy of man for man. The welfare of the wage worker, the welfare of the tiller of the soil, upon these depend the welfare of the entire country; their good is not to be sought in pulling down others; but their good must be the prime object of all our statesmanship.

Materially, we must strive to secure a broader economic opportunity for all men, so that each shall have a better chance to show the stuff of which he is made. Spiritually and ethically we must strive to bring about clean living and right thinking. We appreciate that the things of the body are important; but we appreciate also that the things of the soul are immeasurably more important. The foundation stone of national life is, and ever must be, the high individual character of the average citizen.

SPEECHES ON THE MEDIA

SPIRO AGNEW

1969–1971

Spiro Agnew worked for a man who viscerally disliked the press. In 1962, in California, after he lost a comeback bid for Governor, Richard Nixon held a press conference and bitterly told reporters they no longer had him to kick around any more. But Nixon *did* come back, and his point man against the press was Agnew. In Des Moines in 1969, the Vice President began a bold attack on the press. Years later, in his book *The Impudent Snobs: Agnew v. The Intellectual Establishment,* John R. Coyne, Jr., a conservative admirer of Agnew, called the Des Moines address the "most important vice presidential speech ever given." The speech was drafted by Patrick Buchanan, who was a conservative ideologue then on the President's staff and who later worked in the Reagan White House and as a columnist and commentator. The speech was edited by Nixon himself. It was televised live, highly unusual for a vice presidential address.

Sixteen months after the Des Moines speech, Agnew condemned a CBS documentary in a speech in Boston. He called this "perhaps the most important speech I will deliver in my term as Vice President." Discounting steeply for hyperbole, these speeches—and a dozen that Agnew gave in between—inalterably changed the way the media was viewed and the way the media viewed itself. Agnew raised questions of credibility, fairness, and bias. Two decades later, after scores of studies have been produced on these issues, the questions are still asked.

For a brief period, Agnew became a one-man journalism review, a truth squad from the right, if you will. He became the best-known press basher of a generation. Ironically, while his phrases may have caught on and become part of the nation's vocabulary, his specific criticisms were singularly uninformed and sometimes just plain inaccurate.

For instance, in his Des Moines speech, he singled out for criticism W. Averell Harriman, the veteran diplomat and chief negotiator at the Paris Peace talks, who in response to the President's televised speech on his Vietnam policy concluded by saying: "I wish the President well. I hope he can lead us to peace. But this is not the whole story we've heard tonight." Mild stuff from a mild man, and not, as Agnew said in his speech, words "encouraging the country" not to listen to the President.

A week later, speaking to the Chamber of Commerce in Montgomery, Alabama, Agnew slashed away at the "liberal establishment press," specifically the *New York Times* and *Washington Post.* He excoriated the *Times,* which he said had ignored a Congressional vote that apparently endorsed the administration's position in Vietnam. But he was in error. The *Times* had run the story in detail, but because of the lateness of the vote the story did not appear in the early edition of the paper that Agnew had apparently read in Washington.

SPEECHES ON THE MEDIA

MID-WEST REGIONAL REPUBLICAN COMMITTEE MEETING
DES MOINES, IOWA

NOVEMBER 13, 1969

Tonight I want to discuss the importance of the television news medium to the American people. No nation depends more on the intelligent judgment of its citizens. No medium has a more profound influence over public opinion. Nowhere in our system are there fewer checks on vast power. So, nowhere should there be more conscientious responsibility exercised than by the news media. The question is . . . are we demanding enough of our television news presentations? . . . And, are the men of this medium demanding enough of themselves?

Monday night, a week ago, President Nixon delivered the most important address of his administration, one of the most important of our decade. His subject was Vietnam. His hope was to rally the American people to see the conflict thorugh to a lasting and just peace in the Pacific. For thirty-two minutes, he reasoned with a nation that has suffered almost a third of a million casualties in the longest war in its history.

When the President completed his address—an address that he spent weeks in preparing—his words and policies were subjected to instant analysis and querulous criticism. The audience of seventy million Americans— gathered to hear the President of the United States—was inherited by a small band of network commentators and self-appointed analysts, the *majority* of whom expressed, in one way or another, their hostility to what he had to say.

It was obvious that their minds were made up in advance. Those who recall the fumbling and groping that followed President Johnson's dramatic disclosure of his intention not to seek reelection have seen these men in a genuine state of non-preparedness. This was not it.

One commentator twice contradicted the President's statement about the exchange of correspondence with Ho Chi Minh. Another challenged the President's abilities as a politician. A third asserted that the President was now "following the Pentagon line." Others, by the expressions on their faces, the tone of their questions, and the sarcasm of their responses, made clear their sharp disapproval.

To guarantee in advance that the President's plea for national unity would be challenged, one network trotted out Averell Harriman for the occasion. Throughout the President's address he waited in the wings. When the President concluded, Mr. Harriman recited perfectly. He attacked the Thieu Government as unrepresentative; he criticized the President's speech for various deficiencies; he twice issued a call to the Senate Foreign Relations Committee to debate Vietnam once again; he stated his belief that the Viet Cong or North Vietnamese did not really want a military takeover of South Vietnam; he told a little anecdote about a "very, very responsible" fellow he had met in the North Vietnamese delegation.

All in all, Mr. Harriman offered a broad range of gratuitous advice— challenging and contradicting the policies outlined by the President of the United States. Where the President had issued a call for unity, Mr. Harriman was encouraging the country not to listen to him.

A word about Mr. Harriman. For ten months he was America's chief negotiator at the Paris Peace Talks—a period in which the United States swapped some of the greatest military concessions in the history of warfare for an enemy agreement on the shape of a bargaining table. Like Coleridge's Ancient Mariner, Mr. Harriman seems to be under some heavy compulsion to justify his failures to anyone who will listen. The networks have shown themselves willing to give him all the air time he desires.

Every American has a right to disagree with the President of the United States, and to express publicly that disagreement.

But the President of the United States has a right to communicate directly with the people who elected him, and the people of this country have the right to make up their own minds and form their own opinions about a presidential address without having the President's words and thoughts characterized through the prejudices of hostile critics before they can even be digested.

When Winston Churchill rallied public opinion to stay the course against Hitler's Germany, he did not have to contend with a gaggle of commentators raising doubts about whether he was reading public opinion right, or whether Britain had the stamina to see the war through. When President Kennedy rallied the nation in the Cuban Missile Crisis, his address to the people was not chewed over by a round-table of critics who disparaged the course of action he had asked America to follow.

The purpose of my remarks tonight is to focus your attention on this little group of men who not only enjoy a right of instant rebuttal to every Presidential address, but more importantly, wield a free hand in selecting, presenting, and interpreting the great issues of our nation.

First, let us define that power. At least forty million Americans each

night, it is estimated, watch the network news. Seven million of them view
ABC; the remainder being divided between NBC and CBS. According to
Harris polls and other studies, for millions of Americans the networks are
the sole source of national and world news.

In Will Rogers' observation, what you knew was what you read in the
newspaper. Today, for growing millions of Americans, it is what they see
and hear on their television sets.

How is this network news determined? A small group of men, num-
bering perhaps no more than a dozen "anchormen," commentators, and
executive producers, settle upon the twenty minutes or so of film and commentary that is to reach the public. This selection is made from the ninety
to one hundred eighty minutes that may be available. Their powers of choice
are broad. They decide what forty to fifty million Americans will learn of
the day's events in the nation and the world.

We cannot measure this power and influence by traditional democratic
standards for these men can create national issues overnight. They can
make or break—by their coverage and commentary—a moratorium on the
war. They can elevate men from local obscurity to national prominence
within a week. They can reward some politicians with national exposure
and ignore others. For millions of Americans, the network reporter who
covers a continuing issue, like ABM or Civil Rights, becomes in effect,
the presiding judge in a national trial by jury.

It must be recognized that the networks have made important contri-
butions to the national knowledge. Through news, documentaries, and spe-
cials, they have often used their power constructively and creatively to
awaken the public conscience to critical problems.

The networks made "hunger" and "black lung" disease national issues
overnight. The TV networks have done what no other medium could have
done in terms of dramatizing the horrors of war. The networks have
tackled our most difficult social problems with a directness and immediacy
that is the gift of their medium. They have focused the nation's attention
on its environmental abuses . . . on pollution in the Great Lakes and the
threatened ecology of the Everglades.

But it was also the networks that elevated Stokely Carmichael and George
Lincoln Rockwell from obscurity to national prominence . . . nor is their
power confined to the substantive.

A raised eyebrow, an inflection of the voice, a caustic remark dropped
in the middle of a broadcast can raise doubts in a million minds about the
veracity of a public official or the wisdom of a government policy.

One Federal Communications Commissioner considers the power of the
networks to equal that of local, state, and federal governments combined.

Certainly, it represents a concentration of power over American public opinion unknown in history.

What do Americans know of the men who wield this power? Of the men who produce and direct the network news—the nation knows practically nothing. Of the commentators, most Americans know little, other than that they reflect an urbane and assured presence, seemingly well informed on every important matter.

We do know that, to a man, these commentators and producers live and work in the geographical and intellectual confines of Washington, D.C., or New York City—the latter of which James Reston terms the "most unrepresentative community in the entire United States." Both communities bask in their own provincialism, their own parochialism. We can deduce that these men thus read the same newspapers, and draw their political and social views from the same sources. Worse, they talk constantly to one another, thereby providing artificial reinforcement to their shared viewpoints.

Do they allow their biases to influence the selection and presentation of the news? David Brinkley states, "objectivity is impossible to normal human behavior." Rather, he says, we should strive for "fairness."

Another anchorman on a network news show contends: "You can't expunge all your private convictions just because you sit in a seat like this and a camera starts to stare at you . . . I think your program has to reflect what your basic feelings are. I'll plead guilty to that."

Less than a week before the 1968 election, this same commentator charged that President Nixon's campaign commitments were no more durable than campaign balloons. He claimed that, were it not for fear of a hostile reaction, Richard Nixon would be giving into, and I quote the commentator, "his natural instinct to smash the enemy with a club or go after him with a meat axe."

Had this slander been made by one political candidate about another, it would have been dismissed by most commentators as a partisan assault. But this attack emanated from the privileged sanctuary of a network studio and therefore had the apparent dignity of an objective statement.

The American people would rightly not tolerate this kind of concentration of power in government. Is it not fair and relevant to question its concentration in the hands of a tiny and closed fraternity of privileged men, elected by no one, and enjoying a monopoly sanctioned and licensed by government?

The views of this fraternity do *not* represent the views of America. That is why such a great gulf existed between how the nation received the President's address—and how the networks reviewed it.

As with other American institutions, perhaps it is time that the networks were made more responsive to the views of the nation and more responsible to the people they serve.

I am not asking for government censorship or any other kind of censorship. I am asking whether a form of censorship already exists when the news that forty million Americans receive each night is determined by a handful of men responsible only to their corporate employers and filtered through a handful of commentators who admit to their own set of biases.

The questions I am raising here tonight should have been raised by others long ago. They should have been raised by those Americans who have traditionally considered the preservation of freedom of speech and freedom of the press their special provinces of responsibility and concern. They should have been raised by those Americans who share the view of the late Justice Learned Hand that "right conclusions are more likely to be gathered out of a multitude of tongues than through any kind of authoritative selection."

Advocates for the networks have claimed a first amendment right to the same unlimited freedoms held by the great newspapers of America.

The situations are not identical. Where the *New York Times* reaches 800,000 people, NBC reaches twenty times that number with its evening news. Nor can the tremendous impact of seeing television film and hearing commentary be compared with reading the printed page.

A decade ago, before the network news acquired such dominance over public opinion, Walter Lippmann spoke to the issue. He said:

> There is an essential and radical difference between television and printing. The three or four competing television stations control virtually all that can be received over the air by ordinary television sets. But, besides the mass circulation dailies, there are the weeklies, the monthlies, the out-of-town newspapers, and books. If a man does not like his newspaper, he can read another from out of town, or wait for a weekly news magazine. It is not ideal. But it is infinitely better than the situation in television. There, if a man does not like what the networks offer him, all he can do is turn them off, and listen to a phonograph.

"Networks," he stated, "which are few in number, have a virtual monopoly of a whole medium of communication." The newspapers of mass circulation have no monopoly of the medium of print.

"A virtual monopoly of a whole medium of communication" is not something a democratic people should blithely ignore.

And we are not going to cut off our television sets and listen to the phonograph because the air waves do not belong to the networks; they belong to the people.

As Justice Byron White wrote in his landmark opinion six months ago, "It is the right of the viewers and listeners, not the right of the broadcasters, which is paramount."

It is argued that this power presents no danger in the hands of those who have used it responsibly.

But as to whether or not the networks have abused the power they enjoy, let us call as our first witnesses, former Vice President Humphrey and the City of Chicago.

According to Theodore H. White, television's intercutting of the film from the streets of Chicago with the "current proceedings on the floor of the convention created the most striking and *false* political picture of 1968— the nomination of a man for the American Presidency by the brutality and violence of merciless police."

If we are to believe a recent report of the House Commerce Committee, then television's presentation of the violence in the streets worked an injustice on the reputation of the Chicago police.

According to the Committee findings, one network in particular presented "a one-sided picture which in large measure exonerates the demonstrators and protestors." Film of provocations of police that was available never saw the light of day, while the film of the police response which the protestors provoked was shown to millions.

Another network showed virtually the same scene of violence—from three separate angles—without making clear it was the same scene.

While the full report is reticent in drawing conclusions, it is not a document to inspire confidence in the fairness of the network news.

Our knowledge of the impact of network news on the national mind is far from complete. But some early returns are available. Again, we have enough information to raise serious questions about its effect on a democratic society.

Several years ago, Fred Friendly, one of the pioneers of network news, wrote that its missing ingredients were "conviction, controversy, and a point of view." The networks have compensated with a vengeance.

And in the networks' endless pursuit of controversy, we should ask what is the end value . . . to enlighten or to profit? What is the end result . . . to inform or to confuse? How does the ongoing exploration for more action, more excitement, more drama, serve our national search for internal peace and stability?

Gresham's law seems to be operating in the network news.

Bad news drives out good news. The irrational is more controversial than the rational. Concurrence can no longer compete with dissent. One minute of Eldridge Cleaver is worth ten minutes of Roy Wilkins. The labor crisis settled at the negotiating table is nothing compared to the confrontation that results in a strike—or, better yet, violence along the picket line. Normality has become the nemesis of the evening news.

The upshot of all this controversy is that a narrow and distorted picture of Amierica often emerges from the televised news. A single dramatic piece of the mosaic becomes, in the minds of millions, the whole picture. The American who relies upon television for his news might conclude that the majority of American students are embittered radicals, that the majority of black Americans feel no regard for their country; that violence and lawlessness are the rule, rather than the exception, on the American campus. None of these conclusions is true.

Television may have destroyed the old stereotypes—but has it not created new ones in their place?

What has this passionate pursuit of "controversy" done to the politics of progress through logical compromise, essential to the functioning of a democratic society?

The members of Congress or the Senate who follow their principles and philosophy quietly in a spirit of compromise are unknown to many Americans—while the loudest and most extreme dissenters on every issue are known to every man in the street.

How many marches and demonstrations would we have if the marchers did not know that the ever-faithful TV cameras would be there to record their antics for the next news show.

We have heard demands that Senators and Congressmen and judges make known all their financial connections—so that the public will know who and what influences their decisions or votes. Strong arguments can be made for that view. But when a single commentator or producer, night after night, determines for millions of people how much of each side of a great issue they are going to see and hear; should he not first disclose his personal views on the issue as well?

In this search for excitement and controversy, has more than equal time gone to that minority of Americans who specialize in attacking the United States, its institutions, and its citizens?

Tonight, I have raised questions. I have made no attempt to suggest answers. These answers must come from the media men. They are challenged to turn their critical powers on themselves. They are challenged to direct their energy, talent, and conviction toward improving the quality and objectivity of news presentation. They are challenged to structure their own civic ethics to relate their great freedom with their great responsibility.

And the people of America are challenged too . . . challenged to press for responsible news presentations. The people can let the networks know that they want their news straight and objective. The people can register their complaints on bias through mail to the networks and phone calls to local stations. This is one case where the people must defend themselves . . . where the citizen—not government—must be the reformer . . . where the consumer can be the most effective crusader.

By way of conclusion, let me say that every elected leader in the United States depends on these men of the media. Whether what I have said to you tonight will be heard and seen at all by the nation is not *my* decision; it is not *your* decision; it is *their* decision.

In tomorrow's edition of the *Des Moines Register* you will be able to read a news story detailing what I said tonight; editorial comment will be reserved for the editorial page, where it belongs. Should not the same wall of separation exist between news and comment on the nation's network.

We would never trust such power over public opinion in the hands of an elected government—it is time we questioned it in the hands of a small and unelected elite. The great networks have dominated America's airwaves for decades; the people are entitled to a full accounting of their stewardship.

MONTGOMERY CHAMBER OF COMMERCE
MONTGOMERY, ALABAMA

NOVEMBER 20, 1969

One week ago tonight I flew out to Des Moines, Iowa, and exercised my right to dissent.

There has been some criticism of what I had to say out there.

Let me give you a sampling.

One Congressman charged me with, and I quote, "A creeping socialistic scheme against the free enterprise broadcast industry." That is the first time in my memory anybody ever accused Ted Agnew of entertaining socialist ideas.

On Monday, largely because of this address, Mr. Humphrey charged the Nixon Administration with a "calculated attack" on the right of dissent and on the media today. Yet, it is widely known that Mr. Humphrey himself believes deeply that unfair coverage of the Democratic Convention in Chicago, by the same media, contributed to his defeat in November. Now, his wounds are apparently healed, and he casts his lot with those who were questioning his own political courage a year ago. But let us leave Mr. Humphrey to his own conscience. America already has too many politicians who would rather switch than fight.

Others charged that my purpose was to stifle dissent in this country. Nonsense. The expression of my views has produced enough rugged dissent in the last week to wear out a whole covey of commentators and columnists.

One critic charged that the speech was "disgraceful, ignorant, and base," that it "leads us as a nation into an ugly era of the most fearsome suppression and intimidation." One national commentator, whose name is known to everyone in this room, said "I hesitate to get into the gutter with this guy." Another commentator charges that it was "one of the most sinister speeches I have ever heard made by a public official." The president of one network said it was an "unprecedented attempt to intimidate a news medium which depends for its existence upon government licenses." The president of another charged me with "an appeal to prejudice," and said it was evident that I would prefer the kind of television "that would be subservient to whatever political group happened to be in authority at the time."

And they say *I* have a thin skin.

Here are classic examples of overreaction. These attacks do not address themselves to the questions I have raised. In fairness, others—the majority of critics and commentators—did take up the main thrust of my address. And if the debate they have engaged in continues, our goal will surely be reached—a thorough self-examination by the networks of their own policies—and perhaps prejudices. That was my objective then; it is my objective now.

Now, let me repeat to you the thrust of my remarks the other night, and make some new points and raise some new issues.

I am opposed to censorship of television or the press in any form. I don't care whether censorship is imposed by government or whether it results from management in the choice and the presentation of the news by a little fraternity having similar social and political views. I am against censorship in all forms.

But a broader spectrum of national opinion *should* be represented among the commentators of the network news. Men who can articulate other points of view *should* be brought forward.

And a high wall of separation *should* be raised between what is news and what is commentary.

And the American people *should* be made aware of the trend toward the monopolization of the great public information vehicles and the concentration of more and more power over public opinion in fewer and fewer hands.

Should a conglomerate be formed that tied together a shoe company with a shirt company, some voice will rise up righteously to say that this is a great danger to the economy; and that the conglomerate ought to be broken up.

But a single company, in the nation's capital, holds control of the largest newspaper in Washington, D.C., *and* one of the four major television stations, *and* an all-news radio station, *and* one of the three major national news magazines—all grinding out the same editorial line—and this is not a subject you have seen debated in the editorial pages of the *Washington Post* or the *New York Times*.

For the purpose of clarity, before my thoughts are obliterated in the smoking typewriters of my friends in Washington and New York, let me emphasize I am not recommending the dismemberment of the Washington Post company. I am merely pointing out that the public should be aware that these four powerful voices hearken to the same master.

I am merely raising these questions so that the American people will become aware of—and think of the implications of—that growing monopolization of the voices of public opinion on which we all depend—for our knowledge and for the basis of our views.

When the *Washington Times-Herald* died in the nation's capital, that was a political tragedy; and when the *New York Journal-American,* the *New York World Telegram and Sun,* the *New York Mirror,* and the *New York Herald-Tribune* all collapsed within this decade, that was a great, great political tragedy for the people of New York. The *New York Times* was a better newspaper when they were alive than it is now that they are gone.

What has happened in the city of New York has happened in other great cities in America.

Many, many strong independent voices have been stilled in this country in recent years. Lacking the vigor of competition, some of those that have survived have, let us face it, grown fat and irresponsible.

I offer an example. When three hundred Congressmen and fifty nine Senators signed a letter endorsing the President's policy in Vietnam it was news—big news. Even the *Washington Post* and the *Baltimore Sun*—scarcely house organs of the Nixon administration—placed it prominently on the front page.

Yet the next morning the *New York Times,* which considers itself America's paper of record, did not carry a word. Why?

If a theology student in Iowa should get up at a PTA luncheon in Sioux City and attack the President's Vietnam policy, my guess is that you would probably find it reported somewhere the next morning in the *New York Times*. But when three hundred Congressmen endorse the President's Vietnam policy, the next morning it is apparently not considered news fit to print.

Just this Tuesday, when the Pope, the Spiritual Leader of half a billion Roman Catholics applauded the President's efforts to end the war in Vietnam, and endorsed the way he was proceeding—that news was on page eleven of the *New York Times*. But the same day, a report about some burglars who broke into a souvenir shop at St. Peters and stole $9,000 worth of stamps and currency—that story made page three. How's that for news judgment?

A few weeks ago here in the South, I expressed my views about street and campus demonstrations. Here is how the *New York Times* responded:

> He [that's me] lambasted the nation's youth in sweeping and
> ignorant generalizations, when it is clear to all perceptive ob-
> servers that American youth today is far more imbued with ide-
> alism, a sense of service, and a deep humanitarianism than any
> generation in recent history, including particularly Mr. Agnew's
> [generation].

That seems a peculiar slur on a generation that brought America out of the Great Depression without resorting to the extremes of either fascism or Communism. That seems a strange thing to say about an entire generation that helped to provide greater material blessings and personal freedom—out of that Depression—for more people than any other nation in history. We are not finished the task by any means—but we are still on the job.

Just as millions of young Americans in this generation have shown valor and courage and heroism in fighting the longest and least popular war in our history—so it was the young men of my generation who went ashore at Normandy under Eisenhower and with McArthur into the Phillipines.

Yes, my generation, like the current generation, made its own share of great mistakes and blunders. Among other things, we put too much confidence in Stalin and not enough in Winston Churchill.

But whatever freedom exists today in Western Europe and Japan exists because hundreds of thousands of young men in my generation are lying in graves in North Africa and France and Korea and a score of islands in the Western Pacific.

This might not be considered enough of a "sense of service" or a "deep humanitarianism" for the *"perceptive critics"* who write editorials for the *New York Times,* but it's good enough for me; and I am content to let history be the judge. . . .

One magazine this week said that I will go down as the "great polarizer" in American politics. Yet, when that large group of young Americans marched up Pennsylvania and Constitution Avenues last week—they sought to polarize the American people against the President's policy in Vietnam. And that was their right.

And so it is my right, and my duty, to stand up and speak out for the values in which I believe. How can you ask the man in the street in this country to stand up for what he believes if his own elected leaders weasel and cringe.

It is not an easy thing to wake up each morning to learn that some prominent man or institution has implied that you are a bigot, a racist, or a fool.

I am not asking any immunity from criticism. That is the lot of the man in politics; we would have it no other way in this democratic society.

But my political and journalistic adversaries sometimes seem to be asking something more—that I circumscribe my rhetorical freedom, while they place no restrictions on theirs.

As President Kennedy once observed in a far more serious matter, that is like offering an apple for an orchard.

We do not accept those terms for continuing the national dialogue. The day when the network commentators and even gentlemen of the *New York Times* enjoyed a form of diplomatic immunity from comment and criticism of what they said—that day is over.

Just as a politician's words—wise and foolish—are dutifully recorded by the press and television to be thrown up to him at the appropriate time, so their words should likewise be recorded and likewise recalled.

When they go beyond fair comment and criticism they will be called upon to defend their statements and their positions just as we must defend ours. And when their criticism becomes excessive or unjust, we shall invite them down from their ivory towers to enjoy the rough and tumble of the public debate.

I do not seek to intimidate the press, the networks, or anyone else from speaking out. But the time for blind acceptance of their opinions is past. And the time for naive belief in their neutrality is gone.

But, as to the future, all of us could do worse than take as our own the motto of William Lloyd Garrison who said: "I am in earnest. I will not equivocate. I will not excuse. I will not retreat a single inch. And I will be heard."

MIDDLESEX CLUB
BOSTON, MASSACHUSETTS

MARCH 18, 1971

There is no doubt that the framers of our Constitution considered the vice presidency an office suitable for men of energy. Until the ratification of the twelfth Amendment in 1804, the defeated major presidential candidate was usually elected Vice President. This created some interesting stresses. Over the years, however, the vice presidency has lost its political punch and become the most placid and uncontroversial of political positions. Indeed, as presently structured, it may be compared to an adjustable easy chair. The occupant has his choice of either reclining sleepily or sitting up alertly. The posture adopted is inconsequential, because it is virtually certain that no one will notice which attitude has been selected.

Whatever his decision, however—whether he has dozed amiably or listened attentively—it has been traditional for a Vice President to be indulged by the intellectuals and opinion makers of his time with nothing harsher than a deprecating comment or a condescending joke.

In recent years, the rules have been amended to allow Vice Presidents to talk—so long as they are careful to say absolutely nothing. This privilege was heavily exercised and refined to a high degree during the last administration.

And in regard to vice presidential strictures, it seems appropriate to note—on the occasion of a Lincoln Day address before the oldest Republican organization in Massachusetts—that, following four years of lassitude as Abraham Lincoln's Vice President, Hannibal Hamlin suddenly found himself Collector for the Port of Boston.

In my own case, I found it an onerous choice between the ennui of easy chair existence and pointless verbosity. And so, quick Constitutional research revealing no authoritative reason why a Vice President is required to choose between catalepsy and garrulity, I forsook the comfortable code of many of my predecessors, abandoned the unwritten rules—and said something.

Well, in case you haven't heard, my unorthodoxy produced some rather sharp reverberations. It was as though an earthquake, registering eight on the Richter scale, had disturbed the foundations of the *New York Times,* or the funnel of a tornado had dipped into the editorial offices of *Time-Life.* Everywhere, big media referees were flinging down their handkerchiefs and calling foul. The *Washington Post* stepped off fifteen yards for un-Vice Presidential-like conduct. *Time* magazine waved me to the penalty box. And Eric Sevareid took two free throws at the line—both rolling around the rim and, as usual, dropping out.

Finally the tremors and tumult subsided. Whereupon my critics from all walks of life consulted among themselves and brought forth the strongest indictment they could muster.

"The Vice President," they intoned, "just doesn't seem to understand."

If true, the charge would be a serious enough reflection on the condition of the republic. But worse was yet to come. After my speech on the responsibilities of a free news media in a free society, and after the networks had been deluged with mail in support of my conclusions, a noted network newscaster enlarged the indictment by declaring that, not only the Vice President, but the American people as a whole simply don't understand.

Let me quote that spokesman directly.

"The public," said Walter Cronkite recently, "does not understand journalism. They"—that means you and me—"do not know how we work, they do not believe we can hold strong private thoughts and still be objective journalists."

And that's the way it was—or at least the way he saw it—in November 1970.

Mr. Cronkite has stated the case well. He has discerned and defined the scope of the widening credibility gap that exists between the national news media and the American people—a gap which has simply been reported, not created, by this nonunderstanding Vice President. By "national news media" I mean the powerful news outlet having not just a regional, but a national, impact.

Now, before I proceed further, let me pause to observe that, in all probability, my mere utterance of the words "national news media" has in the past few minutes again set the ideological Richter needles quivering all along the Manhattan-Washington fault line. For "national news media" is, after all, the forbidden phrase of modern American politics.

To be sure, such is the power of the national media today that of all our political, social, and economic institutions, they seem to be able to cloak themselves in a special immunity to criticism. By their lights, it appears, freedom of expression is fine so long as it stops before any question is raised or criticism lodged against national media policies and practices.

Nor is the national media's refusal to abide criticism reserved for utterances of a Vice President or, as I will momentarily point out, a Congressman, or a member of a presidential cabinet. Any citizen who has suffered the frustration of being rebuffed when calling or writing to complain about inaccurate or biased news reporting knows exactly what I mean.

Yet, any extremist who dignifies our adversaries and demeans our traditions is sought out and spotlighted for national attention. He is interviewed as though he were representative of a large following and is treated with the utmost deference as he unloads into millions of American living rooms his imprecations against society and disrespect for civilized law. Such attacks against American institutions are editorially lauded as healthy demonstrations of freedom of expression in a free society.

[At this point, the Vice President's remarks were interrupted momentarily by a young man who was escorted out by the authorities.]

And, incidentally, ladies and gentlemen, in a graphic and personal demonstration, did you notice where the lights and cameras just went?

Again, when the president of a prestigious university assaults our nation's judiciary by declaring that certain defendants cannot receive a fair trial in an American court, he is not charged with attempting to "intimidate the courts." On the contrary, he is praised by important segments of the national news media for contributing to what they term "the dialogue."

And, as I shall discuss in a few moments, when a major television network delivers a subtle but vicious broadside against the nation's defense establishment, accusing it of disseminating deceptive, self-serving propaganda, contrary to the country's interest, that, too, is considered a legitimate exercise of the right to free expression in the public interest.

But let no man be so bold as even to utter the words "national news media." For, as we are forewarned by the national media themselves, the merest mention of the phrase by a man in government somehow constitutes a form of "intimidation" so great as to pose a fundamental threat to the people's right to know.

And so tonight, in once again taking up matters involving an important segment of the national news media, I believe it only fitting to cite some authority within media ranks to reinforce my right to do so.

Hear now the words of Mr. Frank Stanton, president of the Columbia Broadcasting System.

"No American institution," Mr. Stanton has said, "including network news organizations, should be immune to public criticism or public discussion of its performance."

I wholeheartedly agree. Proceeding from this premise, I therefore intend to discuss the public's right to know more about the performance of Mr. Stanton's network news organization in two cases involving documentaries—instances wherein CBS itself has claimed an immunity from criticism ill-becoming one of the country's major institutional critics.

For those who would challenge a Vice President's right to discuss such matters, let me say this: I do so only to raise questions which, if answered, will shed light on an area of network news operations about which the public knows little and needs to know more. These questions do not originate with me, nor do they arise from any partisan political considerations. Others before me, including the Federal Communications Commission, a special subcommittee of the Congress and a former Democratic cabinet member, have asked Mr. Stanton similar questions, to no avail.

However, considering the serious charges leveled recently by the CBS television news organization against the public affairs activities of the Department of Defense, the matter of the network's own record in the field of documentary making can no longer be brushed under the rug of national media indifference.

Little less than a month ago, on the evening of February 23, 1971, CBS television broadcast a one-hour documentary entitled *The Selling of the Pentagon.* The substance of this documentary was that the Department of Defense is subjecting the American people to, I quote, "a propaganda barrage . . . the creation of a runaway bureaucracy that frustrates attempts to control it."

"Nothing is more essential to a democracy," read the CBS script, "than the free flow of information. Misinformation, distortion, and propaganda all interrupt that flow."

No one can disagree with the later statement. But just as he who enters a court of equity should come with clean hands, the news organization that makes such charges should itself be free of any taint of misinformation, distortion, and propaganda in its own operations. In this regard, it is the CBS television network, not the Department of Defense, that leaves much to be desired in terms of "the free flow of information."

Let me be specific. What I cite here is not simply the opinion of a single public official, but conclusions drawn by responsible investigative agencies in the government and the Congress. These conclusions are contained in reports, which in themselves would have made excellent documentary exposés, save for the fact that the national news media have given them scant attention. They concern the production and editing techniques employed by CBS personnel in the making of the documentaries *Hunger in America* and *Project Nassau.*

Many in this audience may have been watching on the evening of May 21, 1968, when the attention of millions of Americans tuned to CBS television was drawn to the onscreen image of an infant receiving emergency treatment while a narrator's offscreen voice said:

> Hunger is easy to recognize when it looks like this. This baby is dying of starvation. He was an American. Now he is dead.

This was compelling film footage and narration designed to awaken the public conscience to a serious social problem. The only thing wrong with it was that it was untrue—but wait, let the official Federal Communications Commission report tell the story. I quote from the official report:

> Our post-broadcast investigation revealed that the infant who was filmed by CBS in the nursery, and who was shown in the relevant segment of the *Hunger in America* program . . . was born prematurely . . . the previous day. . . . The infant died on October 29, 1967, the death certificate shows the cause of death as "Immediate cause: Septicemia. Due to: Meningitis and Peritonitis. Due to: Prematurity." There is no evidence to show that either the mother or father was suffering from malnutrition.

Thus, although the dramatic footage which opened the documentary *Hunger in America* may have served the network's purpose of whetting viewer interest, the baby shown "dying of starvation" in fact died of other causes.

Nor, as investigation of the production revealed, was this distortion only an incidental aspect in the overall production of *Hunger in America.* Evidence was submitted that CBS personnel had, in the words of the report, "paid participants on the program to appear before its cameras and perform as per their instructions"; that the CBS crew "requested that the doors of the commodity distribution office be closed to allow a line of people to form"; that a physician was asked to make "more dramatic statements" and when he refused, the segment of the program featuring his more balanced view of the problem of malnutrition in the area was edited out for being "too technical."

In a letter to Mr. Stanton, then Secretary of Agriculture Orville Freeman cited numerous other instances of factual misrepresentation and distortion contained in the documentary. He asked for equal time to present a Department of Agriculture response to the network program. The network denied his request.

Now, having myself gained some experience in what to expect by way of negative network response to public criticism, I can fairly predict what Mr. Stanton and other CBS spokesmen are likely to say tomorrow morning concerning my recital of the case history on *Hunger in America.* They will ask why this matter should be brought up again at this time.

My answer is that I believe it both timely and in the public interest to point out that the same CBS employee who wrote the script to the 1968 documentary *Hunger in America* wrote the script to the 1971 documentary *The Selling of the Pentagon.*

A second and even more startling case history of a documentary-in-the-making involves the participation of CBS personnel in an aborted effort to film a 1966 invasion of Haiti. The network's role in this effort, called *Project Nassau,* was investigated last year by the Special Subcommittee on Investigations of the House Commerce Committee. Here again, let the report of the investigative body tell the story. I quote:

> The activities preparatory to *Project Nassau* involved more than the filming of sham events, manipulation of sound tracks, and the like. Underlying the whole activity was the earnest endeavor by a group of dangerous individuals to subvert the laws of the United States. Had it been successful, the conspiracy would have produced a crisis for American foreign policy in the sensitive Caribbean area. Six men have now been convicted for their part in this conspiracy.

Continuing with the House Subcommittee report on CBS' participation in *Project Nassau:*

> CBS funds were provided for the leasing of a 67-foot schooner which was to be utilized by the invasion force; expenses were reimbursed for the transportation of weapons which were to be subsequently used by the conspirators; various payments were made to . . . the leader of the invasion conspiracy, with full knowledge of his identity and his criminal intentions. If these acts did not actually involve the network in the conspiracy to violate the U.S. Neutrality Act, they came dangerously close to doing so.

They're not my words, ladies and gentlemen. They're the words of the man of the House of Representatives charged with this investigation.

Concerning such illegal activities, the House subcommittee, in the course of its investigation, made public a CBS policy memorandum which, to quote from the views of a bipartisan group of subcommittee members, "represents a level of irresponsibility which should no longer be tolerated if the public interest is to be served."

Let me read here from that CBS policy statement to its employees and I quote: "CBS personnel will not knowingly engage in criminal activity in gathering and reporting news, nor will they encourage or induce any person to commit a crime."

Now keep in mind, I am directly quoting the network's policy statement to its employees. *"Obviously, there may be exceptions which ought to be made on an ad hoc basis even to so absolute a rule."*

Ladies and gentlemen, exceptions to the prohibition of CBS' employees in engaging in criminal activities, or encouraging or inducing someone to commit a crime. That's unbelievable, but that's what this memorandum says. Small wonder that the House subcommittee termed the results of its *Project Nassau* investigation "disquieting." The subcommittee said, quote:

> To the average viewer, unsophisticated in the intricacies of television production, a network news documentary typically represents a scrupulously objective reporting of actual events shown as they actually transpired. If *Project Nassau* is any indication, this is not always true. During the preparation of this news documentary, CBS employees and consultants intermingled and interacted with personages actively engaged in breaking the law. Large sums of money were made available to these individuals with no safeguards as to the manner in which these funds would be put to use. Events were set up and staged solely for the purpose of being filmed by the CBS cameras. . . .
>
> A disturbing conclusion after the inquiry to date with respect to *Project Nassau* is that the CBS News organization, having become elated at the prospect of a sensational news first—a complete documentary of the forcible overthrow of a foreign government—proceeded in a reckless attempt to capture the hoped-for-film, and that it did so with no great regard for either accuracy or legality.

Here, again, this investigation of the making of a CBS documentary bears on the network's more recent production, *The Selling of the Pentagon.* For the executive producer of the aborted documentary *Project Nassau* also served as executive producer of *The Selling of the Pentagon*—a documentary, keep in mind, that sought to indict the Department of Defense for "misinformation, distortion," and the alleged staging of events.

But disquieting as are the results of these investigations by the FCC and the House subcommittee, there is an even more disturbing note to be added here concerning media treatment of the reports themselves.

Who can doubt that had the evidence uncovered and the conclusions drawn by these investigative bodies related to any other industry or institution they would long ago have become, to coin a phrase, household words? The national news media would have made them so—just as CBS even now seeks to exploit its purported "findings" regarding the Pentagon.

Yet, when the industry and institution involved is itself a part of the national news media, a strange silence and rare restraint inhibits the people's right to know. So powerful is this inhibition that neither a cabinet member, nor an executive agency, nor a Congressional committee was effective in bringing to public attention the serious matters to which I have addressed these remarks. And I have grave doubts about how much of my criticism tonight will be carried in the national media.

My purpose here, however, has not been to pillory or "intimidate" a network or any segment of the national news media in its effort to enhance the people's right to know. Rather it is, once again, to point out to those in positions of power and responsibility that this right to know belongs to the people. It does not belong to the national networks or any other agency, public or private. It belongs *to the people themselves,* and they are entitled to a fair and full accounting of the truth, and nothing but the truth, by those who exercise great influence with their consent.

The House subcommittee concluded:

> We are living through dangerous times. In these days it does not seem too strong a statement to say that the survival of the American society may depend upon the political and social judgments made during the next few years by the American electorate. Sound judgment presupposes valid information. The American public looks in great measure to the electronic news media to provide that information.

Let the people's representatives—not only in their government but in their national news media—also look, listen, and take heed.

A TEST OF THE NEWS

WALTER LIPPMANN AND CHARLES MERZ

The New Republic, August 4, 1920

———

———

———

This article is a stunning, unforgiving indictment of how the country's greatest newspaper, the *New York Times,* short-changed the public in its systematically biased and incomplete reporting of the Russian Revolution. When they wrote this, Walter Lippmann was thirty years old and Charles Merz was twenty-seven. But they had already established themselves as intellectual journalists at the *New Republic* and other publications. Their careers would continue to flourish. In a career that spanned two World Wars, the Korean War, and the Vietnam War, Lippmann became the preeminent columnist in the country for almost half a century. Merz rose to associate editor of the *New York World* before moving to the *Times,* where he became editor of the editorial page.

In 1920, they wrote this blunt analysis of how the *Times* botched its coverage of the Russian Revolution. They studied the *Times* and found a pattern of misstatements and misinformation. In uncovering this embarrassing episode in the history of the *Times,* they created a model of uncompromising press criticism. They decoded the news brilliantly. Their textual analysis covered a three-year period that began in 1917 with the overthrow of Czar Nicholas II. The newspaper cited events that did not happen and atrocities that never took place. On nearly one hundred occasions, the *Times* erroneously reported that the Bolshevik regime was about to collapse.

Lippmann and Merz stressed that the future of democracy rested on the delivery by the press of truthful and accurate information. But in this instance—either out of sloppiness, laziness, bias, or excessive reliance on official sources—the *Times,* in the view of Lippmann and Merz, denied the news to the public. When clear-headed reporting was especially crucial, Lippmann and Merz wrote, the contribution of those articles to public knowledge was about as useful as "that of an astrologer or an alchemist."

What follows is a long excerpt from a near book-length article.

A TEST OF THE NEWS

INTRODUCTION

It is admitted that a sound public opinion cannot exist without access to the news. There is today a widespread and a growing doubt whether there exists such an access to the news about contentious affairs. This doubt ranges from accusations of unconscious bias to downright charges of corruption, from the belief that the news is colored to the belief that the news is poisoned. On so grave a matter evidence is needed. The study which follows is a piece of evidence. It deals with the reporting of one great event in the recent history of the world. That event is the Russian Revolution from March 1917 to March 1920. The analysis covers thirty-six months and over one thousand issues of a daily newspaper. The authors have examined all news items about Russia in that period in the newspaper selected; between three and four thousand items were noted. Little attention was paid to editorials.

The *New York Times* was selected as the medium through which to study the news, first because the *Times*, as great as any newspaper in America, and far greater than the majority, has the means for securing news, second, because the makeup of the news in the *Times* is technically admirable, third, because the *Times* index is an enormous convenience to any student of contemporary history, fourth, because the bound volumes are easily accessible, and fifth, because the *Times* is one of the really great newspapers of the world.

The Russian Revolution was selected as the topic, because of its intrinsic importance, and because it has aroused the kind of passion which tests most seriously the objectivity of reporting.

The first question, naturally, is what constitutes the test of accuracy? A definitive account of the Russian Revolution does not exist. In all probability it will never exist in this generation. After a hundred years there is no undisputed history of the French Revolution, and scholars are still debating the causes and the meaning of the revolt of the Gracchi, the fall of Rome, and even of the American Revolution and the American Civil War. A final history of the Russian Revolution may never be written, and even a tolerably settled account is not conceivable for a long time. It would be footless therefore to propose an absolute measurement of news gathered amid such excitement and confusion. It would be equally vain to accept the account of one set of witnesses in preference to any other set.

The "whole truth" about Russia is not to be had, and consequently no attempt is made by the authors to contrast the news accounts with any other account which pretends to be the "real truth" or the "true truth." A totally different standard of measurement is used here. The reliability of the news is tested in this study by a few definite and decisive happenings about which there is no dispute. Thus there is no dispute that the offensive of the Russian army under Kerensky in July 1917 was a disastrous failure; no dispute that the Provisional Government was overthrown by the Soviet power in November 1917; no dispute that the Soviets made a separate peace with Germany at Brest-Litovsk in March 1918; no dispute that the campaigns of Kolchak, Denikin, and Yudenitch were a failure; no dispute that the Soviet Government was still in existence in March 1920. Against such salient facts the daily reports about Russia in this period are measured. The only question asked is whether the reader of the news was given a picture of various phases of the revolution which survived the test of events, or whether he was misled into believing that the outcome of events would be radically different from the actual outcome.

The question of atrocities and of the merits or demerits of the Soviets is not raised. Thus, for example, there was a Red Terror officially proclaimed by the Soviet Government in the summer of 1918; and apart from the official terror, excesses occurred in many parts of Russia. No attempt is made here to sift the truth of the accounts, to determine whether there were exaggerations, or how far the White Terror equalled the Red Terror. The attempt is not made because no dependable account is available with which to measure the news reports. There was a round measure of truth in the report of terror and atrocity. For analogous reasons no discussion of the virtues and defects of the Soviet system is attempted. There are no authoritative reports. Able and disinterested observers furnish contradictory evidence out of which no objective criteria emerge. Under these circumstances an accurate report of the Soviet Government and the Terror is no doubt more than could have been expected from a newspaper.

But what might more reasonably have been expected, and what was more immediately important for Americans, was to know in the summer of 1917 whether the Russian army would fight, and whether the Provisional Government would survive. It was important to know in the winter of 1917–18 whether the Soviet Government would make a separate peace. It was important to know in the spring and early summer of 1918 whether the Russian people would support allied intervention. It was important to know whether the Soviet Government was bound to collapse soon under

Allied pressure. It was important to know whether the White Generals—
Kolchak, Denikin, Yudenitch—were, or were not, winning their campaigns. It was important to know whether Poland was defending herself
or invading Russia. It was important to know the disposition of the Soviet
Government toward peace at the time of the peace conference. It was
important to know whether there was a Red Peril before Allied troops
entered Russia, or whether that peril dates from the German surrender.
It was important to know whether the Red regime was tottering to its fall
or marching to the military conquest of the world. On each one of these
questions depended some aspect of policy involving lives, trade, finance,
and national honor. It is important now to know what was the net effect
of the news on these points.

For the reader's convenience certain tentative conclusions from the evidence are stated here:

1. From the overthrow of the Czar to the failure of the Galician offensive in July 1917.

> The difficulties in Russia, and especially in the Russian army,
> are not concealed from the attentive reader, but the dominant
> tendency of the captions and the emphasis is so optimistic as
> to be misleading.

2. From the military disaster in July 1917 to the Bolshevik revolution
of November.

> The difficulties of the regime play a bigger part in the news,
> but a misleading optimism still continues. In this period, the
> tendency to seek a solution through a dictator-savior appears
> in the mistaken hope placed upon the Kornilov adventure, a
> hope quickly falsified by his collapse. It may fairly be said that
> the growth of the Bolshevik power from July to November must
> have been seriously underestimated in view of the success of
> the November coup.

3. From the Bolshevik revolution to the ratification of the treaty of Brest-
Litovsk.

> This period is on the whole the best in the three years. Dif-
> ferent points of view are given, and the emphasis is generally
> neutral. After the recovery from the shock of the second rev-
> olution, the reports are inspired by an eager curiosity about the
> diplomatic battle between the Bolsheviks and the enemy. At
> the height of this diplomatic battle the news is handled in a

rather uncritically pro-Bolshevik fashion, as a result of the optimistic assumption that the Soviets would refuse to make peace
with Germany.

4. From the ratification at Brest-Litovsk, which coincided approximately with the Great German offensive in March 1918, to the decision
for Allied intervention in August 1918.

> Under the stress of disappointment and danger the tone and
> quality of the news change radically. Organized propaganda for
> intervention penetrates the news. This propaganda has two
> phases. There is a short and intense period in late March and
> early April, which stops rather suddenly with the announce-
> ment that the President has decided against intervention. There
> is a prolonged and intense period beginning about May which
> culminates in the American approval of intervention.

5. The months immediately following the signing of the armistice.

> The Red Peril, which had hitherto played only an insignifi-
> cant role, now takes precedence in the news from Russia and
> serves as a new motive for Allied intervention.

6. The Spring, Summer, and Autumn of 1919.

> Kolchak, Denikin, and Yudenitch are heralded as dictator-
> saviors of Russia; for their campaigns, extravagant claims are
> made when they are moving forward; in retreat there is a steady
> assurance that a better turn is coming. Meantime the world is
> warned against a Russian invasion of Poland—though Polish
> troops are as a matter of fact deep in Russian soil.

7. The Winter of 1919–20 and the Spring of 1920.

> Once more, with the failure of the White Armies, the Red
> Peril reappears.

The news as a whole is dominated by the hopes of the men who composed the news organization. They began as passionate partisans in a great
war in which their own country's future was at stake. Until the armistice
they were interested in defeating Germany. They hoped until they could
hope no longer that Russia would fight. When they saw she could not fight,
they worked for intervention as part of the war against Germany. When
the war with Germany was over, the intervention still existed. They found
reasons then for continuing the intervention. The German Peril as the rea-

son for intervention ceased with the armistice; the Red Peril almost immediately afterwards supplanted it. The Red Peril in turn gave place to rejoicing over the hopes of the White Generals. When these hopes died, the Red Peril reappeared. In the large, the news about Russia is a case of seeing not what was, but what men wished to see.

This deduction is more important, in the opinion of the authors, than any other. The chief censor and the chief propagandist were hope and fear in the minds of reporters and editors. They wanted to win the war; they wanted to ward off bolshevism. These subjective obstacles to the free pursuit of facts account for the tame submission of enterprising men to the objective censorship and propaganda under which they did their work. For subjective reasons they accepted and believed most of what they were told by the State Department, the so-called Russian Embassy in Washington, the Russian Information Bureau in New York, the Russian Committee in Paris, and the agents and adherents of the old regime all over Europe. For the same reason they endured the attention of officials at crucial points like Helsingfors, Omsk, Vladivostok, Stockholm, Copenhagen, London, and Paris. For the same reason they accepted reports of governmentally controlled news services abroad, and of correspondents who were unduly intimate with the various secret services and with members of the old Russian nobility.

From the point of view of professional journalism the reporting of the Russian Revolution is nothing short of a disaster. On the essential questions the net effect was almost always misleading, and misleading news is worse than none at all. Yet on the face of the evidence there is no reason to charge a conspiracy by Americans. They can fairly be charged with boundless credulity, and an untiring readiness to be gulled, and on many occasions with a downright lack of common sense.

Whether they were "giving the public what it wants" or creating a public that took what it got, is beside the point. They were performing the supreme duty in a democracy of supplying the information on which public opinion feeds, and they were derelict in that duty. Their motives may have been excellent. They wanted to win the war; they wanted to save the world. They were nervously excited by exciting events. They were baffled by the complexity of affairs, and the obstacles created by war. But whatever the excuses, the apologies, and the extenuation, the fact remains that a great people in a supreme crisis could not secure the minimum of necessary information on a supremely important event. When that truth has burned itself into men's consciousness, they will examine the news in regard to other events, and begin a searching inquiry into the sources of public opinion. That is the indispensable preliminary to a fundamental task of the Twentieth Century: the insurance to a free people of such a supply of news that a free government can be successfully administered.

In devoting so long a study to the work of a single newspaper the authors have proceeded without animus against the *Times,* and with much admiration for its many excellent qualities. They trust that the readers of this report, among them the proprietors and editors of the *"Times,"* will not regard it as an "exposure" of the *Times,* but as a piece of inductive evidence on the problem of the news. The authors do not wish to imply, because honestly they do not believe, that the less conservative press is necessarily more reliable. As editors of a liberal weekly journal they know from experience that there are large glass windows in their own house, and they are keenly aware of the fact that reliability is harder to attain in the haste of a daily newspaper than in the greater deliberation of a periodical. If, consequently, nothing were at stake but the question of praise and blame, if nothing were to be accomplished beyond a score in the duel between liberal and conservative, then this report would not have been made. Something much greater is at issue, for the reliability of the news is the premise on which democracy proceeds. A great newspaper is a public service institution. It occupies a position in public life fully as important as the school system or the church or the organs of government. It is entitled to criticism, and subject to criticism, as they are. The value of such criticism is directly proportionate to the steadiness with which the ultimate end of a better news system is clearly and dispassionately kept in mind.

I. TO THE JULY OFFENSIVE

The Russian Revolution occurred during the war with Germany. It was an event that affected immediately and directly the lives, the fortunes, and the dearest hopes of all nations engaged in the war. The Revolution began during the second week of March in the year 1917. This date is highly significant. It is about six weeks after the German Government had announced unlimited submarine war, and six weeks after the rupture of diplomatic relations by America. The Allies were confronted at the same moment by the uncertainty as to what Russia and what the United States would do. The United States was in the act of making up its mind to begin to fight. The question which dominated all the news out of Russia was whether the Russians would continue to fight.

Thus, the circumstances of the Revolution were not such as to invite impartial inquiry. What the reader of newspapers was chiefly concerned about was the fighting power of Russia on the great eastern front. He could hardly have expected a current history of so vast a revolution. He did expect, and he had reason to demand, reliable reports about the morals and strength of Russia's armies. For on those reports he had to arrive at judgments of supreme practical importance.

The reliability of the news for the first four months can fairly be measured by this one concrete test: did it give a tolerably true account of Russia's military strength? Did the news lead to correct or incorrect expectations?

The actual military power of Russia was tested against Germany just once. In July 1917, about three and a half months after the Revolution the army attacked on a wide front in Galicia. After a small initial success the offensive collapsed, the Germans attacked and pierced the Russian front; there were mutinies followed by a rout. The official Russian communiqué (per British Admiralty per Wireless press, Petrograd, July 22) said of the disaster: "This is the result of the instability of our troops, disregard for military orders, and the propaganda of the Maximalists." What had the news for the weeks from March to July been?

TWO VIEWS OF RUSSIA'S POWER

The *Times* of March 16 published the report of the successful revolution. Together with admirably full accounts of events in Petrograd, there began a series of semi-editorial news dispatches. Thus (special cable to the *New York Times,* London, March 16):

> As the situation is explained to the New York Times correspondent, the revolution *simply means* (italics ours) that German sympathizers within the Russian Government have been overthrown, and that no chance remains for a separate peace being secretly arranged with Germany. This, it is felt, is the real basis of the revolution.

Such was the official public British theory. In the same issue Mr. Bonar Law (unidentified dispatch from London, March 15) was quoted as saying that the revolution was due to Russia's purpose to fight the war out. This was, of course, not a statement of fact, but the expression of a wish.

This wish was father to much of the news which followed for several months. Concurrently, there were, however, other interpretations of the Revolution. On March 16 the *Times* published, of course obscurely, an interview with Leon Trotzky:

CALLS PEOPLE WAR WEARY
But Leo Trotzky Says They Do Not Want Separate Peace

Leo Trotzky, a Russian revolutionist now in America, said last night in the office of the *Novy Mir* . . . that the committee which has taken the place of the deposed Ministry in Russia did not represent the interests or the aims of the revolutionists, that it would probably be short lived, and step down in favor of men who would be more sure to carry forward the democratization of Russia . . . . That the cause of the revolution was the unrest of the mass of the people who were tired of war and that the real object . . . was to end war . . . throughout Europe. They do not favor Germany . . . but wish to stop fighting.

Two days later, issue of March 18 (Berlin, March 17, by wireless to the *New York Times* via Tuckerton, N. J.) the *Times* printed a report saying that the general opinion in Berlin was that the new government could not last long and that the lower classes were wishing for peace at any price.

There were thus two alternative theories: one the official Allied theory that Russia would fight; the other, the theory of an unknown Russian revolutionist in New York and of "general opinion in Berlin" that Russia would not fight. The bulk of the news which followed appeared to sustain the official theory.

Three and a half months elapsed to the offensive of July. The reader had by that time perused 107 issues of his paper, practically all of them containing news of the Russian Revolution. He had received hints of profound economic disorder, of demoralization in the army, and of confused dissatisfaction with the Allies. He was in position to guess that the striking power of Russia was not great, if he read all the obscurely placed dispatches, read between the lines of the other dispatches, and sternly declined to let his hopes govern his judgment.

But if he read casually, and chiefly the captions and emphasized news, the impression of hopefulness, or at least of whistling to keep up hope, would have been strong. Captions or prominent news on the following days all of them stated or implied a Russian will to fight.

MARCH	16^2, 19, 20, 21, 23, 27, 28, 29, 30^2—9 issues, 11 items.
APRIL	2, 10, 12, 14, 18, 19^2, 20^2, 21, 22, 24^2, 28, 29, 30^2—13 issues, 17 items.
MAY	3, 4, 7, 9, 12, 13, 17, 18, 19, 20, 21^2, 23, 25, 28^2, 29^2, 31—16 issues, 19 items.

JUNE   2, 3, 4^2, 5, 6^2, 7, 8^2, 9, 11, 13^2, 15, 16, 17, 18^2, 19, 21^2,
          22, 23, 24^2, 25^2, 27^2, 28^2, 29, 30^2—24 issues, 35 items.
Total 62 issues, 82 items.

Thus oftener than every other day for the whole period the reader was
assured that Russia would fight or that the Russian army was strong, or
that the difficulties were being surmounted. Ordeal by battle proved all
these assurances to be false.

Was a darker picture ever suggested? It was. In 49 different issues of
the *Times* were perhaps 66 items of pessimistic character. Numerically this
seems to strike a tolerably even balance:

Optimistic: 62 issues, 82 items
Pessimistic: 49 issues, 66 items

REPUTABLE AND DISREPUTABLE

But closer examination of what has been included under "optimistic" and
"pessimistic" reveals a far greater discrepancy than the figures show. Take
for example the first day's news (March 16). We have called optimistic and
unidentified London dispatch (March 15) quoting Mr. Bonar Law that the
revolution was due to Russia's purpose to fight the war out; we have also
called optimistic the dispatch from London (March 16) printed on the first
page saying:

> As the situation is explained to the *New York Times* cor-
> respondent, the revolution simply means that German sympa-
> thizers within the Russian-Government have been overthrown.

Compare these authoritative pronouncements with the "pessimistic" item
printed at the foot of the fifth column of the fourth page quoting Leo (sic)
Trotzky from his New York office as saying that the people wished to stop
fighting. Trotzky happened to be right, Mr. Bonar Law and the people
who interpreted the Revolution in London to the *Times* correspondent happened to be dead wrong. But which interpretation was emphasized, and
given the authority of the editors? The official and the optimistic, of course,
against the obscure and the unpleasant. The unsatisfactory view was not
suppressed, but it was ignored or played down. This is characteristic of
the news of the period we are considering. The values placed upon news
items were wrong, wrong by the ultimate test of battle.

It is easy to see how this came about. There was an initial desire, shared
by the editors and readers of the *Times,* to have Russia fight, to secure
the military assistance of Russia without opening up contentious questions

of war aims, to smother pacifist agitation. Conflicting estimates of Russian strength and weakness came to the *Times* office. One series was optimistic. The other pessimistic. The optimistic series had the right of way.

Then, too, the sources of the optimistic reports were such as to commend themselves more readily to the credulity of men who have high respect for prestige. Out of 82 optimistic items approximately 49 emanated directly from official sources including the Provisional Government, the American State Department, Ambassador Francis, the Root mission, etc. The remaining 33 are from sources including 4 Reuters, 1 Harold Williams, 2 Herbert Bailey, 1 Special *New York Times,* 1 London *Times,* 5 London *Daily Chronicle,* 13 unidentified, the rest scattering.

When there were at least 49 official assurances and thirty odd more from sources of recognized authority in a period of 107 days it is not surprising that the net tone of the news about Russia was optimistic. It is even less surprising when the character of the 66 pessimistic items is examined. If we add together the distinctly unpopular and therefore incredible sources, that is the German, the Bolshevik, the Council of Workmen's and Soldiers' Deputies, and the items tagged and peppered with epithets, the total is 36.

Thus out of 82 optimistic items, 49 are from friendly official sources, and the rest from respectable ones; out of 66 pessimistic items 36 are distinctly disreputable, and of the thirty remaining practically none contains more than a fragmentary hint of the real difficulty in Russia as later revealed by the collapse of the July offensive, the first Bolshevik rebellion, and the ultimate fall of the Provisional Government.

It remains to be noted however that the optimistic items carried their own antidote to the sophisticated reader. The very fact that it was necessary to proclaim the solidarity and strength of Russia every other day was a suspicious fact. Reiteration emphasized doubt, and trained readers were enabled to reach conclusions quite opposite from those insisted upon in the general intent of the news. But what chance had they of persuading the casual reader that Russian affairs required his earnest attention. Was the casual reader, absorbed in our own war activities, not told about every other day that he could afford to be complacent?

II. THE PRELUDE TO BOLSHEVISM
MISLEADING OPTIMISM

The military weakness of Russia was clear to all observers on the spot after what Kerensky calls the "Tranopol disgrace" of July 19. The condition of the army was explained by the Russian official communiqué (British Admiralty per Wireless press, Petrograd, July 22); the condition behind the lines was indicated by the abortive Bolshevik rebellion of July 16–18. The most obvious facts no longer justified the complacency which had dominated the news. "Something" had to be done by somebody.

There were, roughly speaking, three parties contending for power; the Left led by the Bolsheviks, the Center led by Kerensky, and the Right led by someone in the role of a Dictator-Savior. The Bolshevik uprising of July was suppressed by Kerensky's government. For the next two months the contenders, on the surface at least, are the Right and the Center parties. The Kornilov rebellion in September was the first of the many efforts of the Right to establish a Dictator-Savior. The rebellion was easily put down by Kerensky. The government had thus survived first an attack from the Left, and then an attack from the Right. But within a few days of the supression of Kornilov there is unmistakable evidence of the rise of the third power—that of the Bolsheviki. On September 29, six days after the General's capitulation, the Petrograd Soviet passed from Menshevik and Social Revolutionary control into Bolshevik hands, and the next day (September 20) the Moscow Soviet for the first time refused a vote of confidence in the government of Kerensky. In five weeks that government had fallen.

Every shred of justification for complacent optimism had ceased by July 19. The correspondents in Russia abandoned it. Mr. Harold Williams, in the *Times* of July 28, speaks of "this hour of national disgrace . . . how can Russia be saved . . . the shameful collapse of (the) armies." But though the *Times* of July 23 had printed a three column head saying:

MUTINY ON RUSSIAN FRONT SPREADS
Whole Line Giving Way

Nevertheless the *Times* of July 28 carried the following dispatch from Washington: "The State Department has advices by cable that the defeat of the Russian Army on the Galician front has had a wholesome effect in Petrograd."

Meantime the headlines showed a continued optimism, as the following samples show:

JULY 30	ARMY NOW RECOVERING
JULY 31	RUSSIAN ARMIES NOW STRIKING BACK
AUG. 1	RUSSIANS THROW GERMANS BACK
AUG. 2	RUSSIANS ATTACK ON GALICIAN FRONT

AUG. 4	MINIMIZES CABINET CRISIS
AUG. 5	ROOT HAS FAITH RUSSIA WILL STAND
AUG. 7	TO FIGHT ON, SAYS FRANCIS NO EVIDENCE THAT RUSSIA INTENDS TO QUIT
AUG. 8	SEES RUSSIA SOON AS STRONG AS EVER
AUG. 9	WE CAN DEPEND ON RUSSIA WITH AID FROM US, ROOT SAYS
AUG. 9	RUSSIANS AGAIN ATTACK IN GALICIA
AUG. 9	KORNILOV FIRM FOR WAR
AUG. 14	RUSSO-RUMANIANS TAKE 1,100 TEUTONS
AUG. 15	PRESS TEUTONS BACK ON RUMANIAN FRONT
AUG. 15	TELLS KING GEORGE RUSSIA WILL FIGHT ON
AUG. 18	RUSSO-RUMANIANS REPEL ALL ATTACKS
AUG. 20	RUSSIANS REPULSE ATTACKS EVERYWHERE

Thus from the military rout in July to the verge of the Kornilov conspiracy, on the average once every other day, a certain show of optimism is made. It is derived from official reports of minor engagements, from advices to the State Department, and from the Russian Government. The persistent will to believe is illustrated by the *Times* of July 24. The captions read as follows:

RUSSIANS TAKE 1,000 PRISONERS

BREAK GERMAN LINE IN VILNA REGION
DESPITE DEFECTION OF SOME REGIMENTS

BUT COLLAPSE IN GALICIA

WHOLE FRONT DOWN TO THE CARPATHIANS
IN RETREAT—TARNOPOL GONE

Is it not just to say that the newspaper is a misleading optimist which regards the capture of 1,000 prisoners as of greater significance than the collapse of the whole front down to the Carpathians? It was not always possible, of course, to extract hope out of a desperate situation, but on fourteen days out of twenty-two the captions writer succeeds. On the following dates he announces reverses: July 20, 21, 23, 26, 27, 28, 31, Aug.

2, 17, 23, 24. No doubt there were minor successes, but the net disaster was indisputable. Therefore the interlarding of the news of big defeats with little resistances and verbal optimism must be described as confusing in its total effect. The presentation of news values is eccentric, and distorts the main picture.

THE QUEST OF A DICTATOR-SAVIOR

But parallel with all this runs a great theme of the Russian news: the theme of the Dictator-Savior and the strong man. This quest appears many times throughout the three years of the revolution dealt with in this study. It culminates as all the world knows, in Kolchak, Denikin, and Yudenitch, but it emerges long before. The first choice of the correspondents, curiously enough, is Kerensky himself. The faith in Kerensky is short-lived, but strenuous while it lasts:

JULY 24   KERENSKY MADE DICTATOR OF RUSSIA
               PEASANTS YEARN FOR NEW MONARCHY

> Kerensky, who possesses all Peter the Great's energy and twice his wisdom, is the national hero . . . . It [a new Czardom] would give the imaginative peasants some one in whom to place that loyalty which they could never accord with the same enthusiasm to a blackcoated President. (Herbert Bailey, Special to the *New York Times*, Petrograd, July 21)

That Kerensky did not altogether disdain the role of strong man is indicated by his interview to the Associated Press (issue of July 25) which the *Times* heads:

KERENSKY'S RULE TO BE MERCILESS
WILL BEAT RUSSIA INTO UNITY WITH BLOOD AND
IRON, IF NECESSARY, HE SAYS

Mr. Harold Williams has at this time begun to cast about for a savior. Being better informed than Mr. Bailey, he has never taken very seriously the dictatorship of Kerensky. In the *Times* of July 26, he notes that the Council of Workmen's and Soldiers' Delegates attached a string to Kerensky's unlimited power by demanding an accounting not less than twice a week. And two days later, he is aware of "the brave commander on the southwestern front, General Kornilov." Other correspondents present other guesses as to where the saving force is to be found. Thus in the issue of August 31, the *London Times* correspondent (Moscow, August 28), makes what appears to be the first sketch of the geographical area on which the counter-revolutions of Kolchak and Denikin were later organized. Over a year before the event he discovers that

> The Knights of St. George, representing 80,000,000 acres, (sic) have combined in military leagues . . . here is a *solid* (italics ours) block far exceeding in size and population the combined strength of the Central Empires. From Lake Bikal to the Dniester, from the Don to the Persian border, loyal sons of Russia are ready to rise against the forces of disintegration and defeat.

The *Times* heads this dispatch:

GREAT NEW POWER RISING IN RUSSIA

No less interesting and prophetic is the appearance of the first argument for external military intervention in Russia. While Messrs. Bailey and Williams and the London *Times* correspondent are looking for loyal Russians, the French authorities are thinking of the Japanese army. The *Times* of August 23, in a box on the first page, prints an unidentified dispatch from Paris, August 22, which says:

> The *Figaro* today asks if the moment has not arrived for Japan to take further steps in the war. . . .
> The *Petit Journal, in an editorial along the same lines* . . . adds that never will the Japanese troops be more needed on the Russian front than they are today. (Italics ours.)

The reader will note the common inspiration of these French newspapers and the synchronism of the publication with the bad news of the German offensive against Riga. With such estimates of the Russian problem in their minds, and with such prepossessions, it is not surprising that the newsmen were completely taken in by the Kornilov fiasco.

THE KORNILOV REBELLION

The historical evidence about the affair is still a matter of hot dispute, and there is much mystery about the role of the various personalities who figured prominently in the intrigue. This aspect of the affair the correspondents did not report at length, and could not have been expected to report. But the facts which concerned the American reader were simple. Did Kornilov represent the power of Russia? Were those who gathered about him the effective substance of the nation? Was he, in brief, the real thing, or a flash in the pan?

He was a distinguished officer of the General Staff, a Cossack, who had been appointed commander-in-chief by Kerensky himself after the defeat of July. According to his own proclamation (in *The Prelude to Bolshevism,* by A. F. Kerensky; Dodd, Mead, 1919) issued September 9, his purpose in rebelling against the Provisional Government of Kerensky and starting to march on Petrograd, was "the preservation of a Great Russia." He swore "to carry over the people, by means of a victory over the enemy, to the Constituent Assembly to which it will decide its own fate and choose the order of the new state life." He was, in other words, to be a temporary military dictator acting as a savior of his country. Kerensky in a proclamation (in *The Prelude to Bolshevism*) also issued September 9, denounced him as a counter-revolutionist, representing "a desire of some circles of Russian society to take advantage of the grave condition of the state for the purpose of establishing in the country a state of authority in contradiction to the conquests of the revolution." The rebellion was proclaimed on September 9. By September 12 the Associated Press correspondent in Petrograd described the coup as a failure. Kornilov was suppressed practically without bloodshed.

Nevertheless the special correspondents showed their credulity about the possibilities of a miliary dictator. As early as July 31, the reporter of the *London Morning Post* cables (*New York Times* of August 3) that "from intimations I have received I gather that the fighting Generals have placed before Kerensky what amounts to an ultimatum from the officers of Russia's armies." Note that the soldiers of Russia's armies do not appear. On August 29 the *Times* carried, under headlines announcing "Hailed as Russia's Savior," a Moscow dispatch reporting that "at present the name of General Kornilov is on every tongue." Mr. Harold Williams, to be sure, noted in a cable published the next day that the executives of the Council of Workmen's and Soldiers' Delegates refused to stand or to greet Kornilov at the Moscow Congress.

But the bulk of the dispatches during the two weeks following were highly optimistic. The counter-revolutionists were described as riding on to glory. "Great New Power Rising in Russia" said a headline in the *Times,* August 31. "Kornilov commands confidence in military circles," cabled Mr. Charles H. Grasty on September 11, "not only on his record as an officer, *but because he is a Cossack.* This is the tribe around which *intelligent opinion* in Western Europe has been clustering hopefully *for several months past*" (Italics ours).

News of the actual revolt was cabled that same day from London. "There is yet no indication of General Kornilov's intentions," said a special dispatch to the *Times,* "but it is known that the Cossacks, the backbone of the Russia Army, are his strong adherents."

Yet two days later the Kornilov revolt was a confessed fiasco. "Kornilov

Gives Up, Revolt Ends," said a headline in the *Times*, September 14. Where, one wonders, were the Cossacks who three days before were "known" in London to be Kornilov's "strong adherents" and "the backbone of the Russian Army"? A fortnight later Mr. Harold Williams, in a special to the *Times* from Petrograd dated September 26, blurted out the following:

> *The Kornilov affair has intensified* mutual distrust and *completed the work of destruction.* The Government is shadowy and unreal, and what personality it had has disappeared before the menace of the democratic conference. Whatever power there is, is again concentrated in the hands of the Soviets, and, as always happens when the Soviets secure a monopoly of power, the influence of the Bolsheviks has increased enormously. (Italics ours.)

So runs the obituary by a friend of the first Dictator-Savior.

In view of the fact that the Soviets seized the government six weeks after this dispatch was filed, Mr. Williams had reported news of the first importance. Does the news for the next six weeks, the last weeks before the triumph of Bolshevism, follow the lead given so clearly by Mr. Williams.

THE END OF KERENSKY

The news out of Russia for the first ten days of October does not minimize the increasing difficulties of the existing regime. But the news comment out of Washington on October 10 (unidentified dispatch from Washington, October 9), is this:

> Russian diplomats here appear to be convinced now that the Bolsheviks have been finally overthrown and that Premier Kerensky is once more firmly established in the supreme power.
>
> It was said at the embassy today that the Bolsheviks were greatly discouraged by their first attempt to obtain control of the Government, on July 8, when disturbances caused by them were suppressed by the provisional authorities, and again during the Kornilov movement, when the Bolsheviks seized upon that occasion to overthrow the coalition administration. The action of the democratic conference in upholding the principle of a coalition Cabinet was asserted to reveal the total defeat of the extreme radicals.

Nevertheless the correspondents in Russia are agreed as to the crisis, thus:

OCT. 13   **RUSSIAN CABINET IN HARD POSITION**

OCT. 15   **DISORDERS GROWING AMONG THE PEASANTS**

OCT. 16   **RUSSIAN FLEET IS DEMORALIZED**

OCT. 25   "The evening newspapers which publish the program for the meeting of the Central Council of Soldiers' and Workmen's Delegates on Nov. 2 are filled with rumors of a Bolsheviki demonstration and an attempt to seize the Government. . . ."

OCT. 28   **RUSSIAN ROADS PARALYZED**
              HANDLED LESS TRAFFIC IN SUMMER THAN
                     THEY DID LAST WINTER

NOV. 2   (This was the day on which the *Times* printed briefly Kerensky's historic interview to the Associated Press: Petrograd, November 1. The longer text was printed November 3.)

         RUSSIA WORN OUT, ALLIES MUST TAKE UP
              BURDEN, KERENSKY SAYS

But the State Department in Washington knew better: It issued a statement that:

There has been absolutely nothing in the dispatches received by the Department of State from Russia, nor in information derived from any other source whatever, to justify the impression created by the *Washington Post* today. . . . that Russia is out of the conflict.

NOV. 3   (Special to *New York Times*, Washington, November 2.) "Russia is not out of the war. She is to make no separate peace. The Russian Embassy and the State Department made this clear today."

NOV. 4   From London, Kerensky's interview was deprecated. (London, November 3.)
The Petrograd correspondent of the *Daily Telegraph*, who is now in London, writes: "Premier Kerensky's statement seems to have been taken a little too seriously in some quarters."

The *Graphic* (London) is quoted: *"We should hate to regard the statements as authentic. They have the ring of pro-German propaganda."* (Italics ours.)

NOV. 6 On this day, the *Times* printed obscurely on the fourth column of the fourth page the following news of world-wide importance:

BOLSHEVIK PERIL ACUTE
RUSSIAN RADICAL PACIFISTS
EXPECT TO COME INTO POWER

(London, Nov. 5). At a meeting in Petrograd on Saturday, as reported in an Exchange Telegraph dispatch from that city, representatives of the whole Petrograd garrison passed under the guidance and influence of the Bolsheviks. . . .

The issues of November 7 and 8 carry the news of the Bolshevik Revolution, culminating on November 9, with the six-column headline on the first page:

REVOLUTIONISTS SEIZE PETROGRAD;
KERENSKY FLEES
PLEDGE IS GIVEN TO SEEK "AN IMMEDIATE PEACE"

The reader who had ignored the State Department and the Russian Embassy for the six weeks preceding, and had read the news dispatches from Russia, had no reason to be surprised. The reader who had trusted official pronouncements was misled.

The Provisional Government having been overthrown by the Soviets, he was concerned in the weeks that followed, first, as to whether the Bolsheviks would last, second, as to what they would do about the war.

DEDUCTIONS

Assuming that the preceding chapters constitute at least a prima facie case for saying that the run of the news on one matter of transcendent importance to Americans has been dubious, what deductions are there to be drawn by the constructive critic of the press? Primarily, we believe, that the professional standards of journalism are not high enough, and the discipline by which standards are maintained not strong enough, to carry the press triumphantly through a test so severe as that provided by the Russian Revolution.

First as to standards. The analysis shows how seriously misled was the *Times* by its reliance upon the official purveyors of information. It indicates that statements of fact emanating from governments and the circles around governments as well as from the leaders of political movements cannot be taken as judgments of fact by an independent press. They indicate opinion, they are controlled by special purpose, and they are not trustworthy news. If, for example, the Russian Minister of War says that the armies of Russia were never stronger, that cannot be accepted by a newspaper as news that the armies of Russia *are* stronger than ever. The only news in the statement is that the Minister *says* they are stronger. By any high journalistic standard, the Minister's statement if it deals with a matter of vital importance is a challenge to independent investigation.

The analysis shows that even more misleading than the official statement purporting to be a statement of fact, is the semi-official and semi-authoritative but anonymous statement. Such news is fathered by such phrases as:

Officials of the State Department

government and diplomatic sources

reports reaching here

it is stated on high authority that

Behind those phrases may be anybody, a minor bureaucrat, a dinner table conversation, hotel lobby gossip, a chance acquaintance, a paid agent. Dispatches of this type put the editor at home and the reader at the mercy of opinion that he cannot check, and it is time to demand that the correspondent take the trouble to identify his informants sufficiently to supply the reader with some means of estimating the character of the report. He need not name the individual source but he can "place" him.

The analysis shows that certain correspondents are totally untrustworthy because their sympathies are too deeply engaged. Mr. Harold Williams's reports from Denikin's army were obviously queer at the time and are ridiculous in the light of events. A reporter is not entitled to hold an assignment when his disinterestedness is open to question. One is not able to avoid the impression that in the selection of correspondents the virtue of conformity is at least balanced against the virtues of objectivity, insight, and credibility.

The analysis indicates also that even so rich and commanding a newspaper as the *Times* does not take seriously enough the equipment of the correspondent. For extraordinarily difficult posts in extraordinary times, something more than routine correspondents are required. Reporting is one of the most difficult professions, requiring much expert knowledge and serious eduction. The old contention that properly trained men lack the "news sense" will not stand against the fact that improperly trained men have seriously misled a whole nation. It is habit rather than preference which makes readers accept news from correspondents whose usefulness is about that of an astrologer or an alchemist. Important as it is for the press to read lessons in efficiency to workingmen, employees, and politicians, it is no less important for the press to study those lessons itself. Measured by its responsibility and pretensions the efficiency of the newspapers is not what determined men could make it.

The analysis shows further that at critical periods the time honored tradition of protecting news against editorials breaks down. The Russian policy of the editors of the *Times* profoundly and crassly influenced their news columns. The office handling of the news, both as to emphasis and captions, was unmistakably controlled by other than a professional standard. So obvious in this fact, so blatant is the intrusion of an editorial bias, that it will require serious reform before the code which has been violated can be restored.

Where is the power to be found which can define the standards of journalism and enforce them. Primarily within the profession itself. We do not believe that the press can be regulated by law. Our fundamental reliance must be on the corporate tradition and discipline of the newspaper guild. It is for them to agree on a code of honor, as the Bar Associations and Medical Societies have agreed, and for them to watch vigilantly for infractions of that code. As citizens they cannot escape this duty, and as members of a profession they are forced to it by the growing distrust which everywhere greets them. They know that to-day they are feared but not intimately respected, and the sins of some are visited upon all.

But while the technical code of journalistic standards, the tradition and the discipline belong to the guild, newspapers must be prepared for an increasing supervision from the readers of the press. Those readers will not simply "write letters to the editor," effective as such letters are. They will speak through organizations which will become centers of resistance. The report on the steel strike made by the Inter-church World Movement is an example of such resistance to the newspaper reports of that strike. The report on the activities of the Attorney-General by twelve lawyers for the Popular Government League is an example of resistance to the red hysteria of 1919–20. They illustrate the point that a powerful engine of criticism is appearing in the community which will no longer naively accept the current views on contentious questions. With that fact the profession of journalism will have to make a reckoning.

NATIONAL SECURITY AND THE
BAY OF PIGS INVASION

CLIFTON DANIEL

June 1, 1966

———

———

———

This speech by Clifton Daniel, a courtly editor of the *New York Times*, adds an important footnote to recent history. And it provides important insights into how the press behaves when grave matters of public policy are at stake. Daniel presents information on how the press tried to uncover the fact that the Central Intelligence Agency was helping to train and equip forces of anti-Castro revolutionaries to invade Cuba in 1961. The decision by the *Times* to modify its coverage of the invasion before it occurred has been cited countless times by editors, historians, and press critics as a justification for either withholding information (as the *Times* did) or as a pretext for publishing in the face of government resistance. But most of those who cite the Bay of Pigs do so erroneously.

In brief, editors at the *Times* toned down a lengthy dispatch describing plans for the invasion of Cuba. Initially, the story had been scheduled to lead the paper under a four-column headline, suggesting it contained material of exceptional significance. It still appeared at the top of page one—in the fourth column of a paper that was then eight columns wide. The reference to the CIA and an imminent invasion had been removed from the main story. However, at the end of the lead article, in what is known as a "shirttail," much of the very information that had been excised from the principal account was published! That shirttail said: "The Columbia Broadcasting System issued a report last night saying that there were 'unmistakable signs' that plans for an invasion of Cuba were in their final stages."

That invasion failed. After that, as Daniel disclosed in his speech, President Kennedy told an executive of the *Times* that had the paper printed all it knew about the preparations for the Bay of Pigs invasion the nation would have saved from a "colossal blunder."

Daniel's speech in 1966 followed shortly after the publication of *A*

Thousand Days by Arthur Schlesinger, Jr., who in echoing Kennedy's remarks to the *Times* executive said: "I have wondered whether, if the press had behaved irresponsibly, it would not have spared the country a disaster."

In fact, though, the invasion did not come until *ten days* after the article appeared. The deletions in the *Times* story did not materially alter the main point of the story. And the story's play, while not four columns, was in fact quite prominent. Harrison Salisbury, another *Times* editor, notes in his book *Without Fear or Favor,* "the cat was out of the bag and everyone in and out of Washington knew it."

This, then, is indeed a tale of mixed messages: by censoring itself a little, the press got blamed (or praised) for something it really did not do at all.

NATIONAL SECURITY AND THE
BAY OF PIGS INVASION

This morning I am going to tell you a story—one that has never been told before—the inside story of the *New York Times* and the Bay of Pigs, something of a mystery story.

In its issue of Nov. 19, 1960, the *Nation* published an editorial under the heading, "Are We Training Cuban Guerrillas?"

I had never seen this editorial and had never heard it mentioned until a reader of the *New York Times* sent in a letter to the editor. He asked whether the allegations in the editorial were true, and, if so, why hadn't they been reported by the *New York Times,* whose resources for gathering information were much greater than those of a little magazine like the *Nation.*

The *Nation* said:

> Fidel Castro may have a sounder basis for his expressed fears of a U.S.-financed "Guatemala-type" invasion than most of us realize. On a recent visit to Guatemala, Dr. Ronald Hilton, Director of the Institute of Hispanic-American Studies at Stanford University, was told.
>
> 1. The United States Central Intelligence Agency has acquired a large tract of land, at an outlay in excess of $1-million, which is stoutly fenced and heavily guarded. . . . It is "common knowledge" in Guatemala that the tract is being used as a training ground for Cuban counter-revolutionaries, who are preparing for an eventual landing in Cuba. . . . United States personnel and equipment are being used at the base. . . .
>
> 2. Substantially all of the above was reported by a well-known Guatemalan journalist . . . in *La Hora,* a Guatemalan newspaper. . . .
>
> 3. More recently, the President of Guatemala, forced to take cognizance of the persistent reports concerning the base, went on TV and admitted its existence, but refused to discuss its purpose or any other facts about it.

We believe the reports merit publication: they can, and should, be checked immediately by all U.S. news media with correspondents in Guatemala.

OFF TO GUATEMALA

With that last paragraph, the *New York Times* readily agreed. Paul Kennedy, our correspondent in Central America, was soon on his way to Guatemala.

He reported that intensive daily air training was taking place on a partly hidden airfield. In the mountains, commando-like forces were being drilled in guerrilla warfare tactics by foreign personnel, mostly from the United States.

Guatemalan authorities insisted that the training operation was designed to meet an assault from Cuba. Opponents of the government said the preparations were for an offensive against the Cuban regime of Premier Fidel Castro. Mr. Kennedy actually penetrated two miles into the training area.

His article was published in the *New York Times* on Jan. 10, 1961.

The *Nation* also printed another article in its issue of Jan. 7, 1961, by Don Dwiggins, aviation editor of the *Los Angeles Mirror*.

And now Arthur M. Schlesinger, Jr., takes up the story in *A Thousand Days,* his account of John F. Kennedy's years in the White House. Mr. Schlesinger says:

> On March 31 Howard Handleman of *U.S. News and World Report,* returning from ten days in Florida, said to me that the exiles were telling everyone that they would receive United States recognition as soon as they landed in Cuba, to be followed by the overt provision of arms and supplies. A few days later Gilbert Harrison of the *New Republic* sent over the galleys of a pseudonymous piece called "Our Men in Miami," asking whether there was any reason why it should not be published. It was a careful, accurate and devastating account of CIA activities among the refugees, written, I learned later, by Karl Meyer. Obviously its publication in a responsible magazine would cause trouble, but could the government properly ask an editor to suppress the truth? Defeated by the moral issue, I handed the article to the President, who instantly read it and expressed the hope that it could be stopped. Harrison accepted the suggestion and without questions—a patriotic act which left me oddly uncomfortable.

About the same time Tad Szulc filed a story to the *New York Times* from Miami describing the recruitment drive and reporting that a landing on Cuba was imminent. Turner Catledge, the managing editor, called James Reston, who was in his weekend retreat in Virginia, to ask his advice. Reston counseled against publication: either the story would alert Castro, in which case the *Times* would be responsible for casualities on the beach, or else the expedition would be canceled, in which case the *Times* would be responsible for grave interference with national policy. This was another patriotic act; but in retrospect I have wondered whether, if the press had behaved irresponsibly, it would not have spared the country a disaster.

ARTICLE WAS NOT SUPPRESSED

As recently as last November, Mr. Schlesinger was still telling the same story. In an appearance on "Meet the Press," he was asked about the article in the *New York Times* in which he was quoted as saying that he had lied to the *Times* in April 1961 about the nature and size of the landing in the Bay of Pigs.

Mr. Schlesinger replied that a few days before he misinformed the *Times*, the newspaper had suppressed a story by Tad Szulc from Miami, giving a fairly accurate account of the invasion plans. He said:

If I was reprehensible in misleading the *Times* by repeating the official cover story, the *Times* conceivably was just as reprehensive in misleading the American people by suppressing the Tad Szulc story from Miami. I, at least, had the excuse that I was working for the Government."

I prefer to think that both the *Times* and I were actuated by the same motives: that is, a sense, mistaken or not, that [it] was in the national interest to do so.

Mr. Schlesinger was mistaken, both in his book and in his appearance on "Meet the Press." The *Times* did not suppress the Tad Szulc article. We printed it, and here it is, on page one of the issue of Friday, April 7, 1961.

What actually happened is, at this date, somewhat difficult to say.

None of those who took part in the incident described in Mr. Schlesinger's book kept records of what was said and done. That is unfortunate, and it should teach us a lesson. The Bay of Pigs was not only important in the history of United States relations with Latin America, the Soviet

Union, and world Communism; it was also important in the history of relations between the American press and the United States government.

We owe a debt to history. We should try to reconstruct the event, and
that is what I am attempting to do today.

Late in March and early in April 1961, we were hearing rumors that
the anti-Castro forces were organizing for an invasion. For example, the
editor of the *Miami Herald,* Don Shoemaker, told me at lunch in New York
one day, "They're drilling on the beaches all over southern Florida."

Tad Szulc, a veteran correspondent in Latin America with a well-de-
served reputation for sniffing out plots and revolutions, came upon the
Miami story quite accidentally.

He was being transferred from Rio de Janeiro to Washington and happened to stop in Miami to visit friends on his way north. He quickly discovered that an invasion force was indeed forming and that it was very
largely financed and directed by the CIA. He asked for permission to come
to New York to discuss the situation and was promptly assigned to cover
the story.

His first article from Miami—the one I have just shown to you—began
as follows:

> For nearly nine months Cuban exile military forces dedicated
> to the overthrow of Premier Fidel Castro have been in training
> in the United States as well as in Central America.
>
> An army of 5,000 to 6,000 men constitutes the external
> fighting arm of the anti-Castro Revolutionary Council, which was
> formed in the United States last month. Its purpose is the lib-
> eration of Cuba from what it describes as the Communist rule
> of the Castro regime.

His article, which was more than two columns long and very detailed,
was scheduled to appear in the paper of Friday, April 7, 1961. It was
dummied for page one under a four-column head, leading the paper.

While the front-page dummy was being drawn up by the assistant managing editor, the news editor, and the assistant news editor, Orvil Dryfoos,
then the publisher of the *New York Times,* came down from the fourteenth
floor to the office of Turner Catledge, the managing editor.

He was gravely troubled by the security implications of Szulc's story.
He could envision failure for the invasion, and he could see the *New York
Times* being blamed for a bloody fiasco.

He and the managing editor solicited the advice of Scotty Reston, who
was then the Washington correspondent of the *New York Times* and is
now an associate editor.

RECOLLECTIONS CONFLICT

At this point, the record becomes unclear. Mr. Reston distinctly recalls that Mr. Catledge's telephone call came on a Sunday, and that he was spending the weekend at his retreat in the Virginia mountains, as described by Arthur Schlesinger. As there was no telephone in his cabin, Mr. Reston had to return the call from a gas station in Marshall, Virginia. Mr. Catledge and others recall, with equal certainty, that the incident took place on Thursday and that Mr. Reston was reached in his office in Washington.

Whichever was the case, the managing editor told Mr. Reston about the Szulc dispatch, which said that a landing on Cuba was imminent.

Mr. Reston was asked what should be done with the dispatch.

"I told them not to run it," Mr. Reston says.

He did not advise against printing information about the forces gathering in Florida; that was already well known. He merely cautioned against printing any dispatch that would pinpoint the time of the landing.

Others agree that Szulc's dispatch did contain some phraseology to the effect that an invasion was imminent, and those words were eliminated.

Tad Szulc's own recollection, cabled to me from Madrid the other day, is that "in several instances the stories were considerably toned down, including the elimination of statements about the 'imminence' of an invasion."

> Specifically, a decision was made in New York not to mention the CIA's part in the invasion preparations, not to use the date of the invasion, and, on April 15, not to give away in detail the fact that the first air strike on Cuba was carried out from Guatemala.

After the dummy for the front page of the *Times* for Friday, April 7, 1961, was changed, Ted Bernstein, who was the assistant managing editor on night duty at the *Times,* and Lew Jordan, the news editor, sat in Mr. Bernstein's office fretting about it. They believed a colossal mistake was being made, and together they went into Mr. Catledge's office to appeal for reconsideration.

Mr. Catledge recalls that Mr. Jordan's face was dead white, and he was quivering with emotion. He and Mr. Bernstein told the managing editor that never before had the front-page play in the *New York Times* been changed for reasons of policy. They said they would like to hear from the publisher himself the reasons for the change.

ANGRY AT INTERVENTION

Lew Jordan later recalled that Mr. Catledge was "flaming mad" at this intervention. However, he turned around in his big swivel chair, picked up the telephone, and asked Mr. Dryfoos to come downstairs. By the time he arrived, Mr. Bernstein had gone to dinner, but Mr. Dryfoos spent ten minutes patiently explaining to Mr. Jordan his reasons for wanting the story played down.

His reasons were those of national security, national interest, and, above all, concern for the safety of the men who were preparing to offer their lives on the beaches of Cuba. He repeated the explanation in somewhat greater length to Mr. Bernstein the next day.

I describe the mood and behavior of the publisher and editors of the *New York Times* only to show how seriously and with what intensity of emotion they made their fateful decisions.

Mr. Bernstein and Mr. Jordan now say, five years later, that the change in play, not eliminating the reference to the imminence of the invasion, was the important thing done that night.

"It was important because a multi-column head in this paper means so much," Mr. Jordan told me the other day.

Mr. Reston, however, felt that the basic issue was the elimination of the statement that an invasion was imminent.

Ironically, although that fact was eliminated from our own dispatch, virtually the same information was printed in a shirttail on Tad Szulc's report. That was a report from the Columbia Broadcasting System. It said that plans for the invasion of Cuba were in their final stages. Ships and planes were carrying invasion units from Florida to their staging bases in preparation for the assault.

When the invasion actually took place ten days later, the American Society of Newspaper Editors happened to be in session in Washington, and President Kennedy addressed the society. He devoted his speech entirely to the Cuban crisis. He said nothing at that time about press disclosures of invasion plans.

APPEAL BY PRESIDENT

However, a week later in New York, appearing before the Bureau of Advertising of the American Newspaper Publishers Association, the President asked members of the newspaper profession "to re-examine their own responsibilities."

He suggested that the circumstances of the cold war required news-papermen to show some of the same restraint they would exercise in a shooting war.

He went on to say, "Every newspaper now asks itself with respect to every story, 'Is it news?' All I suggest is that you add the question: 'Is it in the interest of national security?'"

If the press should recommend voluntary measures to prevent the pub-lication of material endangering the national security in peacetime, the President said, "the Government would cooperate wholeheartedly."

Turner Catledge, who was the retiring president of the A.S.N.E., Felix McKnight of the *Dallas Times-Herald,* the incoming president, and Lee Hills, executive editor of the Knight newspapers, took the President's statement as an invitation to talk.

Within two weeks, a delegation of editors, publishers, and news agency executives was at the White House. They told President Kennedy they saw no need at that time for machinery to help prevent the disclosure of vital security information. They agreed that there should be another meet-ing in a few months. However, no further meeting was ever held.

That day in the White House, President Kennedy ran down a list of what he called premature disclosures of security information. His examples were mainly drawn from the *New York Times.*

He mentioned, for example, Paul Kennedy's story about the training of anti-Castro forces in Guatemala. Mr. Catledge pointed out that this infor-mation had been published in *La Hora* in Guatemala and in the *Nation* in this country before it was ever published in the *New York Times.*

"But it was not news until it appeared in the *Times,*" the President replied.

While he scolded the *New York Times,* the President said in an aside to Mr. Catledge, "if you had printed more about the operation you would have saved us from a colossal mistake."

"SORRY YOU DIDN'T TELL IT"

More than a year later, President Kennedy was still talking the same way. In a conversation with Orvil Dryfoos in the White House on Sept. 13, 1962, he said: "I wish you had run everything on Cuba. . . . I am just sorry you didn't tell it at the time."

Those words were echoed by Arthur Schlesinger when he wrote, "I have wondered whether, if the press had behaved irresponsibly, it would not have spared the country a disaster."

They are still echoing down the corridors of history. Just the other day in Washington, Senator Russell of Georgia confessed that, although he was chairman of the Senate Armed Forces Committee, he didn't know the timing of the Bay of Pigs operation.

"I only wish I had been consulted," he said in a speech to the Senate, "because I would have strongly advised against this kind of operation if I had been."

It is not so easy, it seems, even for Presidents, their most intimate advisers and distinguished United States Senators to know always what is really in the national interest. One is tempted to say that sometimes—sometimes—even a mere newspaperman knows better.

My own view is that the Bay of Pigs operation might well have been canceled and the country would have been saved enormous embarrassment if the *New York Times* and other newspapers had been more diligent in the performance of their duty—their duty to keep the public informed on matters vitally affecting our national honor and prestige, not to mention our national security.

Perhaps, as Mr. Reston believes, it was too late to stop the operation by the time we printed Tad Szulc's story on April 7. Mr. Reston says:

> If I had it to do over, I would do exactly what we did at the time. It is ridiculous to think that publishing the fact that the invasion was imminent would have avoided this disaster. I am quite sure the operation would have gone forward.
>
> The thing had been cranked up too far. The CIA would have had to disarm the anti-Castro forces physically. Jack Kennedy was in no mood to do anything like that.

PRELUDE TO GRAVER CRISIS

The Bay of Pigs, as it turned out, was the prelude to an even greater crisis—the Cuban missile crisis of 1962.

In Arthur Schlesinger's opinion, failure in 1961 contributed to success in 1962. President Kennedy had learned from experience, and once again the *New York Times* was involved.

On May 28, 1963, the President sat at his desk in the White House and with his own hand wrote a letter to Mrs. Orvil Dryfoos, whose husband had just died at the age of fifty. The letter was on White House stationery, and the President used both sides of the paper.

The existence of this letter has never been mentioned publicly before.

I have the permission of Mr. Dryfoos' widow, now Mrs. Andrew Heiskell, to read it to you today:

Dear Marian:

I want you to know how sorry I was to hear the sad news of Orvil's untimely death.

I had known him for a number of years and two experiences I had with him in the last two years gave me a clear insight into his unusual qualities of mind and heart. One involved a matter of national security—the other his decision to refrain from printing on October 21st the news, which only the man for the *Times* possessed, on the presence of Russian missiles in Cuba, upon my informing him that we needed twenty-four hours more to complete our preparations.

This decision of his made far more effective our later actions and thereby contributed greatly to our national safety.

All this means very little now, but I did want you to know that a good many people some distance away, had the same regard for Orvil's character as did those who knew him best.

I know what a blow this is to you, and I hope you will accept Jackie's and my deepest sympathy.

Sincerely,
JOHN F. KENNEDY.

In the Cuban missile crisis, things were handled somewhat differently than in the previous year. The President telephoned directly to the publisher of the *New York Times*.

He had virtually been invited to do so in their conversation in the White House barely a month before.

That conversation had been on the subject of security leaks in the press and how to prevent them, and Mr. Dryfoos had told the President that what was needed was prior information and prior consultation. He said that when there was danger of security information getting into print, the thing to do was to call in the publishers and explain the matters to them.

In the missile crisis, President Kennedy did exactly that.

Ten minutes before I was due on this platform this morning Mr. Reston telephoned me from Washington to give me further details of what happened that day. Mr. Reston said:

The President called me . . . He understood that I had been talking to Mac Bundy and he knew from the line of questioning

that we knew the critical fact—that Russian missiles had indeed been emplaced in Cuba. . . .

The President told me that he was going on television on
Monday evening to report to the American people. He said that
if we published the news about the missiles Khrushchev could
actually give him an ultimatum before he went on the air. Those
were Kennedy's exact words.

I told him I understood. . . . but I also told him I could not
do anything about it. And this is an important thought that you
should convey to those young reporters in your audience.

I told the President I would report to my office in New York
and if my advice were asked I would recommend that we not
publish. It was not my duty to decide. My job was the same
as that of an ambassador—to report to my superiors.

I recommended to the President that he call New York. He
did so.

That was the sequence of events as Mr. Reston recalled them this
morning. The President telephoned the publisher of the *New York Times*.
Mr. Dryfoos in turn put the issue up to Mr. Reston and his staff.

And the news that the Soviet Union had atomic missiles in Cuba only
ninety miles from the coast of Florida was withheld until the Government
announced it.

What conclusion do I reach from all these facts? What moral do I draw
from my story?

My conclusion is this: Information is essential to people who propose
to govern themselves. It is the responsibility of serious journalists to supply that information—whether in this country or in the countries from which
our foreign colleagues come.

Still, the primary responsibility for safeguarding our national interest must
rest always with our Government, as it did with President Kennedy in the
two Cuban crises.

Up until the time we are actually at war or on the verge of war, it is
not only permissible—it is our duty as journalists and citizens to be constantly questioning our leaders and our policy, and to be constantly informing the people, who are the masters of us all—both the press and
the politicians.

3

THE POWER AND LIMITATIONS
OF THE PRESS

Throughout the century, there has been a strong undercurrent of dissatisfaction with the performance of the press. A string of critics—many from the left, some from the right, and others from the center—have suggested that the press is giving the public something other than the unvarnished truth about politics and business. These four selections present different appraisals of how journalists deal with the world of public affairs.

In fifteen installments in *Collier's* in 1911, Will Irwin, the muckraker, described the power and the limitations of the press. He was a skeptic, but he held an essentially romantic notion of reporting: "Truth, fogged by the imperfections of human sight, hidden under the wrappings of lies, stands the final aim of a reporter when he goes out on a news tip."

In his 1919 book *The Brass Check* (named after the token given to a man who had paid for the services of a prostitute), Upton Sinclair, the novelist and reformer, wrote: "Just imagine if the newspapers of America were to print the truth for ten days! The truth about poverty and the cause of poverty; the truth about corruption in politics and in all branches of government, in journalism, and throughout the business world . . . "

In answering charges often leveled against the press, at the 1933 meeting of the American Society of Newspaper Editors, Carl Ackerman, the dean of the Columbia Journalism School, pragmatically observed: "What our critics desire is a superhuman institution." These critics, he said, would create a newspaper "which only a perfect philanthropist could finance and edit."

Finally, in 1947, the Hutchins Commission, a group of thirteen intellectuals, outlined the dangers facing the press and offered suggestions "of freeing the press from the influences which now prevent it from supplying the communication of news and ideas needed by the kind of society we have and the kind of society we desire." The report of the Hutchins Commission, which resembles in many ways the articles written by Will Irwin, was generally denounced by editors when it was first published. But its impact has been enduring, if subtle.

THE AMERICAN NEWSPAPER

WILL IRWIN

Collier's, 1911

———

———

———

Will Irwin, a former *San Francisco Chronicle* and *New York Sun* reporter and editor at *McClure's,* belonged to the small group of muckrakers who flourished from 1902 to 1914. In 1911 he completed an exhaustive fifteen-part series on journalism. The series, he said, dealt with "the whole subject of American journalism—the most powerful extrajudicial force in society, except religion." In his wide-ranging articles, he grappled with a definition of news, he examined the ethics of his colleagues, he decried sensationalism (a newspaper, he said, should behave like a "gentleman"), and he took on cowardly publishers who were wedded to wealth.

His series rambled at times, but he differed from other early critics in that he suffused his articles with specific examples of misdeeds by journalists and publishers. His ambitious criticism, which holds up surprisingly well today, was the first comprehensive look at press practices. "I had no precedents to go by," Irwin noted in his memoirs, which appeared in 1942. His criticism established a framework for later press critics. For instance, there are strong similarities between his series and the Hutchins Commission report. He influenced a generation of critics, including George Seldes, who in his memoirs, published in 1987, singled out the outstanding work done by Irwin.

Excerpts from the series follow.

THE AMERICAN NEWSPAPER

*A Study of Journalism in Its
Relation to the Public*

THE POWER OF THE PRESS

When the investigator looks for some formulation of the larger principles of journalism in relation to its times, he finds nothing. Try all the books listed under "Journalism" in the Astor Library in New York or the Congressional Library in Washington. You will discover only a few treaties on the making of newspapers, a few volumes of pleasant reminiscences, one interesting but incomplete and shallow history. Dig further; the great social philosophers, who have worked out the relations of law, religion, commerce, of all the other permanent human forces, to the modern organization of society, mention journalism only in passing or not at all. Of the subtler modern philosophers, Robert Louis Stevenson presents a type. Democratic as he was in sentiment and practise, he touched journalism only to revile it as the worthless imitator of his own higher art.

Now, religion, law, science, art, infused the ancient world as well as the modern; we had recognized them, had worked out their principles and their relation to society, before the great flowering of the human spirit in the nineteenth century. Their maturity goes back always to a formative youth. But this alone of our intellectual forces is new. Two centuries ago there was no such thing. A century ago we had newspapers so-called, but they were only infant second cousins to the modern newspaper. A generation still lives which saw the birth of journalism in its present form. It has burst into the world with a flare of trumpets, but it has not even crept into the slow consciousness of the philosophers. . . .

POWER THROUGH THE NEWS

In this series, and in later articles by other hands, *Collier's* sets about to explore the uncharted country. That we shall say any final word upon journalism, we are not so egregious as to believe. But it is perhaps the first attempt, in the United States at least, to study the subject fully and candidly. Mainly, it will be a piece of reporting; on the lamp of civilization, itself hidden behind the brilliance of its own rays, we are about to turn our

rushlight. Others, we hope, will follow with larger philosophies of the subject, with the creation of laws, the formulation of public sentiment, which
shall turn this new intellectual force, at present so wasteful and uncon-
trolled, into its proper relation toward progressive civilization. We are looking
only for the truth, so far as our point of view permits us to perceive the
truth. The work will be limited by our capacities; it will not be limited by
any passion other than the passion for truth, by any desire other than the
desire to know.

We shall arrive at few conclusions; but one I would better state in the
beginning, that we may have done with it. The "power of the press" is
greater than ever before. They who deny this are looking back to the old
age when all party lines were definite, when men first swallowed a formula
and then bent their intellectual powers to prove it. That was the golden
age of the editorial; and these panegyrists of older times assume that the
editorial page still swings all the power of the press. The world runs differently now since Darwin. The power of the press has shifted. . . . Indeed,
line for line, it is greater, if for no other reason than that in the last generation not every one was a newspaper reader, while now the audience of
the daily press includes all human beings with two eyes and an elementary
education.

This has come to be the age of the reporter. In even its simplest form,
news is the nerves of the modern world. Because of the press in its news
function, San Diego, Seattle, and Boston, days apart by the swiftest trains,
know as soon as New York and Washington that the insurance companies
are under fire, that the Government has been swindled on glove contracts.
So, and only so, is democracy possible in this immense country. Stated
otherwise, the newspaper, in this simplest activity, furnishes the raw material for public opinion. If you want a concrete comparison, put our own
small cities beside the Stratford of Shakespeare's time. Four or five days
from London by existing means of travel, the intelligent burgher of Stratford had only the dimmest notion of events at the capital or on the far
borders. His news came by inaccurate word of mouth from late visitors to
London, or by an occasional royal proclamation tainted with the Government point of view. His mind was the prey of rumors and extravagant
reports. From his very ignorance about the larger world, he would have
been an impossible unit in a democracy. Perhaps I only state the obvious
here; but I do it that we may keep fairly before us the newspaper's most
important public function.

So much for colorless news; but, as we shall see when we come to
considered reporting, colorless news is an impossible ideal. When Pilate
asked: "What is truth?" he expressed the eternal quandary of the news

editor. Truth, absolute truth, is a hypothesis. No man, from a cub reporter writing a dog-fight to a star writing a political convention, but puts into his work a point of view. Yielding to that tendency, newspapers, good and bad, honest and venal, have come more and more to put their views into their news columns, to relate events from a basis of opinion. The *Chicago Tribune,* in its late exposé of Senator Lorimer, went far beyond a simple statement of the facts—that popular Representatives had taken money to vote for a United States Senator. Every paragraph in that story, as told by the *Tribune,* was infused with moral indignation. When the Insurgents forced Speaker Cannon from the Committee on Rules, but did not pass the resolution calling for his resignation, the *San Francisco Bulletin,* Insurgent in opinion, announced in its news headlines: "Corrupt Wealth Loses Control of the House of Representatives—Cannon Is At Last Repudiated—Great Demonstration Follows the Victory." In neighboring Los Angeles is the *Times,* firm for the Republican organization. "Speaker Cannon Triumphant in Defeat," announced its headlines—"Insurgents Lose Nerve in the Heat of Battle—Mercerized Republicans Dare Not Support an Attempt to Dislodge Uncle Joe." In fact, there is no colorless newspaper, though a few approximate it; every news report has some point of view, expresses some mission of God or of the Devil. . . .

WHAT IS NEWS?

News is the main thing, the vital consideration to the American newspaper; it is both an intellectual craving and a commercial need to the modern world. In popular psychology, it has come to be a crying primal want of the mind, like hunger of the body. Tramp windjammers, taking on the pilot after a long cruise, ask for the papers before they ask, as formerly, for fresh fruit and vegetables. Whenever, in our later Western advance, we Americans set up a new mining camp, an editor, his type slung on burro-back, comes in with the missionaries, evangel himself of civilization. Most dramatically the San Francisco disaster illuminated this point. On the morning of April 20, 1906, the city's population huddled in parks and squares, their houses gone, death of famine or thirst a rumor and a possibility. The editors of the three morning newspapers, expressing the true soldier spirit which inspires this most devoted profession, had moved their staffs to the suburb of Oakland, and there, on the presses of the *Tribune,* they had issued a combined *Call-Chronicle-Examiner.* When, at dawn, the paper was printed, an editor and a reporter loaded the edition into an automobile and drove it through the parks of the disordered city, giving copies away. They were fairly mobbed; they had to drive at top speed, casting out the sheets as they went, to make any progress at all. No bread wagon, no supply of blankets, caused half so much stir as did the arrival of the news.

We need it, we crave it; this nerve of the modern world transmits thought and impulse from the brain of humanity to its muscles; the complex organism of modern society could no more move without it than a man could move without filaments and ganglia. On the commercial and practical side, the man of even small affairs must read news in the newspapers every day to keep informed on the thousand and one activities in the social structure which affect his business. On the intellectual and spiritual side, it is—save for the Church alone—our principal outlook on the higher intelligence. The thought of legislature, university, study, and pulpit comes to the common man first—and usually last—in the form of news. The tedious business of teaching reading in public schools has become chiefly a training to consume newspapers. We must go far up in the scale of culture before we find an intellectual equipment more a debtor to the formal education of school and college than to the haphazard education of news.

Axiomatically, then, the quality of news, its freedom from undue bias and taint, is supremely important. Could one slant or taint all news at its source, he would vitiate all public intelligence. Could one raise the standard of all news at its source, he would correspondingly elevate public intelligence. And since it is so vital, we must stop here to consider what news is, before we consider what, in the ideal, should be the attitude of writer and editor toward his product.

It looks simple at first sight. News is a report of just what occurs in the world, or rather what has just occurred. But a million billion things occur hourly in the world, from the movement of the finger by which I write this line to the surging of the crowd which is at this minute harrying strike-breakers along the Canadian border. The movement of this finger is not news, while the surge of that crowd is; and something more than importance divides them. My neighbor, John Smith, a virtuous man of well-conducted life, is just going to his office. He will do business honorably all day, come home, eat his dinner, enjoy the evening with his family, and go to bed. That, again, is not news. The world is working hard today on a million mighty labors. Tomorrow will be Sunday; most of the million on million human units in it will listen to sermon or mass, and rest and be virtuous and reasonably happy. And that is not news, while the raging of a thousand men along our border is—decidedly. Tell the former fact to a man and he is bored; tell the latter, and he stops to listen.

Here lies the distinction, and it is also a definition: The beating of strike-breakers is news because it is a departure from the established order. . . .

With our education in established order we get the knowledge that man-kind in bulk obeys its ideals of that order only imperfectly. When something brings to our attention an exceptional adhesion to religion, virtue, and truth, that becomes in itself a departure from regularity, and therefore news. The knowledge that most servants do their work conscientiously and many stay long in the same employ is not news. But when a committee of house-wives presents a medal to a servant who has worked faithfully in one em-ploy for fifty years, that becomes news, because it calls our attention to a case of exceptional fidelity to the ideals of established order. The fact that mankind will consume an undue amount of news about crime and dis-order is only a proof that the average human being is optimistic, that he believes the world to be true, sound, and working upward. Crimes and scandals interest him most because they most disturb his picture of the established order.

That, then, is the basis of news. The mysterious news sense which is necessary to all good reporters rests on no other foundation than acquired or instinctive perception of this principle, together with a feeling for what the greatest number of people will regard as a departure from the estab-lished order. In Jesse Lynch Williams' newspaper play, "The Stolen Story," occurs this passage:

(*Enter Very Young Reporter; comes down to city desk with air of excitement.*)

VERY YOUNG REPORTER (*considerably impressed*): Big story. Three dagoes killed by that boiler explosion!

THE CITY EDITOR (*reading copy. Doesn't look up*): Ten lines. (*Continues reading copy.*)

VERY YOUNG REPORTER (*looks surprised and hurt. Crosses over toward reporters' tables. Then turns back to city desk. Casual conversational tone*): By the way. Funny thing. There was a baby in a baby carriage within fifty feet of the explosion, but it wasn't upset.

THE CITY EDITOR (*looks up with professional interest*): That's worth a dozen dead dagoes. Write a half column.

(*Very Young Reporter looks still more surprised, perplexed. Suddenly the idea dawns upon him. He crosses over to table, sits down, writes.*)

Both saw news; but the editor went further than the reporter. For cases of Italians killed by a boiler explosion are so common as to approach the commonplace; but a freak explosive chemistry which annihilates a strong man and does not disturb a baby departs from it widely.

Last year Porter Charlton, rich and well connected, murdered his wife, a woman who had given up "society" to go on the stage, crammed the body into a trunk which he sunk in Lake Como, and fled to America. In the same week several other men in humble circumstances murdered their wives. Why did the Charlton case get so much more attention and interest from writers and readers? Mainly because it departed further from the customs of the established order. The "upper class," having a better opportunity, is supposed to be less given to the greater crimes than the "lower." Women in "society" do not generally go on the stage. Wife murderers are not generally so hardened as to cram the body into a trunk and sink it in a lake. Of course, since mankind is complex, other factors entered into the case, such as that basic instinct of snobbery which makes us like to contemplate beings greater and more esteemed than ourselves. But the deepest reason for interest in the Charlton case was the wide departure which it presented from the normal.

This interest is in itself a progressive force; it lies close to the noblest practical activities of the human spirit. Invention, moral heroism, and genius in art are nothing but the discovery of something useful or fine apart from the established order.

The subject-matter of which it treats greatly modifies news interest in the masses and in the individual. First of all: We prefer to read about the things we like.

The chief business of a true yellow journalist is to find the class of news which will interest the greatest number of people; and to this end yellow journalism has made a formula: "Sport for the men, love and scandal for the women," says an executive of the Scripps papers. "Power for the men, the affections for the women," expresses it better. Power is a man's business, his chief intellectual liking; politics, wealth, and sport are all different manifestations of it. Affection is a woman's business; love is affection at its height; scandal, affection gone wrong. Every trained journalist understands that no minor news succeeds better than a story about an animal— as the dog who rescued his master from fire or drowning. Aside from the basic news interest which they represent, their departure from the accepted order, these stories "go" because most people like animals; else we should have no cats but mousers and no dogs but hunters. The rule holds with stories about little children and, especially, those about beautiful women. Herein the yellow editor who sprinkles his pages with the phrase "pretty girl," lays hold on the universal, since both sexes, from different causes, glory in the beauty of woman. As I have hinted before, interest in the doings of high society, which get so much space in our sensational publications, and so much more in the English press, proceeds from that instinct of snobbery which democracy can not cure. The under stratum yearns to those brighter beings and would like to resemble them. Even when it envies, it pays tribute to the principle, since envy is only liking and disappointment mixed in bad chemical combination.

Theatrical managers are still citing, for amusement and instruction, the great interest which New York took in the third act of Denman Thompson's *Old Homestead*. The scene was the thing; it represented the exterior of Grace Church at night. Every New Yorker had seen the real Grace Church, yet people crowded the theater to witness its canvas counterfeit. Their motive introduces the second factor which intensifies news interest in the individual:

Our interest in news increases in direct ratio to our familiarity with its subject, its setting, and its dramatis personae.

Nor is this an outgrowth of the first principle, that liking governs news interest. While by nature we characteristically like our relatives, and by association and man's free choice our friends and environment, this principle goes deeper. For example, we do not love our enemies, in spite of Christianity's two thousand years; and yet a piece of news which relates either the good fortune or the disaster of an enemy is most important to any normal man.

The interest in familiar things, people, and places—publications have waxed greater on no other policy. To-morrow you may open your newspaper and discover that your next door neighbor has been arrested for speeding his automobile or has fallen from a scaffold and broken his leg. Though the item occupy only an inch in the column, it will probably cause more discussion at the breakfast table than two columns about an earthquake in Peru, a famine in Russia, or a rebellion in the Sudan. Of course, with increase of intelligence and education, with mental broadening, the circle of familiarity widens; the man of culture may care as much to read of the Russian famine as of his neighbor's arrest; but that is because he has read of Russia or studied the wheat supply. . . .

THE SELFISH INTEREST

News is a commercial necessity as well as an intellectual satisfaction, part of our business as well as part of our thought. And so:

Our interest in news is in direct ratio to its effect on our personal concerns.

The fact that Reading common stock has dropped two points is hardly news at all in the absolute, so slight a variation from the regular and accepted does it proclaim. To the man who holds ten thousand shares of

Reading common, it may be the most important news in any paper. The *Leadville Herold-Democrat* and the *Butte Miner* publish daily columns of "notes from the mines," just as the *New York Sun* publishes a Wall Street edition. Not once a week does anything happen in the mines which rises to news in the absolute by presenting a striking departure from routine and custom. Unilluminated by personality or color, these notes make little appeal to that interest in familiar things which the *Boston Globe*'s suburban notes satisfy. The people of Leadville and Butte want them because mining, their only industry, affects the fortunes of all, and the slightest change in the policy or conduct of a mine may take away the individual's employment or increase the receipts of his grocery.

THE SENSE OF PROPORTION

Finally comes the most obvious factor of all, but no means the least influential.

Our interest in news increases in direct ratio to the general importance of the persons or activities which it affects.

This principle is hardly worth examples. News about President Taft is more interesting than news about John Smith, because Taft is more important in the world than Smith. So Taft's sore throat is "worth" a paragraph to every newspaper in the United States, while Smith's broken leg draws scarcely a line in his country weekly. A dramatic change in the fortunes of the Standard Oil Company is supremely interesting; the unexpected foreclosure on Baccigalupi's corner grocery gets rightly no space in the newspapers. This is merely the working of man's sense of proportion.

THE FEELING FOR THE DRAMATIC

These are not the only factors that intensify news interest, but they are the chief ones. Sense for the clash and adjustment of character and incident which we call drama is a factor. That a woman finds her long-lost child after ten years' search is mild news; that she finds him in the next hospital cot, fellow victim of a train wreck, is great news. So with the sense of humor. Such newspapers as the *Kansas City Star,* the *New York Sun,* and the *Chicago Tribune,* daily print stories which have only slight interest through departure from the accepted order, through popular liking for their subject matter, through self-interest, or through the importance of the persons and interests involved. But they fall naturally into such form, or the skillful reporter casts them in such form that they amuse. . . .

THE EDITOR AND THE NEWS

Every night there happen in New York, Philadelphia, and Chicago a thousand events which fit the definition of news; and information on most of them reaches the newspaper offices. Not one-tenth of them, however, get into print. The editor's work, therefore, is always selective. According to his point of view as transmitted through the trained men under him, he prints certain things and omits certain things, uses one item as a "front-page feature" and another as a "filler." If you live in the radius of four or five big city newspapers, compare, to-morrow, the right-hand or "outside" column of their front pages. This column, by the immemorial custom of American journalism, holds the day's most important piece of news, as the editor sees news. Unless there is something exceptionally important afoot, you will find one printing in that column a social scandal or an episode which drags in society by the heels; another political story; another movement in high finance. A Scripps newspaper, with the Scripps outlook on economic and social questions, has in that preferred position an account of a working man's strike in Sweden, a Hearst newspaper a breach of promise suit, an Ochs newspaper a railway merger.

THE QUANDARY OF THE EDITOR

Now, in making this selection, two lights guide the honest editor. In the first place, he must sell his newspaper. He, like any one else not wholly an artist who ministers to the intellectual needs of the populace, must consider not only what he would give the public, but what the public will take. He himself may be scholarly in his tastes; the discovery of a Sapphic ode in a Greek excavation, or the fact that Professor Wallace has found another document concerning the life of Shakespeare, may be to him the most highly important news of the day. He knows, however, that a hundred potential readers will be far more interested in the latest picturesque murder. Editors exist who have naturally the popular point of view, whose interests are those of the man in the street. They are the born commercial successes of the craft; of such, for example, are many of the best Hearst editors—like Andrew Lawrence.

The other light to his feet is his conception of what the public should want; and there are men in the profession who are guided by this light alone. They will make no concessions to popularity for revenue's sake. Such men, if they manage to remain in the business, never achieve heavy financial success, although they may, through their limited circulations among highly intelligent people, have great personal and professional influence. . . .

FACT OR GOSSIP?

"Most news," says Tiffany Blake, "is not fact, anyway. It is gossip about facts." In this, I think, he has said a wise and final word. News, as it works out in newspaper practise, amounts to gossip, the impressionist picture of truth. It is gossip organized to our uses, subdued to our hand, and raised to both a science and an art. For before journalism was, the town or tribal gossip discharged in irregular and primitive fashion most lower functions of a newspaper and some higher ones. He "mixed," he found by force of his prying curiosity the things which were his business as a member of the tribe, and the things which were no one's business. After that, he circulated through town or settlement, telling. And I conceive of one gossip, expressing most closely the bad sense we have come to feel in that word, whose tongue wagged on the hinges of malice and vanity, who spread no good thing about his enemies, and who made a mountain of rumor from a molehill of fact for the satisfaction of attracting attention. To him tribe or town listened, though they despised. He was a curse to his world. Foolish rumor and baseless report play a large part in the history of all ages down to the one which brought accurate journalism, and the springs of destructive rumor were such tribal gossips.

Another kind of gossip there must have been. I imagine a man of ready speech, rolling and curious eye and attractive manner, an ornament to any fireside, who came with his mouth full of greater and better things. The chiefs and the council had decided to change the spring planting from the east field to the west; that was a good thing; he had dug into the land and found it rich. Rab had wounded Ush and stolen away his wife; that was a pity, and Rab had his hands full with her, which served him right. A sickness was on the cattle in the northern fold; let those in other parts of the village keep their cows away lest the devil get them also. The chief's counselor had been caught stealing. Many thought that the tribe should exercise its immemorial right of deposing the unfit leader. I imagine him telling these tales of the day with the narrative gift, but also with a ripe philosophy and a point of view as high and progressive as the age knew. I think of him as ignoring the trivial things, the mere surmises, the facts which, spread abroad, would have injured individuals without benefitting the tribe. Such as he helped the upward march from tool to machinery, tribe to nation.

THE POINT OF VIEW

Each of these gossips had the eager curiosity and the burning desire to communicate its results which mark the real journalist. The difference between them consisted partly in moral intention, but mainly in point of view. And that necessity for approaching truth from a point of view rules us of the twentieth century A.D. as it did them of the twentieth century B.C., though they spoke simple things by word of mouth to one full fireside, and we complex things by word of pen and type and lightning press to a hundred thousand firesides. Nothing above a market report, or a tabulation of stock fluctuations, but shows the point of view of him who wrote.

Picking at random, as a Scotch soothsayer pricks his Bible for a sign, I lay my finger on a piece of news in this morning's *Boston Post*. It is an item, a "stick" long, from Lynn; it relates to a young girl who went to sleep with a revolver under her pillow. The revolver exploded in the night, wounding her in the shoulder. As you read it, you find the reporter's point of view. It was a "regrettable accident." "Restlessness in sleep" was the probable cause. A reader sympathizes with the young woman. I imagine its treatment from other points of view. First, the flippant and jocular— the girl who went "heeled" for that old fetish of humor, the man under the bed, and shot only herself. Then the sensational, hinting, by a twist here and a turn of phrase there, that there was more in the case than the girl told. Then the heavy monitory, implying—if only by inserting the adverb "carelessly"—that girls should not keep revolvers under their pillows. Be a journalist anything more than a clod, anything less than an archangel, he must have a human point of view; be his work any warm expression of himself, anything beyond a dry, unreadable lump, he must throw on it that light which is an expression of character and belief.

The old editor, feeling about for proper use of the news-force, either overemphasized this factor or ignored it. The blatant old party organ published, if Democratic, only the Democratic rallies and speeches, ignoring the Republican or sneering at their meetings in little ten-line reports. The point of view was there, but bigoted, narrow, and unfair. Another kind of editor, who left no descendants to this generation, held, as the fettered English do, that news should be colorless, that all expression should come in the editorial columns. So he killed art in reporting, reducing it to a mechanical formula, thereby dulling the minds of his readers and forfeiting some of his hold on his public. . . .

THE REPORTER AND THE NEWS

Truth, fogged by the imperfections of human sight, hidden under the wrappings of lies, stands the final aim of a reporter when he goes out on a news tip. It is the working hypothesis of a reporter, "Why don't our newspapers tell the truth?" ask politicians and excellent ladies of women's clubs. Could they only know the difficulty of reaching an approximation to the hidden fact! Accurate perception of the event which has just happened before the eyes of flesh is so exceptional as to be almost unknown. Hugo Munsterberg tried an experiment once before his Harvard class in psychology. As the students settled themselves to the lecture, two men rose from the front seat and started to fight. Others joined in to separate or to assist them. A minute of lively action followed. "Gentlemen," said Dr. Munsterberg, when the disturbance was quelled, "we have only been acting for your benefit, a little drama, rehearsed beforehand. We know, for we followed our lines, just what happened. Please write down all you saw." The resultant papers differed ridiculously from each other; and all differed materially from fact. Later, Munsterberg produced another such drama, this time warning the class, asking them in advance to observe, and to write out their observations. The results were only a little less inaccurate. A professor at a Kansas university, imitating the Munsterberg experiment, staged a pretended "shooting scrape." One of the actors sprang into the melee flourishing a monkeywrench. Not a member of the class but saw it as a pistol. The streamer Rio de Janeiro struck the reef off Fort Point in the Golden Gate, ran out toward the sea in the darkness and ebb tide, and sank, blowing her whistle until the water drowned her steam. In the subsequent inquiry the duration of her whistle blasts became important. A company of soldiers was quartered just above Fort Point; most of them heard the blasts. Part of their drill in soldiering had consisted in counting off seconds. Yet some said that the blasts were ten seconds long, some two minutes, and some that there was just one continuous blast.

Now the reporter really approaches accuracy of perception. Daily training has made him so. Had Professor Munsterberg produced his drama before a body of journalists, I venture that their reports would have varied but little in statement of fact; I venture that certain individuals among a body of reporters watching the Kansas experiment, would have detected the monkeywrench, and that had there been a trained journalist in the barracks over Fort Point we should know more than the Government ever learned about the means the Rio took to save herself.

But the reporter sees few of his comedies, tragedies, dramas, and little novels of the street firsthand. He is not there when the trains collide, the mania shoots, or the thief escapes. He must take his information second-hand from witnesses with untrained and imperfect eyes. The courts, when they come to adjudicate these matters, will have trouble enough and to spare in getting at the probable truth; yet lawyers and detectives have weeks to weigh, sift, and correct by that circumstantial evidence which is often the best evidence, where reporters have but minutes.

This would be difficult enough were all the witnesses of the events which he sets about to chronicle disingenuous and truthful. But no one is so beset by the falsity of man as this same reporter. "Half the population," some one says, "is trying to keep out of the newspapers and half trying to get in." And both these classes lie consistently, or employ press-agents to do the lying for them. In unraveling these tangled things, in arriving at his results—marvel of accuracy in view of his difficulties—the reporter's feet, like Patrick Henry's, are guided by the one lamp of experience. Roughly acquainted with all classes of men, all kinds of human institutions—for each day brings him in contact with a fresh aspect of life—he develops an intuition, which is only crystalized experience, for the probable fact hidden under human contradictions and lies. You, reader, as a consumer of newspapers, do not often see a newspaper story about a little girl lured away from home and imprisoned in a dark cellar by a villain. Yet cases of that kind are commonly reported to the police. How experience has shown that a certain kind of hysterical girl who has played truant from home for a day or so usually falls back on her Laura Jean Libbey and invents such an excuse to her family. The girl's assertion is uncontradicted; but the reporter, remembering previous cases, does not accept the story unless it has strong circumstantial corroboration. Here we have an obvious case of experience in action.

In this elemental function of finding just what happened, reporters and those editors in most immediate touch with them are, by and large, about as sincere as we may expect imperfect humanity to be. The untruth in our journalism resides elsewhere. William Jennings Bryan once raised the question: "Have we an honest press?" Were news investigation all of journalism, the answer would need be a strong affirmative. Excepting for the very "yellow" reporter, who has lost his sense of truth and proportion, these men are after the fact and nothing else. Indeed, reporting is an unsurpassed training in sincerity. And where news results seem untruthful, the fault lies often with the reporter's judgment, not his intentions. He may accept, in the first excitement following disaster, the statement of some hysterical official that twenty people are dead, may telephone in this estimate for an extra, and may find later that the victims number only two or three. Here the public is partly to blame, since it demands immediate

information. News editors, in throwing out extras while the event is still
fresh, generally make allowance for this tendency and cut down the first
figures. "Halve 'em," is the rule of a great press bureau. And in late years
the roster of victims grows rather than diminishes with succeeding extras. . . .

ALL THE NEWS THAT'S FIT TO PRINT
THE CODE OF ETHICS

Now, strangely, these men at the bottom of the profession—if we measure standing by salary and public esteem—have come nearest of all
American journalists to forming a professional spirit and formulating an ethical code. Not all reporters hold that code, of course, but the best, the
directing journalists of to-morrow, do. These are its main articles:

First—Never, without special permission, print information which you
learn at your friend's house, or in your club. In short, draw a strict line
between your social and professional life. The journalist must keep such a
line if he is to be anything but a pariah. The layman generally does not
understand this. The remark, thrown at him across a dinner table, "Of
course, this is not for publication," offends the very young reporter; later,
iteration breeds indifference.

Second—Except in the case of criminals, publish nothing without full
permission of your informant. The caution, "But this is not for publication,"
stands between every experienced reporter and a world of live, sensational
matter. As a rule, reporters and their directing editors abide by this article
of the code to the last item. It is a question not so much of morals as of
convenience. In news-gathering, acquaintance is half the battle.

A man once betrayed goes forever off your calling list; continue the
process, and you lose all acquaintance. Politicians, popular clergymen,
police officials, and others who have daily contact with reporters understand this working agreement. The Washington corps has called Theodore
Roosevelt "the greatest journalist of us all." He showed this in his confi-
dences to the newspaper men. Again and again he told the reporters, at
his daily interviews, the whole secret of a blind event. "This is for your
own information. Don't print it until I tell you," he would say. And wo to
the wight who did it! Seldom was Roosevelt betrayed, and then only on
minor points.

Not only convenience holds good reporters to this article of faith, but
also a real sense of morals. I know a reporter who was ostracized for years
by his fellows because he published matter after the admonition of secrecy

from his informants. The breaking-point came when seven men from as many newspapers went to interview a politician under fire. He gave them the formal news, and later the story of his private relation to the event. "But you won't print *that*, of course," he added. "Oh, no!" responded all the reporters except this one. He published it; the story was a fine beat. "You didn't notice that I didn't say 'No,'" he said in extenuation. This read him out of the craft.

Third—Never sail under false colors. State who you are, what newspaper you represent, and whether or not your informant is talking for publication. If there is keyhole work to be done, leave that to the detectives, who work inside the law.

Fourth (and to Henry Watterson, the cardinal article in the code)— Keep this side of the home boundary. Remember that when the suicide lies dead in the chamber there are wretched hearts in the hall, that when the son is newly in jail intrusion is torment to the mother. Nearly all reporters who expect to remain in the business respect articles one and two. Articles three and four most of them would like to respect. They can not do so, however, without permission of their directing editors and of the publisher, a court of last resort. Half the reporting staffs are forced to do distasteful things because the publisher needs the news and does not care how the mere agent gets it. Yet with the passing of yellow journalism, and the contemporaneous passing of the craze for beats, publishers begin to see that enlightened self-interest may demand observance of even these articles. The reporter is, to the plain citizen, the visible representative of his newspaper. A violated home becomes a hostile home; and certain journals owe their special facilities for newsgetting to the decency and acceptability of their reporters. There are city editors as scrupulous about the methods of their men as any reporter could wish. On the *New York Sun* and *Post*, the *Kansas City Star*, the *Chicago Post*, the *Boston Transcript*, and the *Washington Star*, the reporter who presented information plucked from a wastebasket, or bullied from a woman at the back door, would be presenting an application for discharge. Most of these newspapers have their shortcomings; in some, the vices may be more harmful to the body politic and social than any lapse in manners. But they do insist on decent relations between the reporter and his public.

THE LIMITS OF GENTILITY

The newspaper should be a gentleman—such is the whole formula. However, some arbiter of manners has said: "It is never gentlemanly to knock a man down, but sometimes a gentleman must do it, nevertheless." When the law is not the regulator of society but its disturber, not the protector of the weak but the bulwark of the brutal strong, then the newspaper, chief expression of public opinion, becomes agent of a justice higher than formal law. Justice is grim business; its processes from arrest to execution are not pretty. And in such a fight as that with the Quy gang in Philadelphia or Tammany in New York, a few breaches of mere manners count for little beside the ultimate object. When Watterson made his criticism of our press, several American editors expressed themselves in approval or opposition. Ernest S. Simpson, editor of the *San Francisco Call*, stated the other side. He said:

> It is a well-recognized function of American journalism to play the part of an electric light in a dark alley. The light exposes ugliness, and until it is exposed ugliness will not be cleaned up. The people who most fear publicity talk most of sensational journalism. Let Colonel Watterson take care that he is not charged hereafter with trying to turn off the electric light in the dark alley.

THE VOICE OF A GENERATION

Logically, I should close this series with a view of the present state of American journalism. It is impossible, however, to do that with fairness and certitude. No one can state his own period in terms of time and eternity. His eyes are too near the object. Then, too, there is a special difficulty. This is a transition period. In American journalism, as in American statecraft, we are sloughing off dead skin and the new is not yet hardened to use. In spite of the evils and excesses in our journalism, the curve of progress appears to run upward. . . .

In the profession itself lies our greatest hope. In spite of all commercial tendencies, its personnel and intelligence are improving year by year. Visiting from newspaper shop to newspaper shop last year, I was struck with the general and noble dissatisfaction of the men over the present condition in their craft. It was not the whine of the half-baked old-time newspaper man—"this is a rotten business!" They are coming to realize the importance of their profession, its usefulness, its potential standing. Their dissatisfaction is only disgust for a control which forces the reporter to drop a "good story" because it leads to the iniquity of some "friend" of the paper, which forces the editorial writer to write against all his opinions because the source of income is involved. The sentiment is young, but growing; it has not yet crystallized in results. In ten years of journalism, I have not known five writers for the daily press who left their employment over a matter of opinion. . . .

Most of the faults which I have enumerated in showing the darker side of our wonderfully able, wonderfully efficient, and wonderfully powerful daily journalism, might all be gathered under the cover of this one generic fault— take it by and large, *it does not speak to its generation.* It is the mouthpiece of an older stock; it lags behind the thought of its times.

For in the uninterrupted flow of the coming and going of men, time somehow arranges generations like the generations of a family. We had one such after the Civil War. The men of that day broke ground. They performed miraculous labors; they tamed a continent. In the dust and scuffle of their war with unharnessed nature, they took little time to analyze the nicer moral questions, or to consider the ends to which their warfare led. They worshiped success and its rewards; the stories which made their hearts glow were stories of poor boys grown rich and great—they never inquired how. John D. Rockefeller was long, to his own generation, the pattern for youth that he is to himself.

"WE OF THE THIRTIES"

Then, after that little Spanish War, so poor in action, so rich in consequences, a new earth held up its smoky hands to the same old heaven. We in our thirties and forties, who are now doing and directing that work of America, are not nearly so respectful toward immediate success. We found the continent broken and tamed; we are considering the new forces loosed by the work of the nineteenth century, and wondering how we may reduce them to the power of law before they overwhelm us. It may be a less able generation; it is surely a more moral one. And our chief concern with such a phenomenon as John D. Rockefeller is to see that no one ever repeats his kind of success.

To us of this younger generation our daily press is speaking, for the most part, with a dead voice, because the supreme power resides in men of that older generation. Could the working journalists of our own age tell us as frankly as they wished what they think and see and feel about the times, we should have only minor points to criticize in American journalism.

SELECTION FROM
THE BRASS CHECK

UPTON SINCLAIR

1919

———

———

———

Upton Sinclair was one of the most prolific writers of his age and was equally comfortable crafting novels and turning out nonfiction. In 1906 *The Jungle,* an unremitting attack on the meatpacking industry, became a best-selling novel. In 1919, in *The Brass Check,* in raw, staccato prose, Sinclair painted a picture of a false, cowardly press dominated by its business offices and its advertisers. He could not find a publisher for the book, so he published it himself, and it too became a best-seller, with 300,000 copies in print in its first year of publication. He called the press a slave to capitalism, which was engaged in suppressing truth and spreading falsehoods. As an alternative to control by the media barons, he proposed public ownership.

Just as *The Jungle* had appeared first in the widely circulated socialist weekly *Appeal to Reason,* so did *The Brass Check.* In his 1962 memoirs, Sinclair recalled how much difficulty he had in coming up with a title. He toyed with such possibilities as *Typhoid Mary, The Poison Square, The Gas Attack, The Daily Lie, Give Us This Day Our Daily Lie,* and *The Madam Kept.* Then, he wrote in his memoirs, "it struck me that *The Brass Check* was a fine title for a book about the prostitution of the press." (At brothels in the early part of this century, men paid money to a cashier who handed them a brass check which they then gave to the prostitutes.)

His book was generally shunned by the mainstream press of his day, and it received only a handful of reviews. The *New York Times* did not review it, but it did carry an article about a speech given by James Melvin Lee, a professor of journalism at New York University, on "The Fallacies of the *Brass Check.*" When Sinclair asked for space to reply to this attack, he was denied it, and the *Times* editorialized: "We find that Mr. Lee speaks the truth and Mr. Sinclair does not. . . . It may be mildly interesting to watch Mr. Lee swatting a fly, but there is no reason why any of the spectators should open the house as refuge for the pestiferous and defiling insect."

SELECTION FROM
THE BRASS CHECK

THE STORY OF THE BRASS CHECK

Once upon a time there was a little boy; a nice little boy, whom you would have liked if you had known him—at least, so his mother says. He had been brought up in the traditions of the old South, to which the two most important things in the world were good cooking and good manners. He obeyed his mother and father, and ate his peas with a fork, and never buttered the whole slice of his bread. On Sunday mornings he carefully shined his shoes and brushed his clothes at the window, and got into a pair of tight kid gloves and under a tight little brown derby hat, and walked with his parents to a church on Fifth Avenue. On week-days he studied hard and obeyed his teachers, and in every field of thought and activity he believed what was told him by those in authority. He learned the catechism and thought it was the direct word of God. When he fell sick and the doctor came, he put himself in the doctor's hands with a sense of perfect trust and content; the doctor knew what to do, and would do it, and the little boy would get well.

The boy's grandfather had been a Confederate naval officer, drowned at sea. The boy's father had spent his youth in Virginia during the agonies of the Civil War, thus missing most of his education. After the war the family was ruined, and the father had to enter into competition with Yankee "hustle," handicapped by a Southern gentleman's quaint notions of dignity, and also by a Southern gentleman's weakness for mint-juleps. So the last week's board bill was generally a matter of anxiety to the family. But always, no matter how poor the family might be, the little boy had a clean white collar, and a copy of the *New York Sun* every morning. This paper was beautifully printed, smooth and neat; the little boy knew all its peculiarities of type, and he and his father and his mother accepted every word they read in it, both the news-columns and the editorial page, precisely as they accepted the doctor's pills and the clergyman's sermons, the Bible and the multiplication table and Marian Harland's cookbook.

The *New York Sun* was edited by one of the bitterest cynics that ever lived in America. He had been something of a radical in his early days, and

had turned like a fierce wolf upon his young ideals. He had one fixed opinion, which was that everything new in the world should be mocked at and
denounced. He had a diabolical wit, and had taught a tradition to his staff,
and had infected a good part of American journalism with the poison of his
militant cynicism. Once every twenty-four hours the little boy absorbed
this poison, he took it for truth, and made all his ideas of it.

For example, there were women who were trying to be different from
what women had always been. There was a thing called "Sorosis." The
boy never knew what "Sorosis" was; from the *Sun* he gathered that it was
a collection of women who wanted to have brains, and to take part in public
affairs—whereas the *Sun* acidly considered that woman's place was the
home. And the boy found it easy to agree with this. Did not the boy's
grandmother make the best ginger-cakes of any grandmother in the whole
city of Baltimore? Did not his mother make the best chocolate-cake and
the best "hot short-cake"—that is, whenever the family could escape from
boarding-houses and have a little kitchen of its own. The boy was enor-
mously fond of chocolate-cake and short-cake, and of course he didn't want
women neglecting their duties for fool things such as "Sorosis."

Also there were the Populists. The little boy had never seen a Populist,
he had never been given an opportunity to read a Populist platform, but
he knew all about the Populists from the funny editorials of Charles A.
Dana. The Populists were long-haired and wild-eyed animals whose habit
was the corn-fields of Kansas. The boy knew the names of a lot of them,
or rather the nicknames which Dana gave them; he had a whole portrait-
gallery of them in his mind. Once upon a time the *Sun* gave some statistics
from Kansas, suggesting that the Populists were going insane; so the boy
took his pen in hand and wrote a letter to the editor of the *Sun,* gravely
rebuking him. He had never expected to read in the columns of the *Sun*
a suggestion that Populists might go insane. And the *Sun* published this
feeble product of its own "smartness."

Later on the boy discovered the *New York Evening Post,* the beau ideal
of a gentleman's newspaper, and this became for years his main source of
culture. The *Evening Post* was edited by E. L. Godkin, a scholar and a
lover of righteousness, but narrow, and with an abusive tongue. From him
the boy learned that American politics were rotten, and he learned the
cause of the rottenness: First, there was an ignorant mob, composed mainly
of foreigners; and second, there were venal politicians who pandered to
this mob. Efforts were continually being made by gentlemen of decency
and culture to take the government away from these venal politicians, but
the mob was too ignorant, and could not be persuaded to support a clean
government. Yet the fight must be kept up, because conditions were going

from bad to worse. The boy witnessed several "reform campaigns," conducted mainly by the *Evening Post* and other newspapers. These campaigns consisted in the publication of full-page exposures of civic rottenness, with denunciations of the politicians in office. The boy believed every word of the exposures, and it never occurred to him that the newspapers might be selling more copies by means of them; still less did it occur to him that anybody might be finding in these excitements a means of diverting the mind of the public from larger and more respectable forms of "graft."

There was a candidate for district attorney, William Travers Jerome by name; a man with a typical *Evening Post* mind, making an ideal *Evening Post* candidate. He conducted a "whirlwind" campaign, speaking at half a dozen meetings every evening, and stirring his audience to frenzy by his accounts of the corruption of the city's police-force. Men would stand up and shout with indignation, women would faint or weep. The boy would sit with his finger-nails dug into the palms of his hands, while the orator tore away the veils from subjects which were generally kept hidden from little boys.

The orator described the system of prostitution, which was paying its millions every year to the police of the city. He pictured a room in which women displayed their persons, and men walked up and down and inspected them, selecting one as they would select an animal at a fair. The man paid his three dollars, or his five dollars, to a cashier at the window, and received a brass check; then he went upstairs, and paid this check to the woman upon receipt of her favors. And suddenly the orator put his hand into his pocket and drew forth the bit of metal. "Behold!" he cried. "The price of a woman's shame!"

To the lad in the audience this BRASS CHECK was the symbol of the most monstrous wickedness in the world. Night after night he would attend these meetings, and next day he would read about them in the papers. He was a student at college, living in a lodging-house room on four dollars a week, which he earned himself; yet he pitched in to help this orator's campaign, and raised something over a hundred dollars, and took it to the *Evening Post* candidate at his club, interrupting him at dinner, and no doubt putting a strain on his patience. The candidate was swept into office in a tornado of excitement, and did what all *Evening Post* candidates did and always do—that is, nothing. For four long years the lad waited, in bewilderment and disgust, ending in rage. So he learned the grim lesson that there is more than one kind of parasite feeding on human weakness, there is more than one kind of prostitution which may be symbolized by the BRASS CHECK.

THE STORY OF A POET

The boy, now become a youth, obtained a letter of introduction from his clergyman to the editor of his beloved *Evening Post,* and at the age of sixteen was given a trial as reporter. He worked for a week collecting odd scraps of news, and when the week was over he had earned the generous sum of two dollars and sixty-seven cents. This was his first and last experience as newspaper reporter, and it confirmed his boyish impression of the integrity of the journalistic profession. His work had consisted of compiling obituary notices about leading citizens who had died. "John T. McGurk, senior partner of McGurk and Isaacson, commission-merchants of 679 Desbrosses Street, died yesterday of cirrhosis of the liver at his home, 4321 George Washington Avenue, Hoboken. Mr. McGurk was 69 years of age, and leaves a widow and eleven children. He was a member of the Elks, and president of the North Hoboken Bowling Association." And these facts the *Evening Post* printed exactly as he had written them. In a book which will not have much to say in favor of American journalism, let this fidelity to truth, and to the memory of the blameless McGurk, have its due meed of praise.

The youth took to writing jokes and jingles, at which he earned twice as much as the *Evening Post* had paid him. Later he took to writing dime-novels, at which he made truly fabulous sums. He found it puzzling that this cheap and silly writing should be the kind that brought the money. The editors told him it was because the public wanted that kind; but the youth wondered—might not at least part of the blame lie with the editors, who never tried giving anything better? It was the old problem—which comes first, the hen or the egg?

We have spoken jestingly of the traditions of the old South, in which the youth was brought up; but the reader should not get a false impression of them—in many ways they were excellent traditions. For one thing, they taught the youth to despise a lie; also to hate injustice, so that wherever in his life he encountered it, his whole being became a blaze of excitement. Always he was striving in his mind to discover the source of lies and injustice—why should there be so much of them in the world? The newspapers revealed the existence of them, but never seemed to know the causes of them, nor what to do about them, further than to support a reform candidate who did nothing but get elected. This futility in the face of the world's misery and corruption was maddening to the youth.

He had rich relatives who were fond of him, so that he was free to escape from poverty into luxury; he had the opportunity to rise quickly in the world, if he would go into business, and devote his attention thereto.

But would he find in business the ideals which he craved? He talked with business men, also he got the flavor of business from the advertisements in the newspapers—and he knew that this was not what he was seeking. He cultivated the friendship of Jesus, Hamlet, and Shelley, and fell in love with the young Milton and the young Goethe; in them he found his own craving for truth and beauty. Here, through the medium of art, life might be ennobled, and lifted from the muck of graft and greed.

So the youth ran away and buried himself in a hut in the wilds of Canada, and wrote what he thought was the great American novel. It was a painfully crude performance, but it had a new moral impulse in it, and the youth really believed that it was to convert the world to ways of love and justice. He took it to the publishers, and one after another they rejected it. They admitted that it had merit, but it would not sell. Incredible as it seemed to the youth, the test by which the publishers judged an embryo book and its right to be born, was not whether it had a vision and beauty and a new moral impulse; they judged it as the newspapers judged what they published—would it sell? The youth earned some money and published the book himself, and wrote a preface to tell the world what a wonderful book it was, and how the cruel publishers had rejected it. This preface, together with the book, he sent to the leading newspapers; and thus began the second stage of his journalistic experiences!

Two newspapers paid attention to his communication—the *New York Times,* a respectable paper, and the *New York American,* a "yellow" paper. The *American* sent a woman reporter, an agreeable and friendly young lady, to whom the author poured out his soul. She asked for his picture, saying that this would enable her to get much more space for the story; so the author gave his picture. She asked for his wife's picture; but here the author was obdurate. He had old-fashioned Southern notions about "newspaper notoriety" for ladies; he did not want his wife's picture in the papers. There stood a little picture of his wife on the table where the interview took place, and after the reporter had left, it was noticed that this picture was missing. Next day the picture was published in the *New York American,* and has been published in the *New York American* every year or two since. The author, meantime, has divorced his first wife and married a second wife—a fact of which the newspapers are fully aware; yet they publish this picture of the first wife indifferently as a picture of the first wife and of the second wife. When one of these ladies says or does a certain thing, the other lady may open her paper in the morning and receive a shock!

Both the *New York Times* and the *New York American* published interviews with the young author. It had been his fond hope to interest people in his book and to cause them to read his book, but in this he failed; what both the interviews told about was his personality. The editors had been amused by the naive assumption of a young poet that he might have something of importance to say to the world; they had made a "human interest" story out of it, a journalistic tidbit to tickle the appetites of the jaded and worldly-wise. They said scarcely anything about the contents of the book, and as a result of the two interviews, the hungry young author sold precisely two copies!

Meantime he was existing by hack-work, and exploring the world in which ideas are bought and sold. He was having jokes and plots of stories stolen; he was having agreements broken and promises repudiated; he was trying to write worth-while material, and being told that it would not sell; he was trying to become a book reviewer, and finding that the only way to succeed was to be a cheat. The editor of the *Independent* or the *Literary Digest* would give him half a dozen books to read, and he would read them, and write an honest review, saying that there was very little merit in any of them: whereupon, the editor would decide that it was not worthwhile to review the books, and the author would get nothing for his work. If, on the other hand, he wrote an article about a book, taking it seriously, and describing it as vital and important, the editor would conclude that the book was worth reviewing, and would publish the review, and pay the author three or four dollars for it.

This, you understand, was the "literary world," in which ideas, the most priceless possession of mankind, were made the subject of barter and sale. In every branch of it there were such petty dishonesties, such tricks of the trade. There were alway ten times as many people trying to get a living as the trade would support. They were clutching at chances, elbowing each other out of the way; and their efforts were not rewarded according to their love of truth and beauty, but according to quite other factors. They were dressing themselves up and using the "social game," they were exposing and pretending, the women were using the sex lure. And everywhere, when they pretended to care about literature and ideas, they were really caring about money, and "success" because it would bring money. Everywhere, above all things else, they hated and feared the very idea of genius, which put them to shame, and threatened with annihilation their petty gains and securities.

From these things the youth fled into the wilderness again, living in a tent with his young wife, and writing a story in which he poured out his contempt upon the great Metropolis of Mammon. This was "Prince Hagen," and he sent it to the *Atlantic Monthly,* and there came a letter from the editor, Professor Bliss Perry, saying that it was a work of merit and that he would publish it. So for weeks the young author walked on the top of the clouds. But then came another letter, saying that the other members of the *Atlantic* staff had read the story, and that Professor Perry had been unable to persuade them to see it as he saw it. "We have," said he, "a very conservative, fastidious and sophisticated constituency."

The young author went back to his "pot-boiling." He spent another winter in New York, wrestling with disillusionments and humiliations, and then, fleeing to that wilderness for a third summer, he put his experience into "The Journal of Arthur Stirling," the story of a young poet who is driven to suicide by neglect and despair. The book was given to the world as a genuine document, and relieved the tedium of a literary season. Its genuineness was accepted almost everywhere, and the author sat behind the scenes, feeling quite devilish. When the secret came out, some critics were cross, and one or two of them have not yet forgiven the writer. The *New York Evening Post* is accustomed to mention the matter every once in a while, declaring that the person who played that trick can never receive anyone's confidence. I will not waste space discussing this question, save to point out that the newspaper reviewers had set the rules of the game — that love and beauty in art were heeded only in connection with personalities and sensation; so, in order to project love and beauty upon the world, the young author had provided the personalities and sensation. As for the *Evening Post* and its self-righteousness, before I finish this book I shall tell of things done by that organ of Wall Street which qualify decidedly its right to sit in judgment upon questions of honor.

THE MENTAL MUNITION-FACTORY

A solution that comes at once to mind is state-owned or municipal-owned newspapers. This is the orthodox Socialist solution, and is also being advocated by William Jennings Bryan. Fortunately, we do not have to take his theories, or anyone's theories; we have facts — the experience of Los Angeles with its public paper, the *Municipal News,* which was an entire success. I inquire of the editor of the paper, Frank E. Wolfe, and he writes:

> The *Municipal News?* There's a rich story buried there. It was established by an initiative ordinance, and had an ample appropriation. It was launched in the stream with engines going full steam ahead. Its success was instantaneous. Free distribution; immense circulation; choked with high-class, high rate advertising; well edited, and it was clean and immensely popular.

Otis said: "Every dollar that damned socialistic thing gets is a dollar out of the *Times* till." Every publisher in the city re-echoed, and the fight was on. The chief thing that rankled, however, was the outgrowth of a clause in the ordinance which gave to each political party polling a three per cent vote a column in each issue for whatsoever purpose it might be used. The Socialist Labor Party nosed out the Prohibitionists by a fluke. The Socialists had a bit margin in the preceding elections, so the Reds had two columns, and they were quick to seize the opportunity for propaganda. The Googoos, who had always stoutly denied they were a political party, came forward and claimed space, and the merry war was on. Those two columns for Socialist propaganda were the real cause for the daily on-slaught of the painted ladies of Broadway (newspaper district of Los Angeles). There were three morning and three evening papers. Six times a day they whined, barked, yelped, and snapped at the heels of the *Municipal News.* Never were more lies poured out from the mouths of these mothers of falsehood. The little, weakly whelps of the pornographic press took up the hue and cry, and Blanche, Sweetheart and Tray were on the trail. Ad-vertisers were cajoled, browbeaten, and blackmailed, until nearly all left the paper. The *News* was manned by a picked staff of the best newspaper men on the coast. It was clean, well edited, and gave both sides to all controversies—using the parallel col-umn system. It covered the news of the municipality better than any paper had ever covered it. It was weak and ineffective editorially, for the policy was to print a newspaper. We did not indulge in a clothes-line quarrel—did not fight back.

The *News* died under the axe one year from its birth. They use the initiative to kill it. The rabble rallied to the cry, and we foresaw the end.

The paper had attracted attention all over the English-read-ing world. Everywhere I have gone I have been asked about it, by people who never dreamed I had been an editor of the paper. Its death was a triumph for reaction, but its effect will not die. Some day the idea will prevail. Then I might want to go back into the "game."

City-owned newspapers are part of the solution, but not the whole part. As a Socialist, I advocate public ownership of the instruments and means of production; but I do not rely entirely upon that method where intellectual matters are concerned. I would have the state make all the steel and coal and oil, the shoes and matches and sugar; I would have it do the distributing of newspapers, and perhaps even the printing; but for the editing of the newspapers I cast about for a method of control that allows free play to the development of initiative and the expression of personality.

In a free society the solution will be simple; there will be many groups and associations, publishing their own papers, and if you do not like the papers which these groups give you, you can form a group of your own. Being in receipt of the full product of your labor, you will have plenty of money, and will be surrounded by other free and independent individuals, also receiving the full product of their labor, and accustomed to combining for the expression of their ideas. The difference is that today the world's resources are in the hands of a class, and this class has a monopoly of self-expression. The problem of transferring such power to the people must be studied as the whole social problem, and not merely as the problem of the press.

Fortunately there are parts of America in which the people have kept at least a part of their economic independence, and have gone ahead to solve the problem of the "kept" press in true American fashion—that is, by organizing and starting honest newspapers for themselves. The editor of the *Nonpartisan Leader,* Oliver S. Morris, has kindly written for me an account of the experiences of the Nonpartisan League, which I summarize as follows:

The League commenced organization work early in 1915 in North Dakota. By the summer of the next year it had forty thousand members, yet no newspaper in the state had given, even as news, a fair account of the League's purposes. Every daily paper in the state was filled with "gross misinformation and absurd lies." So the League started a little weekly paper of its own. With this single weekly, against the entire daily press of the state, it swept the primaries in June 1916.

Then the League decided to have a daily paper. The *Courier-News* of Fargo had been for sale, but the owners would not sell to the League. The League went ahead to start a new paper, actually buying machinery and taking subscriptions; then the *Courier-News* decided to sell, and its circulation under League ownership now exceeds the total population of Fargo.

The League at present has weekly papers in seven states, with a total circulation of two hundred thousand, and another weekly, the *Non-partisan Leader,* published in St. Paul, with a circulation of two hundred and fifty thousand. It is starting co-operative country weekly papers, supervising their editorial policy and furnishing them news and editorial service; over one hundred of these weekly papers are already going. There is another League daily in Grand Forks, North Dakota, and one at Nampa, Idaho. Finally, the League is going ahead on its biggest venture, the establishment of a daily in Minneapolis. This paper is to be capitalized at a million dollars, and the stock is being sold to farmer and labor organiations throughout the state. Says Mr. Morris: "Many wealthy professional and business men, disgusted with the controlled press, have purchased stock, and are warm boosters for the League publications." Also he says:

> One of the chief result of the establishment of a League press is a different attitude on the part of many existing papers. With competition in the field, many publishers who have hitherto been biased and unfair have been forced to change their tactics. Few of these papers have gone over to the League side of political and economic questions, but they have been forced at least to print fair news reports on both sides of the question in their news columns, reserving their opposition to the movement for their editorial columns. That, of course, is fair enough. The menace of the controlled press in America is due to the fact that as a rule this press does not confine its arguments and opposition to the editorial columns, but uses the news columns for propaganda, and, failing to print the news, printing only a part of it, distorting it or actually lying, sways opinion through the news columns.

Such is the procedure in places where Americans are free. But what about our crowded cities, with their slum populations, speaking forty different languages, illiterate, unorganized, and dumb? Even in these cities there have been efforts made to start newspapers in the interest of the people. I know few more heroic stories than the twenty-year struggle to establish and maintain the *New York Call*. It began as a weekly, *The Worker*. Even that took endless campaigns of begging, and night labor of devoted men and women who earned their livings by day-time labor under the cruel capitalist grind. At last they managed to raise funds to start a daily, and then for ten years it was an endless struggle with debt and starvation. It was a lucky week when the *New York Call* had money enough to pay its printing force; the reporters and editors would sometimes have to wait for months. A good part of the space in the paper had to be devoted to ingenious begging.

The same attempt was made in Chicago, and there bad management and factional quarrels brought a disastrous failure. At the time of writing, there are Socialist dailies in Butte, in Seattle, and in Milwaukee, also a few foreign-language Socialist dailies. There are numerous weeklies and monthlies; but these, of course, do not take the place of newspapers, they are merely a way of pamphleteering. The people read falsehoods all week or all month, and then at last they get what portion of the truth the *Appeal to Reason* or the *Nation* or the *Liberator* or *Pearson's* can find room for. In the meantime the average newspaper reader has had his whole psychology made of lies, so that he cannot believe the truth when he sees it.

There are a few millionaires in America who have liberal tendencies. They have been willing to finance reform campaigns, and in great emergencies to give the facts to the people; they have been willing now and then to back radical magazines, and even to publish them. But—I state the fact, without trying to explain it—there has not yet appeared in America a millionaire willing to found and maintain a fighting daily paper for the abolition of exploitation. I have myself put the proposition before several rich men. I have even known of cases where promises were made, and plans drawn up. My friend Gaylord Wilshire intended to do it with the proceeds of his gold-mine, but the gold-mine has taken long to develop. I had hopes that Henry Ford would do it, when I read of his purchase of the *Dearborn Independent.* I urged the matter upon him with all the eloquence I could muster; he said he meant to do it, but I have my fears. The trouble is his ignorance; he really does not know about the world in which he finds himself, and so far the intellectual value of the *Dearborn Independent* has been close to zero.

So our slum proletariat is left to feed upon the garbage of yellow journalism. Year by year the cost of living increases, and wages, if they move at all, move laggingly, and after desperate and embittered strife. In the midst of this strife the proletariat learns its lessons; it learns to know the clubs of policemen and the bayonets and machine-guns of soldiers; it learns to know capitalist politicians and capitalist judges; also it learns to know Capitalist journalism! Wherever in America the workers organize and strike for a small portion of their rights, they come out of the experience with a bitter and abiding hatred of the press. I have shown you what happened in Colorado; in West Virginia; in Paterson, New Jersey; in Calumet, Michigan; in Bisbee, Arizona; in Seattle, Washington. I could show you the same thing happening in every industrial center in America.

The workers have come to realize the part which the newspapers play; they have come to know the newspapers as the crux of the argument, the key to the treasure-chamber. A modern newspaper, seen from the point of view of the workers, is a gigantic munition-factory, in which the propertied class manufactures mental bombs and gas-shells for the annihilation of its enemies. And just as in war sometimes the strategy is determined by the location of great munition-factories and depots, so the class-struggle comes to center about newspaper offices. In every great city of Europe where the revolution took place, the first move of the rebels was to seize these offices, and the first move of the reactionaries was to get them back. We saw machine-guns mounted in the windows of newspaper-offices, sharp-shooters firing from the roofs, soldiers in the streets replying with shrap-nel. It is worth noting that wherever the revolutionists were able to take and hold the newspapers, they maintained their revolution; where the newspapers were retaken by the reactionaries, the revolution failed.

In Petrograd the *Little Gazette,* organ of the "Black Hundreds," became the *Red Gazette,* and has remained the *Red Gazette.* The official military organ, the *Army Fleet,* became the *Red Army and Fleet.* The *Will of Rus-sia,* organ of Protopopov, last premier of the Tsar, became the *Pravda,* which means "Truth." In Berlin, on the other hand, the *Kreuz-Zeitung,* organ of black magic and reaction, became for a few days *Die Rothe Fahne,* the "Red Flag"; but, alas, it went back to *Kreuz-Zeitung* again!

Will it come this way in America? Shall we see mobs storming the offices of the *New York Times* and *World,* and *Chicago Tribune,* the *Los Angeles Times?* It depends entirely upon the extent to which these capitalist news-papers continue to infuriate the workers, and to suppress working-class propaganda with the help of subservient government officials. I personally am not calling for violent revolution; I still hope for the survival of the American system of government. But I point out to the owners and man-agers of our great capitalist news-organs the peril in which they place themselves, by their system of organized lying about the radical move-ment. It is not only the fury of resentment they awaken in the hearts of class-conscious workingmen and women; it is the condition of unstable equilibrium which they set up in society, by the mass of truth they sup-press. Today every class-conscious workingman carries about with him as his leading thought, that if only he and his fellows could take the printing-offices and hold them for ten days, they could end forever the power of Capitalism, they could make safe the Co-operative Commonwealth of America.

I say ten days, and I do not speak loosely. Just imagine if the news-papers of America were to print the truth for ten days! The truth about poverty, and the causes of poverty; the truth about corruption in politics and in all branches of government, in Journalism, and throughout the busi-ness world; the truth about profiteering and exploitation, about the banking graft, the plundering of the railroads, the colossal gains of the Beef Trust and the Steel Trust and the Oil Trust and their hundreds of subsidiary organizations; the truth about conditions in industry, the suppression of labor-revolts and the corrupting of labor movements; above all, the truth about the possibilities of production by modern machinery, the fact that, by abolishing production for profit and substituting production for use, it would be possible to provide abundance. . . .

THE PROBLEM OF THE REPORTER

. . . Must a reporter be a cringing wretch, or else a man of honor in search of a job? Might not a reporter be a member of an honored profession, having its own standards, its sense of duty to the public? Obviously, the first trouble is that in his economic status the reporter is a sweated wage slave. If reporting is to become a profession, the reporters must organize, and have power to fix, not merely their wage-scale, but also their ethical code. I wrote an article calling for a "reporters' union," and [Isaac] Russell [a reporter for the *New York Times*] began to agitate among New York newspaper-men for this idea, which has now spread all over the country.

What would be the effect upon news-writing of a reporters' union? What assurance have we that reporters would be better than owners? Well, in the first place, reporters are young men, and owners are nearly always old men; so in the newspaper-world you have what you have in the world of finance, of diplomacy, of politics and government—a "league of the old men," giving orders to the young men, holding the young men down. The old men own most of the property, the young men own little of the property; so control by old men is property control, while control by young men would be control by human beings.

I have met some newspaper reporters who were drunken scoundrels. I have met some who were as cruel and unscrupulous as the interests they served. But the majority of newspaper reporters are decent men, who hate the work they do, and would gladly do better if it were possible. . . .

THE PRESS SET FREE

Some years ago Allan Benson told me of his troubles as an honest journalist; I asked him to repeat them for this book, and he answered:

> I doubt if my experiences as a daily newspaper editor would serve your purpose. When I was a daily editor I edited. I printed what I pleased. If I could not do so, I resigned. I didn't resign with a bank account to fall back upon—I resigned broke.

I am sorry that I struck my friend Benson in an uncommunicative mood. It doesn't in the least interfere with my thesis to learn that some editors resign; it is plain enough to the dullest mind that it doesn't help the public when an honest man resigns, and a rogue or a lickspittle takes his place. . . .

Here, as everywhere, the salvation of the world rests upon you, the workers of hand and brain. I took up half this book telling how the capitalist press lied about one man; you said, perhaps, that I liked to be in the "lime-light"; anyhow, I was only one writer-fellow, and it didn't matter to you what the newspaper did to a writer-fellow. But now I make my appeal for yourself, for your wives and your children. I have shown you how this knavish press turns the world against you; I have shown how it turns you against yourself—how it seduces you, poisons your mind, breaks your heart. You go on strike, and it plays upon your fears, it uses your hunger and want as weapons against you; it saps your strength, it eats out your soul, it smothers your thinking under mountain-loads of lies. You fall, and the chariot of Big Business rolls over you.

These men who own the world in which you struggle for life—what is it that they want? They want power, power to rule you. and what is it that you want? You want power to rule yourself. Between those two wants there is eternal and unending and irreconcilable war—such is the class struggle, and whether you will or not, you take your part in it, and I take mine. I, a writer-fellow who wants to write the truth, appeal to you, the laboring fellows of hand and brain, who want to read the truth, who *must* read the truth, if civilization is not to perish. I cry to you: "Help! Help against the lying, kept press!"

I cry to you for the integrity of your calling, for the honor and dignity of Journalism. I cry to you that Journalism shall no longer be the thing described by Charles A. Dana, master-cynic of the *New York Sun,* "buying white paper at two cents a pound and selling it at ten cents a pound." I cry to you that Journalism shall be a public ministry, and that you who labor in it shall be, not wage-slaves and henchmen of privilege, but ser-vants of the general welfare, helping your fellow-men to understand life, and to conquer the evils in nature outside them, and in their own hearts. Why cannot the men and women of this great profession form a society with a common mind and a common interest and a common conscience, based upon the fact that they are all necessary, they have each, down to the humblest office-boy, their essential part in a great social service?

By the blindness and greed of ruling classes the people have been plunged into infinite misery; but that misery has its purpose in the scheme of na-ture. Something more than a century ago we saw the people driven by just such misery to grope their way into a new order of society; they threw off the chains of hereditary monarchy, and made themselves citizens of free republics. And now again we face such a crisis; only this time it is in the world of industry that we have to abolish hereditary rule, and to build an industrial commonwealth in which the equal rights of all men are recognized by law. Such is the task before us; go to it with joy and certainty, playing your part in the making of the new world, in which there shall be neither slavery nor poverty, in which the natural sources of wealth belong to all men alike, and on one lives in idleness upon the labor of his fellows. That world lies just before you, and the gates to it are barred only by ignorance and prejudice, deliberately created and maintained by prostitute journalism.

A FRAME-UP THAT FELL DOWN

When I first talked over this book with my wife, she gave me a bit of advice: "Give your facts first, and then call your names." So throughout this book I have not laid much stress on the book's title. Perhaps you are wondering just where the title comes in!

What is the Brass Check? The Brass Check is found in your pay-envelope every week—you who write and print and distribute our newspapers and magazines. The Brass Check is the price of your shame—you who take the fair body of truth and sell it in the market-place, who betray the virgin hopes of mankind into the loathsome brothel of Big Business. And down in the counting-room below sits the "madame" who profits by your shame; unless, perchance, she is off at Palm Beach or Newport, flaunting her jewels and her feathers.

Please do not think that I am just slinging ugly words. Off and on for years I have thought about this book, and figured over the title, and what it means; I assert that the Brass Check which serves in the house of ill-fame as "the price of a woman's shame" is, both in its moral implications and in its social effect, precisely and identically the same as the gold and silver coins and pieces of written paper that are found every week in the pay-envelopes of those who write and print and distribute capitalist publications.

The prostitution of the body is a fearful thing. The young girl, trembling with a strange emotion of which she does not know the meaning, innocent, confiding and tender, is torn from her home and started on a road to ruin and despair. The lad, seeking his mate and the fulfilment of his destiny, sees the woman of his dreams turn into a foul harpy, bearer of pestilence and death. Nature, sumptuous, magnificent, loving life, cries: "Give me children!" And the answer comes: "We give you running sores and bursting glands, rotting lips and festering noses, swollen heads and crooked joints, idiot gabblings and maniac shrieks, pistols to blow out your brains and poisons to still your agonies." Such is the prostitution of the body.

But what of the mind? The mind is master of the body, and commands what the body shall do and what it shall become; therefore, always, the prostitution of the mind precedes and causes the prostitution of the body. Youth cries: "Life is beautiful, joyous! Give me light, that I may keep my path!" The answer comes: "Here is darkness, that you may stumble, and beat your face upon the stones!" Youth cries: "Give me Hope." The answer comes: "Here is Cynicism." Youth cries: "Give me understanding, that I may live in harmony with my fellow-men." The answer comes: "Here are lies about your fellow-men, that you may hate them, that you may cheat them, that you may live among them as a wolf among wolves!" Such is the prostitution of the mind.

When I planned this book I had in mind a sub-title: *A Study of the Whore of Journalism*. A shocking subtitle; but then, I was quoting the Bible, and the Bible is the inspired word of God. It was surely one of God's prophets who wrote this invitation to the reading of *The Brass Check:*

> Come hither; I will shew unto thee the judgment of the great whore that sitteth upon many waters;
> With whom the kings of the earth have committed fornication, and the inhabitants of the earth have been made drunk with the wine of her fornication.

For eighteen hundred years men have sought to probe the vision of that aged seer of the lonely isle of Patmos. Listen to his strange words:

> So he carried me away in the spirit into the wilderness: and I saw a woman sit upon a scarlet colored beast, full of names of blasphemy, having seven heads and ten horns. And the woman was arrayed in purple and scarlet color, and decked with gold and precious stones and pearls, having a golden cup in her hands full of abominations and filthiness of her fornication:
> And upon her forehead was a name written, MYSTERY, BABYLON THE GREAT, THE MOTHER OF HARLOTS AND ABOMINATIONS OF THE EARTH.

Now, surely, this mystery is a mystery no longer! Now we know what the seer of Patmos was foreseeing—Capitalist Journalism! And when I call upon you, class-conscious workers of hand and brain, to organize and destroy this mother of all iniquities, I do not have to depart from the language of the ancient scriptures. I say to you in the words of the prophet Ezekiel:

So the spirit took me up, and brought me into the inner court;
and behold, the glory of the Lord filled the house.
And I heard him speaking unto me out of the house:
Now let them put away their whoredom, and the carcasses
of their kings, far from me, and I will dwell in the midst of them
forever.

As I am about to send this book to press, I take one last look at the world around me. Half a million coal-miners have struck, a court injunction has forced the leaders to call off the strike, the miners are refusing to obey their leaders—and the newspapers of the entire United States are concealing the facts. For a week it has been impossible for me to learn, except from vague hints, what is happening in the coal-strike. And at the same time, because of false newspaper stories from Centralia, Washington, a "white terror" reigns in the entire West, and thousands of radicals are beaten, jailed, and shot.

I have pleaded and labored long to avoid a violent revolution in America; I intend to go on pleading and laboring to the last hour. I know that thousands of my readers will, like myself, be desperately anxious for something they can do. I decided to work out a plan of action; something definite, practical, and immediate.

I propose that we shall found and endow a weekly publication of truth-telling, to be known as "The National News." This publication will carry no advertisements and no editorials. It will not be a journal of opinion, but a record of events pure and simple. It will be published on ordinary news-print paper, and in the cheapest possible form. It will have one purpose and one only, to give to the American people once every week the truth about the world's events. It will be strictly and absolutely nonpartisan, and never the propaganda organ of any cause. It will watch the country, and see where lies are being circulated and truth suppressed; its job will be to nail the lies, and bring the truth into the light of day. I believe that a sufficient number of Americans are awake to the dishonesty of our press to build up for such a paper a circulation of a million inside of a year. . . .

Our editor will not give much space to the news that all other papers publish. The big story for him will be what the other papers let alone. He will employ trained investigators, and set them to work for a week, or maybe for several months, getting the facts about the lobby of the Beef Trust in Washington, the control of our public schools in the interest of militarism, the problem of who is paying the expenses of the American railway mission in Siberia. Needless to say, the capitalist press will provide the "National News" with a complete monopoly of this sort of work. Also it will provide the paper with many deliberate falsehoods to be nailed. When this is done, groups of truth-loving people will buy these papers by the thousands, and blue-pencil and distribute them. So the "National News" will grow, and the "kept" press will be moved by the only force it recognizes — loss of money.

There are in America millions of people who could not be persuaded to read a Socialist paper, or a labor paper, or a single tax paper; but there are very few who could not be persuaded to read a paper that gives the news and proves by continuous open discussion that it really does believe in "the truth, the whole truth, and nothing but the truth." I do not think I'm too optimistic when I say that such a publication, with a million circulation, would change the whole tone of American public life.

THE CHALLENGE TO THE PRESS

CARL ACKERMAN

Speech to the American Society of Newspaper Editors, April 29, 1933

―――――
―――――
―――――

Carl Ackerman, a member of the first graduating class of Columbia Journalism School, guided the school as its dean from 1931 to 1956. From 1913 to 1921, he was a foreign correspondent for several different publications. Then, in 1921, he left journalism to open up a public relations firm in New York in which he represented some of the leading corporations of the country. When he was named dean of the school, he had been serving as assistant to the president of the General Motors Corporation.

As dean, he was popular with publishers and editors. At the school he stiffened admissions standards—a move hailed by the American Society of Newspaper Editors as tending to eliminate "the drones and the unfit." As dean, he had a bully pulpit, and he used it frequently, often in support of traditional press practices. In this speech to newspaper editors, he tried to deflect common criticisms brought against the press. One of those criticisms had been leveled by George Bernard Shaw, the Irish author, who had charged that "in all civilized countries at present newspapers exist for the purpose of concealing the truth." This, said Ackerman, was a "deliberate lie."

THE CHALLENGE TO THE PRESS

The challenge to the press today is the private criticism of the press by intelligent men and women. It is not a by-product of the depression. Much of it existed before 1929 and continues today. It hurts those of us who are sensitive and it injures the profession we represent. I sense it keenly in my present post because so many people, within and without our ranks, speak to me specifically and freely about their concern and their disappointments in the press. They do so for various reasons. They think the so-called sheltered environment of a university makes me a free agent to look objectively upon our work. Actually they are inspired also by a desire to be helpful to a profession upon which they must depend for information and understanding of public affairs.

Today, for the purpose of this meeting, I shall appear as their spokesman to lay before you nineteen charges which they have formulated. I shall analyze these indictments, consider sympathetically those which are constructive and reply to those which are based upon a lack of knowledge of our practices, our limitations, or our aims. I shall nail to the mast one of the current lies and rest the case with you, confident that in the discussion which follows the American Society of Newspaper Editors will reflect the judgment of newspaper men who are striving to promote the welfare and the progress of a profession upon which rests today the destiny of representative governments.

One of the basic criticisms of the press is that newspaper men close their minds to the faults of their profession. We are accused of criticizing public and private citizens and institutions without heeding their criticisms of us. We are attacked for our unwillingness to examine our own practices and policies critically and we are condemned for retaliating with attacks, when others point out our weakness and our failures. Your society has met this challenge before and in meeting it again today you pass on to the next generation the oldest tradition of the art of printing. "Fiat lux"—"let there be light"—is said to have been the first line of type in history. Let us therefore turn the light on our profession and on the daily newspaper and give our critics a day in court.

Today's challenge to the press comes chiefly from one group of citizens. Included are many distinguished men and women. I shall not mention names, but I shall identify their characters or the business or profession which they represent. With few exceptions I shall not identify their criticisms because it is neither your wish nor my desire that this should be personal. The challenge from this group particularly must be weighed impersonally and impartially—for their motives, in most instances, cannot or should not be discredited.

In this group are such representative and distinguished men and women as high officials of our government, executive heads of large businesses and industries, a distinguished novelist, two Nobel prize winners, the presidents of two large universities, leading historians and economists, a banker who has not as yet been discredited, two nationally known clergymen, army and navy officers and others, all of whom I have interviewed personally since last fall.

These men and women represent the intelligent minority. They are specifically informed in special fields of human endeavor. Most of them have high regard for single newspapers or for the press as an institution.

What are the most important charges against the press made by this interested and educated minority?

1. That newspaper standards are determined by circulation. That the press gives the public what it wants, rather than what the public needs.

2. That the newspaper violates the individual right of privacy.

3. That financial news is promotional rather than informative.

4. That news values are often superficial and trivial.

5. That most reporters are inaccurate when reporting interviews.

6. That newspapers do not lead in public affairs, but follow the leadership of organized minorities.

7. That the newspapers make heroes of criminals by their romantic accounts of gang activities.

8. That headlines frequently do not correctly reveal the facts and the tenor of the articles.

9. That newspapers are interested primarily in day by day news developments and do not follow through to give the reader a continuous and complete account of what is happening.

10. That the weekly newspapers are subservient to local political machines.

11. That the press utilizes its freedom as a license to exploit policies which make for circulation rather than for service.

12. That the press is not sincere in its attack upon special privilege because it accepts a subsidy from the Post Office Department.

13. That the basic fault with the press is its ownership; that the press cannot be an impartial and true advocate of public service so long as its owners are engaged or involved in other businesses.

14. That news and photographs are sometimes deliberately falsified.

15. That many men and women hesitate to express their real opinions of the press because of the uncharitable attitude of editors toward criticism and because of the fear of retaliation.

16. That in reporting Sunday sermons and religious meetings the press seeks sensation rather than knowledge.

17. That corporations, private and public organizations, are compelled by self-interest to maintain publicity departments to insure accurate reporting of their affairs and policies.

18. That the press overemphasizes irrational statements of public officials, particularly members of Congress.

19. That "in all civilized countries at present newspapers exist for the purpose of concealing the truth."

What our critics desire is a superhuman institution. They would create a newspaper which only a perfect philanthropist could finance and edit. They would distribute the paper everywhere and place it on sale at a low price. They would employ reporters possessing the skill and precision of a surgeon, the patience and resourcefulness of chemists, the spiritual idealism of the church, the unhurried study and the power of reflection of an educator; men or women having a thorough knowledge of history and an understanding of public affairs possessed at present only by members the "brain trust." Our critics would engage as editorial writers only men capable of being President of the United States in the millennium. Headlines, news, and editorials would be passed upon before press time by men sitting as a supreme court, selected for their ability to make instantaneous decisions without making mistakes.

Obviously, this is an ideal quite beyond human realization. Even if such a group of specialists could be assembled, it would be doubtful whether they could work together in a cooperative effort essential in every newspaper office to insure the publication of a daily paper.

Granting that their conception of a perfect newspaper cannot be realized, what are the merits of their criticisms as applied to the press today?

Let us recognize at the beginning a fact upon which most of us would agree with our critics, that is, that only a few general indictments of the press can be made to apply to all newspapers or to all newspaper men.

For example, when a distinguished international representative of women in public life writes to me: "If there's anything in the world that needs purifying it's journalism—and yet what can we do until we get at the source of the trouble, which is the owners"—I know, as you do, that there are outstanding exceptions to her general criticism.

There are many important newspaper publishers and editors in this country who have no outside financial or personal interest—whose sole object is the publication of the best newspaper possible within physical and human limitations. We know also that there are other owners who are heavily involved in business, industry, or banking. We know there are exceptions among these men. Even the great majority of those who have outside interests cannot be corrupted or influenced by private interests. Nevertheless, as long as there are owners of newspaper properties whose motives can be questioned by critical readers, this criticism of the press will remain to color the confidence and respect of some influential readers.

The dangers of general observations in regard to the ownership of newspapers was brought to my attention last fall after the publication of my annual report to President Butler. I said:

> There have been fewer mergers and failures, proportionally, in the newspaper field than in any other organized business and no scandals or financial losses to large bodies of individual investors. Newspapers have been singularly free from speculation.

This statement was used publicly by Hearst Consolidated Publications, Inc., to promote the sale of 7 per cent preferred stock. Letters, clippings, and comments came from all parts of the country questioning first whether this was an authorized use of my report, and asking secondly, whether I knew about the depreciation in the market value of the common stock of the Curtis Publishing Company on the New York Stock Exchange. In the first instance this was a misuse of my statement and secondly, I knew that the market quotations of the Curtis Company securities had declined.

Now neither of these exceptions disproved my general statement as far as the press of the nation is concerned, but they did give our critics an opportunity, and a fair one, to challenge the accuracy of my assertion as applied to specific newspaper groups.

As long as there are exceptions to the public hope and the working newspaper man's ideal that the motives and private interests of newspaper owners must be above criticism, there will be criticism of the press and intelligent critics will discount our assertion that the newspaper exists primarily to perform a public service.

One of the most common charges against the press is that it gives the public what it wants in order to maintain or increase circulation. To the journalist circulation is an evidence of public interest and influence primarily. The financial consideration is largely secondary because one of the fundamental principles of journalism today, one which most newspaper editors are conscious of, but which others do not recognize, is that the success of the newspaper as a business depends entirely upon its progress as a profession. The publisher's over-all viewpoint is that while circulation is necessary both for income and in order to maintain advertising revenues, his primary concern is with a news and editorial policy, which, over a period of years, will increase the importance and usefulness of his property. This is good business as well as good journalism. While the newspaper as a business must be a profit-making institution, the profit motive has not been the underlying reason for the success or the progress of American journalism.

The charge that the press gives the public what it wants, rather than what it needs, has been disproved by the action of the press during the depression. Where editorial control has been exercised, it has been based upon the editor's judgment of what would best serve the public interest. Editors have explored every possible source of information and printed endless comments and opinions of men and women in every field of work and thought, whose viewpoint could have been of help to the public in understanding and interpreting economic and social changes. If bankers, businessmen, educators, and public officials had exercised similar care and judgment in their personal conversations, gossip which finally reached ruinous proportions would have been dried up at the source.

In this connection we must recognize the existence of a few sensational sheets, commonly called tabloids by the public, although only a few are tabloid in size and not all tabloids, by any means, belong in this group. These products of the printing press are survivals of the day of opportunism in journalism. They are owned or dominated by men who traffic in news for selfish political and business reasons. When this form of sensationalism appears in other journals it is a temporary infection, not an epidemic, for sensationalism in journalism has been on the toboggan for many years.

Journalism today is not only attracting but newspapers are demanding men of character and when we reach that stage in our relations with public men where they recognize reporters and correspondents as men and discard the patronizing appellation "boys," we shall be treated with more respect. This will have some influence upon sensationalism in journalism because a man cannot be sensational and be respected at the same time.

The charge that the newspaper violates the individual right of privacy is one that can lead to a real controversy. A distinguished historian is in the habit of referring to newspaper men as "murderers of character." Another distinguished economist, who recently assumed a governmental position, has told photographers that he would shoot them if the newspapers published pictures of his children. These extreme cases are only two of the many which have come to my attention. The attack of Mitchell Dawson in the *Atlantic* expressed the views of hundreds of intelligent newspaper readers. There is a persisting conviction that the reporter, representing the press as an institution, pries into private affairs where he has not the right to be inquisitive.

This criticism strikes at the foundations of journalism. Has the reporter the right to question any citizen on any subject which the press believes is of news interest? Some months ago, I asserted that the time was coming when the rights of the reporter would be considered paramount to the private rights of the individual. This assertion was widely challenged by men and women outside of the press although generally upheld by editorial writers.

Let me cite specific instances aside from the Lindbergh case.

A leading clergyman in a large Middle Western city, who declines to give copies of his sermons to the local newspapers on the ground that they are written to be spoken and not read, told me the following story:

The owner of one of the leading newspapers of that city is a Baptist and a good newspaper editor. The editor insists that he has the right to publish the sermons and he does so, relying upon his own reporters to attend and report the sermon. One Sunday the rector preached on the Virgin Birth and the report of the sermon was so unintelligible that the managing editor killed it.

The owner, missing the sermon in the Monday paper, asked the managing editor how he happened to leave out a sermon of one of the leading ministers in the city. The reporter's story was recalled and the owner ordered the editor to send a reporter to the rector for an interview.

On Monday afternoon, a Jewish reporter appeared at an Episcopal Cathedral to interview the rector for a daily newspaper owned by a Baptist layman! The rector, having a sense of humor, welcomed the reporter to his study, explained that he had spent years of study and had one of the most complete libraries on this subject in the United States. He took three hours to explain his ideas with the deliberate object of confusing the reporter. He did this so effectively that no interview was published and the schism between the rector and the press still continues.

The second instance refers to a missionary whose reported unorthodox views are to be examined by the church concerned. It is this missionary's conviction that if the press would drop its interest in the reported charges they would disappear as an issue in the course of time and both she and the church would be benefited by bringing an end to the controversy.

In this case both the religious organization and the missionary involved have legitimate news interest and the press has an inalienable right to both facts and opinions.

I shall appreciate the opinion of this Society, or of its members, on this controversial subject. Is there any rule of reason which we can apply? Where the public welfare is involved the press has an obvious right to inquire, but how far can this be extended? May we interpret the public welfare to include also anything of public interest, of news or feature value? To what extent is this a matter of good manners and good taste? Sometimes it seems to me that if all reporters and photographers had the qualifications and the high standards of Washington correspondents, there would be no real issue in this criticism.

One of the indictments, which it is difficult to defend, is that financial news is promotional rather than informative. Wall Street is not only the headquarters but the paradise of promoters. Stock and commodity markets reflect, with the sensitiveness of a thermometer, the promotional influences of all those impelled by the instinct of speculation, which Arthur Brisbane once defined as being greater than reason, custom, or law.

Throughout the boom days financial writers reflected accurately the promotion psychology of Wall Street until it became a national and international infection. While it is true that they reported, from time to time, the cautious viewpoints of those who questioned or doubted the wisdom and effect of stock market exploitation, it is generally true that financial writers rode the wave of financial promotions and accepted day by day, largely without question, the optimistic and extravagant opinions of so-called financial and business leaders. The newspapers exercised little supervision and less care over the financial advertisements which were offered for publication. The result was a boom and a collapse which cannot be defended by bankers, economists, educators, or newspaper men. This indictment is sound and just and must be taken to heart by the press.

It is asserted by our critics that news values are often superficial and trivial; that the press reports what has happened without explaining and knowing the significance of the events; that many reporters who interview, do so in a hit-and-miss, catch-as-catch-can fashion; that crime news makes heroes of criminals and inspires others to commit crimes; that headlines frequently are misleading; that the freedom of the press is misused to exploit events which make for increased circulation; that some news and photographs are distorted or falsified and that the press overemphasizes irrational statements by erratic public officials.

These are serious charges. If all of them, or any portion of them, could be applied honestly to a majority of the two thousand daily newspapers this would be an indictment of the press which would shake the foundations of the institution we represent. Fortunately for us and for the nation, there is an element of truth in each criticism only when applied to a few specific newspapers. They cannot be applied either honestly or fairly to the press as a whole.

Granted that some items are superficial and trivial, the "diary of mankind" would not be a true record if it eliminated the superficial or the trivial. The great majority of newspaper readers are superficial. At times even the great men of the world are not high-minded and serious. I recall an interview with Thomas A. Edison. It was on a technical subject, but at the close of the conversation he left the house before I did, and, as he entered his car to depart for what I thought was to be an hour of reflection upon some profound scientific subject, he called to his wife and asked, "Did you say a quart of 'Grade A' milk?"

That was trivial, but true, and it belonged rightly in the news record of the day.

I am certain that we would all agree that there are times when newspaper writers do not understand the significance of many public developments. What editor or writer, for example, can today appraise the significance or meaning of the confidential conversations during the current week at the White House? At best only limited information is given to the press at all international conferences. The governmental leaders control the sources of information and they alone can and do decide what to reveal officially and explain privately.

This situation prevails at all sources of important information, whether governmental, financial, industrial, religious, or educational. The press does not always have access to the whole truth and the entire responsibility for a lack of complete information or a lack of understanding of the significance of events cannot justly be placed upon the press. The truth is controlled in the first instance by those at the source of events, but once an arc of the circle of truth reaches the attention of newspaper men no effort is spared to verify and interpret what has happened, is happening, or is projected.

Much of the criticism above is directed at reporting and editing. While we might honestly retaliate by comparing reporting and editing with teaching and preaching, with business and bank management, with unquestionable medical and engineering practices, no useful purpose can be served. Although, in my opinion, the work of reporters and editors can be compared favorably with any profession our duty is not to compare ourselves with others, but to set standards for ourselves which others must accept. The press has the inherent responsibility to lead.

We do not need to reply to criticism by a counter-attack. Reporters and editors, as a rule, are as eager and anxious to benefit by criticism and to improve their methods and practices as men and women of any other profession. In fact, they are more open-minded because they are engaged in the most competitive activity in the world. They cannot conceal their mistakes or their faults. They must be prepared to face and meet every error openly and aboveboard every day. Their ethics must be tested in the laboratory of public opinion every hour.

If, as is frequently the case, the newspaper appears to give prominence to the murder of a gangster or racketeer, it is not because the newspaper has made him a hero, but because there are thousands of citizens who were hero worshippers of the notoriety and wealth which it has been all too possible for criminals to achieve in a corrupt modern society.

T. R., the famous fifth cousin of the present President of the United States, made a remark to Paul Morton in 1907, which applies to this condition. "If trouble comes from having the light turned on," Theodore Roosevelt said, "remember that it is not really due to the light, but to the misconduct which is exposed."

When George Bernard Shaw states publicly, for example, as he did in New York, that "in all civilized countries at present newspapers exist for the purpose of concealing the truth" he states a deliberate lie. If all men and women were intelligent and knew how to draw a distinction between Shaw, the dramatist, and Shaw, the publicist, it would not be necessary for us to mention this indictment. But there are far too many Americans who believe the rumors they hear rather than the news they read and these people believe Shaw. I think we should nail his lies, or the lies of any other critic, when they are malicious or deliberate. . . .

Journalism today is news as much as medicine, law, education, or any other profession and it is part of our function as newspaper men to recognize, at all times, the increasing public interest in our work, our problems, and our aims.

When an aviator flies four hundred miles an hour, it is news, and the world marvels at the speed and achievement made possible by scientific investigation and research. Readers are awed by experiments which break the atom and realize new possibilities of energy. These physical developments, as important and significant as they are to humanity, are no greater than the transmission of facts and ideas which create the sinews of public opinion.

Just as the public today demands an explanation and an interpretation of news, so it needs and will welcome facts and opinions about journalism.

At the beginning of this paper I asserted that the destiny of representative governments depends upon the progress of journalism. There is more at stake than the survival of a form of government. There are the rights of millions of men and women to work, and to a decent living. These people are our readers. They still have faith in the daily newspaper. Despite the criticism of the press sponsored by their intellectual superiors they look to the press as their reliable and incorruptible friend and counsellor.

SELECTION FROM THE
REPORT OF THE COMMISSION ON
FREEDOM OF THE PRESS

ROBERT MAYNARD HUTCHINS

1947

———

———

———

Rarely had a group of outstanding intellectuals gathered to discuss any topic for such an extended period. Never had such a collection of minds focused exclusively on the press. The chairman of the grandly titled Commission on Freedom of the Press was Robert Maynard Hutchins, the chancellor of the University of Chicago. Among the dozen other members were Zechariah Chafee, Jr., a law professor at Harvard; Archibald MacLeish, the poet and former assistant secretary of state; Reinhold Niebuhr, the theologian; Beardsley Ruml, the chairman of the Federal Reserve Bank of New York; and Arthur M. Schlesinger, the historian.

The inquiry into the press was suggested in 1942 by Henry R. Luce of Time, Inc., which along with the *Encyclopedia Britannica* financed the project. In 1947 the commission issued a report that challenged many of the sacred cows of journalism, including this one—that the press had a right to reject any kind of examination of its performance. The report was either vilified or ignored by editors. Luce himself criticized the report for what he called its "appalling lack of even high school logic."

Four decades after it was published it is only infrequently cited. But its significance has been immense: it provided the intellectual underpinning out of which has grown the campaign to upgrade the ethical standards of journalists. It sounded an important alarm that the power of the press giants was growing. It established a theoretical framework of discussion of what the proper role of the press should be. From the report emerged what is known as the "social responsibility theory" of the press—that it is the media's duty to act responsibly and to serve society.

One of the report's specific recommendations called for the es-

tablishment of a new and independent agency to review the performance of the press. Finally, after years of false starts, a national
press council similar to one envisaged by the Hutchins Commission
began operations in 1973. But the National News Council enjoyed
uneven support among the nation's editors, publishers, and broadcasters, and after accomplishing little, the council folded in 1984.

SELECTION FROM THE
REPORT OF THE COMMISSION ON
FREEDOM OF THE PRESS

WHAT CAN BE DONE

The thirteen recommendations made in this chapter reflect the conviction, stated at the beginning of this report, that there are no simple solutions of the problem of freeing the press from the influences which now prevent it from supplying the communication of news and ideas needed by the kind of society we have and the kind of society we desire.

These recommendations have been grouped according to the source from which action must come—government (including the courts), the press itself, and the public. We consider it particularly important to lay before the press and the public the measures which each of them may take in order that the press may give the service which the country requires and which newspapers, magazines, books, motion pictures, and radio, as now technically equipped, are capable of furnishing. The more the press and the public are willing to do, the less will be left for the state; but we place our recommendations as to legal action first because freedom of the press is most commonly thought of in relation to the activities of government.

We do not believe that the fundamental problems of the press will be solved by more laws or by governmental action. The Commission places its main reliance on the mobilization of the elements of society acting directly on the press and not through governmental channels.

No democracy, however, certainly not the American democracy, will indefinitely tolerate concentrations of private power irresponsible and strong enough to thwart the aspirations of the people. Eventually governmental power will be used to break up private power, or governmental power will be used to regulate private power—if private power is at once great and irresponsible.

Our society requires agencies of mass communication. They are great concentrations of private power. If they are irresponsible, not even the First Amendment will protect their freedom from governmental control. The amendment will be amended.

In the judgment of the Commission everyone concerned with the freedom of the press and with the future of democracy should put forth every effort to make the press accountable, for, if it does not become so of its own motion, the power of government will be used, as a last resort, to force it to be so.

The American people recognize that there are some things the government should do. For example, Americans place their trust in private enterprise, but they do not object to having the government run the post office. They believe in individual initiative, but they do not carry the doctrine of self-help so far as to dispense with courts of law. Though we may like to think of government merely as a policeman, we know that it does play a positive role at many points in our society and that in any highly industrialized society it must do so.

Under our system the legislature may pass no law abridging the freedom of the press. But this has never been thought to mean that the general laws of the country were inapplicable to the press. The First Amendment was intended to guarantee free expression, not to create a privileged in dustry. Nor has the First Amendment been interpreted to prevent the adoption of special laws governing certain types of utterance. Nor is there anything in the First Amendment or in our political tradition to prevent the government from participating in mass communications: to state its own case, to supplement private sources of information, and to propose standards for private emulation. Such participation by government is not dangerous to the freedom of the press.

The principal aim of this section of our report is not to recommend more governmental action but to clarify the role of government in relation to mass communication.

1. We recommend that the constitutional guarantees of the freedom of the press be recognized as including the radio and motion pictures.

In view of the approaching advent of the broadcast facsimile newspaper and the development of the newsreel and the documentary film, constitutional safeguards for the radio and the motion picture are needed more than ever. We believe that such regulation of these media as is desirable can and should be conducted within the limitations which the federal and state constitutions now place upon the regulation of newspapers and books. . . .

In the case of radio this recommendation would give constitutional support to the prohibition against censorship in the Communications Act. It would not prevent the Federal Communications Commission from denying a license on the ground that the applicant was unprepared to serve the public interest, convenience, and necessity. Nor would it prevent the Commission from considering, in connection with an application for renewal, whether the applicant had kept the promises he made when the license was granted and had actually served the public interest, convenience, and necessity. This recommendation is intended to strengthen the prohibition against censorship, not to guarantee licensees a perpetual franchise regardless of their performance. The air belongs to the public, not to the radio industry.

2. We recommend that government facilitate new ventures in the communications industry, that it foster the introduction of new techniques, that it maintain competition among large units through the antitrust laws, but that those laws be sparingly used to break up such units, and that, where concentration is necessary in communications, the government endeavor to see to it that the public gets the benefit of such concentration.

We accept the fact that some concentration must exist in the communications industry if the country is to have the service it needs. People need variety and diversity in mass communication; they must also have service, a quantity and quality of information and discussion which can often be supplied only by large units.

The possibilities of evil inherent in concentration can be minimized by seeing to it that no artificial obstructions impede the creation and development of new units. In the communications industry it is difficult to start new units because of the large investment required and because of the control of the existing units over the means of distribution.

Little can be done by government or any other agency to reduce the cost of entering the industry except to adjust governmental charges, such as tax laws and postal rates, to facilitate new enterprises, and to prevent established interests from obstructing the introduction of new techniques. Tax laws and postal rates should be restudied with a view to discovering whether they do not discriminate against new, small businesses and in favor of large, well-established ones.

As for new techniques, an invention like FM radio offers the possibility of greatly increasing quantity and diversity in broadcasting. The cost of the equipment is low, and the number of frequencies large. We believe that the Federal Communications Commission should fully exploit the opportunity now before it and should prevent any greater concentration in FM radio than the service requires.

Government can stop the attempt by existing units of the press to monopolize distribution outlets. The types of governmental action called for range from police protection and city ordinances which would make it possible for new newspapers and magazines to get on the newsstands to antitrust suits against motion picture companies which monopolize theaters.

The main function of government in relation to the communications industry is to keep the channels open, and this means, in part, facilitating in every way short of subsidy the creation of new units in the industry.

The Commission believes that there should be active competition in the communications industry. It inclines to the view that the issue of the size of the units competing is not one which can best be dealt with by law. The antitrust laws can be invoked to maintain competition among large units and to prevent the exclusion of any unit from facilities which ought to be open to all; their use to force the breaking-up of large units seems to us undesirable.

Though there can be no question that the antitrust laws apply to the communications industry, we would point out that these laws are extremely vague. They can be very dangerous to the freedom and the effectiveness of the press. They can be used to limit voices in opposition and to hinder the processes of public education.

Since the Commission looks principally to the units of the press itself to take joint action to provide the diversity, quantity, and quality of information and discussion which a free society requires, it would not care to see such action blocked by the mistaken application of the antitrust laws. Honest efforts to raise standards, such as we suggest elsewhere in this chapter, would not be thwarted, even though they result in higher costs.

Since the need for service is the justification for concentration, the government should see to it that, where concentration exists, the service is rendered; it should see to it that the public gets the benefit of the concentration. For example, the Federal Communications Commission should explore the possibilities of requiring the radio networks to increase the number of their affiliated stations and of using clear-channel licenses as a means of serving all the less populous regions of the country. The extension of radio service of the quality supplied by the networks and the maintenance and multiplication of local stations are of the first importance. There are only two ways of obtaining these results: they can be achieved by the acceptance of responsibility by the industry, or they can be achieved by government ownership. We prefer the former.

3. As an alternative to the present remedy for libel, we recommend legislation by which the injured party might obtain a retraction or a restatement of the facts by the offender or an opportunity to reply.

The only legal method by which a person injured by false statements in the press may vindicate his reputation is a civil action for damages. The remedy is expensive, difficult, and encumbered with technicalities. Many injured persons hesitate to sue because of the "shadow of racketeering and blackmail which hangs over libel plaintiffs."

The proposed remedy should operate quickly while the issue is before the public. It should lead to an increase in the practice, now common among the responsible members of the press, of voluntarily correcting misstatements. It ought to diminish lying in the press.

We are opposed to the group libel laws now under discussion in several states. We believe that an action for libel should be a civil suit brought by a person who can show that he, as an individual, was damaged by a false statement about him. We fear that, if an individual may sue or initiate a criminal prosecution, because a group he belongs to has been criticized falsely, the law might be used to suppress legitimate public controversy.

The Commission has given extensive consideration to numerous suggested methods of reducing lying in the press by law. We insist that, morally considered, the freedom of the press is a conditional right—conditional on the honesty and responsibility of writer, broadcaster, or publisher. A man who lies, intentionally or carelessly, is not morally entitled to claim the protection of the First Amendment. The remedy for press lying, however, must go deeper than the law can go. We are reluctant to suggest governmental interference with the freedom of the press; we see many difficulties of enforcement; we do not find in the present situation justification for stronger legislation than that which we here propose.

4. We recommend the repeal of legislation prohibiting expressions in favor of revolutionary changes in our institutions where there is no clear and present danger that violence will result from the expressions.

The Supreme Court has held that expressions urging the overthrow of the government by force are within the protection of the First Amendment unless there is a clear and present danger that these expressions will lead to violence. We believe that this sound principle is violated by the peacetime sedition clauses of the Alien Registration Act of 1940 and by the various state syndicalism acts which make it a crime to advocate the overthrow of the government by force, irrespective of the probable effect of the statements. The really dangerous persons within the scope of these laws can be reached by the conspiracy statutes and the general criminal law. As applied to other persons, which is most likely to be the case, these laws are of dubious constitutionality and unwise. Yet only a few of the agitators who are prosecuted can succeed in getting before the Supreme Court. Consequently, so long as this legislation remains on the statutebooks, its intimidating effect is capable of stifling political and economic discussion. These acts ought to be repealed.

5. We recommend that the government, through the media of mass

communication, inform the public of the facts with respect to its policies and of the purposes underlying those policies and that, to the extent that private agencies of mass communication are unable or unwilling to supply such media to the government, the government itself may employ media of its own.

We also recommend that, where the private agencies of mass communication are unable or unwilling to supply information about this country to a particular foreign country or countries, the government employ mass communication media of its own to supplement this deficiency.

We should not think it worthwhile to make the recommendations if it were not for the fact that in recent years there have been increasingly strident charges that the government is exceeding its proper functions and wasting the taxpayers' money when it undertakes to inform the people in regard to its program or to supplement and correct the picture of this country which the press has projected to other parts of the world or which results from misinformation or lack of information.

Doubtless some governmental officers have used their publicity departments for personal or partisan aggrandizement. But this evil is subject to correction by normal democratic processes and does not compare with the danger that the people of this country and other countries may, in the absence of official information and discussion, remain unenlightened on vital issues.

In addition to supplying information at home and abroad, the government has special obligations in international communications, which are elaborated in *Peoples Speaking to Peoples*: to use its influence to reduce press rates all over the world; to obtain equal access to the news for all; to break down barriers to the free flow of information; and to collaborate with the United Nations in promoting the widest dissemination of news and discussion by all the techniques which become available.

WHAT CAN BE DONE BY THE PRESS

The recommendations we have made for action by government, though they are minimal, could be reduced still further in the domestic field, at least, by the action of the press itself. Existing units of the press could abstain from attempts to monopolize distribution outlets; they could insist that new techniques be made available and freely used; the press could of its own motion make it a rule that a person injured by a false statement should have an opportunity to reply. We believe that these changes are bound to come through legislation if they do not come through the action of the press and that it would be the part of wisdom for the press to take these measures on its own initiative.

The communications industry in the United States is and, in the opinion of the Commission, should remain a private business. But it is a business affected with a public interest. The Commission does not believe that it should be regulated by government like other businesses affected with a public interest, such as railroads and telephone companies. The Commission hopes that the press itself will recognize its public responsibility and obviate governmental action to enforce it.

It may be argued that the variety, quantity, and quality of information and discussion which we expect from the press cannot be purveyed at a profit and that a business which cannot operate at a profit cannot last under a system of private enterprise. It has been said that, if the press is to continue as a private business, it can succeed only as other retailers succeed, that is, by giving the customers what they want. On this theory the test of public service is financial success. On this theory, too, the press is bound by what it believes to be the interests and tastes of the mass audience; these interests and tastes are discovered by finding out what the mass audience will buy. On this theory, if the press tries to rise higher than the interests and tastes of the mass audience as they are revealed at the newsstands or at the box office, it will be driven into bankruptcy, and its existence as a private business will be at an end.

We have weighted the evidence carefully and do not accept this theory. As the example of many ventures in the communications industry shows, good practice in the interest of public enlightenment is good business as well. The agencies of mass communication are not serving static wants. Year by year they are building and transforming the interests of the public. They have an obligation to elevate rather than to degrade them.

The gist of the recommendations in this section of our report is that the press itself should assume the responsibility of providing the variety, quantity, and quality of information and discussion which the country needs. This seems to us largely a question of the way in which the press looks at itself. We suggest that the press look upon itself as performing a public service of a professional kind. Whatever may be thought of the conduct of individual members of the older, established professions, like law and medicine, each of these professions as a whole accepts a responsibility for the service rendered by the profession as a whole, and there are some things which a truly professional man will not do for money.

1. We recommend that the agencies of mass communication accept the responsibilities of common carriers of information and discussion.

Those agencies of mass communication which have achieved a dominant position in their areas can exert an influence over the minds of their audience too powerful to be disregarded. We do not wish to break up these agencies, because to do so would break up the service they can render. We do not wish to have them owned or controlled by government. They must therefore themselves be hospitable to ideas and attitudes different from their own, and they must present them to the public as meriting its attention. In no other way can the danger to the mind of democracy which is inherent in the present concentration be avoided.

2. We recommend that the agencies of mass communication assume the responsibility of financing new, experimental activities in their fields.

Here we have in mind activities of high literary, artistic, or intellectual quality which do not give promise of immediate financial return but which may offer long-term rewards. Only in a few metropolitan areas can the citizen easily gain access to a wide variety of motion pictures and radio programs. Elsewhere discriminating, serious minorities are prisoners of the estimate of mass taste made by the industry. Motion pictures, radio programs, newspapers, and magazines aimed at these minorities may not make money at the beginning. They require a considerable investment. They do not attract capital seeking quick profits. Nonprofit institutions can do something in this field, but they should not be expected to do the whole job. The responsibility of the industry for diversity and quality means that it should finance ventures of this kind from the profits of its other business.

3. We recommend that the members of the press engage in vigorous mutual criticism.

Professional standards are not likely to be achieved as long as the mistakes and errors, the frauds and crimes, committed by units of the press are passed over in silence by other members of the profession. As we indicated in Chapter 5, the formal organization of the press into a profession, with power in the organization to deprive an erring member of his livelihood, is unlikely and perhaps undesirable. We have repeatedly evidenced our desire that the power of government should not be invoked to punish the aberrations of the press. If the press is to be accountable— and it must be if it is to remain free—its members must discipline one another by the only means they have available, namely, public criticism.

Professional standards are not likely to be achieved as long as the mistakes and errors, the frauds and crimes, committed by units of the press are passed over in silence by other members of the profession. As we indicated in Chapter 5, the formal organization of the press into a profession, with power in the organization to deprive an erring member of his livelihood, is unlikely and perhaps undesirable. We have repeatedly evidenced our desire that the power of government should not be invoked to

punish the aberrations of the press. If the press is to be accountable—
and it must be if it is to remain free—its members must discipline one
another by the only means they have available, namely, public criticism.

4. We recommend that the press use every means that can be devised
to increase the competence, independence, and effectiveness of its staff.

The quality of the press depends in large part upon the capacity and
independence of the working members in the lower ranks. At the present
time their wages and prestige are low and their tenure precarious. Adequate compensation, adequate recognition, and adequate contracts seem
to us an indispensable prerequisite to the development of a professional
personnel.

Elsewhere in this chapter we shall refer to education for journalism.
Here we would merely indicate that the press can do a good deal to improve the quality of its staff by promoting an intelligent educational program, both for young people and for men and women who are already at
work in the field. The type of educational experience provided for working
journalists by the Nieman fellowships at Harvard seems to use to deserve
extension, if not through private philanthropy, then with the financial assistance of the press itself.

5. We recommend that the radio industry take control of its programs
and that it treat advertising as it is treated by the best newspapers.

Radio cannot become a responsible agency of communication as long as
its programming is controlled by the advertisers. No newspaper would call
itself respectable if its editorial columns were dominated by its advertisers
and if it published advertising, information, and discussion so mixed together that the reader could not tell them apart. The importance and va-
lidity of this recommendation seem to us so obvious as not to require argument. Radio is one of the most powerful means of communication known
to man. With the advent of facsimile and television, it will become more
powerful still. The public should not be forced to continue to take its radio
fare from the manufacturers of soap, cosmetics, cigarettes, soft drinks,
and packaged foods.

WHAT CAN BE DONE BY THE PUBLIC

The people of this country are the purchasers of the products of the press.
The effectiveness of buyers' boycotts, even of very little ones, has been
amply demonstrated. Many of these boycotts are the wrong kind for the
wrong purposes; they are the work of pressure groups seeking to protect

themselves from justifiable criticism or to gain some special advantage. The success of their efforts indicates what a revolt of the American people against the service given them by the press might accomplish.

We are not in favor of a revolt and hope that less drastic means of improving the press may be employed. We cannot tell what direction a revolt might take; it might lead to government control or to the emasculation of the First Amendment. We want the press to be free, and a revolt against the press conducted for the purpose of giving the country a truly free press might end in less freedom than we have today.

What is needed, first of all, is recognition by the American people of the vital importance of the press in the present world crisis. We have the impression that the American people do not realize what has happened to them. They are not aware that the communications revolution has occurred. They do not appreciate the tremendous power which the new instruments and the new organizations of the press place in the hands of a few men. They have not yet understood how far the performance of the press falls short of the requirements of a free society in the world today. The principal object of our report is to make these points clear.

If these points are clear, what can the people do about them? They have, or they can create, agencies which can be used to supplement the press, to propose standards for its emulation, and to hold it to its accountability.

1. We recommend that nonprofit institutions help supply the variety, quantity, and quality of press service required by the American people.

We have indicated our belief that the agencies of mass communication have a responsibility to the public like that of educational institutions. We now wish to add that educational institutions have a responsibility to the public to use the instruments employed by the agencies of mass communications. The radio, the motion picture, television, and facsimile broadcasting are most powerful means of molding the minds of men. That is why we worry about their exclusive appropriation by agencies engaged in the pursuit of profit. Not that educational institutions are free from financial problems and the pressures associated with them. But the nonprofit corporation does not exist for the purpose of making profits. It is peculiarly able to enlist the cooperation of all who are interested in the cultural development of the country. Hence it can render those services which commercial enterprise cannot offer on a profit-making basis.

It can restore an element of diversity to the information and discussion reaching the public by organizing the demand for good things and by putting out good things itself. A chain of libraries, schools, colleges, and universities, together with the various religious organizations, could establish the documentary film in mass communication. A chain of educational FM stations could put before the public the best thought of America and could make many present radio programs look as silly as they are.

The business of organizing demand requires nothing but realization of the importance of the opportunity and cooperation, to which educational institutions are notoriously averse. The business of putting out good things requires in addition a determined effort to acquire the professional skill that is needed if the efforts of nonprofit corporations are not to be scorned as the work of second-rate amateurs.

We cannot believe that nonprofit institutions will continue to fail to grasp the opportunity they have before them. It has always been clear that education is a process which goes on through the whole of life. It has always been clear that, as working hours diminished and leisure increased, a responsibility devolved upon educators to help people make wise use of their leisure. Now a new urgency is added to this duty. The world seems on the brink of suicide, and the ultimate catastrophe can be avoided only if the adult citizens of today can learn how to live together in peace. It will not be enough to educate the rising generation; the time is too short. The educators have the enormous task of trying to make the peoples of the earth intelligent now. It is fortunate that, as their task has grown greater and more pressing, technology has given them new instruments of incredible range and power.

2. We recommend the creation of academic-professional centers of advanced study, research, and publication in the field of communications. We recommend further that existing schools of journalism exploit the total resources of their universities to the end that their students may obtain the broadest and most liberal training.

The importance of the field of communications does not seem to us to have been adequately recognized by the educational institutions of the country. We doubt that new professional or technical training schools should be established in this area. We do see, however, a need for centers of investigation, graduate study, and critical publication. These are, in fact, so important that without them it is unlikely that the professional practices and attitudes which we recommend to the press can ever become characteristic of the communications industry.

Preparation for work in the press seems to us to require the best possible general education. It is important that students who enter schools of journalism should not be deprived of liberal education because they have made up their minds that they want to work in the press. Few schools of journalism can develop a liberal curriculum within their own faculties. It is therefore imperative that they associate themselves as closely as possible with other departments and schools of their universities.

3. We recommend the establishment of a new and independent agency to appraise and report annually upon the performance of the press.

The public makes itself felt by the press at the present time chiefly through pressure groups. These groups are quite as likely to have bad influence as good. In this field we cannot turn to government as the representative of the people as a whole, and we would not do so if we could. Yet it seems to us clear that some agency which reflects the ambitions of the American people for its press should exist for the purpose of comparing the accomplishments of the press with the aspirations which the people have for it. Such an agency would also educate the people as to the aspirations which they ought to have for the press.

The Commission suggests that such a body be independent of government and of the press; that it be created by gifts; and that it be given a ten-year trial, at the end of which an audit of its achievement could determine anew the institutional form best adapted to its purposes.

The activities of such an agency would include:

1. Continuing efforts, through conference with practitioners and analysis by its staff, to help the press define workable standards of performance, a task on which our Commission has attempted a beginning.

2. Pointing out the inadequacy of press service in certain areas and the trend toward concentration in others, to the end that local communities and the press itself may organize to supply service where it is lacking or to provide alternative service where the drift toward monopoly seems dangerous.

3. Inquiries in areas where minority groups are excluded from reasonable access to the channels of communication.

4. Inquiries abroad regarding the picture of American life presented by the American press; and cooperation with agencies in other countries and with international agencies engaged in analysis of communication across national borders.

5. Investigation of instances of press lying, with particular reference to persistent misrepresentation of the data required for judging public issues.

6. Periodic appraisal of the tendencies and characteristics of the various branches of the communications industry.

7. Continuous appraisal of governmental action affecting communications.

8. Encouragement of the establishment of centers of advanced study, research, and criticism in the field of communications at universities.

9. Encouragement of projects which give hope of meeting the needs of special audiences.

10. The widest possible publicity and public discussion on all the foregoing.

The above recommendations taken together give some indication of methods by which the press may become accountable and hence remain free. We believe that if they are carried out, press performance will be brought much closer to the five ideal demands of society for the communication of news and ideas which were set forth in the second chapter: (1) a truthful, comprehensive, and intelligent account of the day's events in a context which gives them meaning; (2) a forum for the exchange of comment and criticism; (3) the projection of a representative picture of the constituent groups in the society; (4) the presentation and clarification of the goals and values of the society; (5) full access to the day's intelligence.

Plainly, each of these five ideals will be served by more than one of our recommendations. Instead of stating those relationships in detail, we think that it will be more helpful to point out how the various recommendations will supplement each other in remedying some aspects of the press as it now exists which have constantly disturbed the members of the Commission during our investigation.

The failure of radio to reach all citizens adequately can be relieved through the licensing policy of the F.C.C., while the international coverage of American news and opinions can be extended by various measures proposed in *Peoples Speaking to Peoples*.

Deliberate falsifications and reckless misstatements of fact will be lessened by a new legal remedy compelling the publication of a retraction or reply and, even more, by the assumption of a greater responsibility for accuracy on the part of the press, by the readiness of newspapers and other agencies of communication to criticize one another for gross departures from truthfulness, and by periodic appraisals of press accuracy issuing from a body of citizens.

The inclination of the press to adapt most of its output to the supposed desires of the largest possible number of consumers and the resulting trends toward sensationalism and meaninglessness can be reduced by similar periodical appraisals from citizens and by the initiation of new activities for the benefit of specialized audiences on the part of the press itself as well as nonprofit institutions. In the case of radio, the quality of output can be improved through organizations of listeners in the communities and through the determination of the industry to take control of its programs out of the hands of the advertisers and their agents.

The greatest difficulty in preserving free communications in a technical society arises from the concentration of power within the instruments of communication. The most conspicuous example of this is in the ownership of instrumentalities, but the concentration also exists in the power of advertisers, of labor organizations, of organized pressure groups—all capable of impairing the free interchange of news and ideas. The danger is that the entire function of communications will fall under the control of fewer and fewer persons.

Among the consequences of this concentration, the output of the press reflects the bias of owners and denies adequate expression to important elements in communities.

In order to counteract the evil effects of concentration, we have urged that newspapers and other agencies of mass communication regard themselves as common carriers of information and discussion, that the entry of new units into the field be facilitated, and that the government prevent monopolistic control of outlets by the sources of production.

Finally, members of the Commission were disturbed by finding that many able reporters and editorial writers displayed frustration—the feeling that they were not allowed to do the kind of work which their professional ideals demanded, that they were unable to give the service which the community needs from the press. A continuation of this disturbing situation will prevent the press from discharging its responsibilities toward society. As remedies we have urged the press to use every means that can be devised to increase the competence and independence of the staff, and we have urged universities and schools of journalism to train existing or potential members of the press in the exercise of judgment on public affairs. In many different ways the rank and file of the press can be developed into a genuine profession.

The outside forces of law and public opinion can in various ways check bad aspects of press performance, but good press performance can come only from the human beings who operate the instrumentalities of communication.

We believe that our recommendations, taken together, give some indication of methods by which the press may become accountable and, hence, remain free. The urgent and perplexing issues which confront our country, the new dangers which encompass our free society, the new fatefulness attaching to every step in foreign policy and to what the press publishes about it, mean that the preservation of democracy and perhaps of civilization may now depend upon a free and responsible press. Such a press we must have if we would have progress and peace.

ROBERT M. HUTCHINS   CHARLES E. MERRIAM
ZECHARIAH CHAFEE, JR.   REINHOLD NIEBUHR

JOHN M. CLARK   ROBERT REDFIELD
JOHN DICKINSON   BEARDSLEY RUML
WILLIAM E. HOCKING   ARTHUR M. SCHLESINGER
HAROLD D. LASSWELL   GEORGE N. SHUSTER
ARCHIBALD MACLEISH

4

MAKING REPORTERS BETTER

J ournalists have long argued among themselves over how best they should be trained. Unlike lawyers or doctors or architects, journalists are not required to attend a special school, although many of them have done so. It was not until the early 1900s that these special schools began to spring up, and there has never been a period when they have not been viewed suspiciously either by journalists or outsiders.

Within the field of journalism, an anti-intellectual strain runs deep. In the 1860s, for instance, Horace Greeley, the powerful New York Republican editor, had dismissed a university education—of any sort—with the comment that he would "not hire a college graduate who did not show he could overcome the handicap of a college education." The press critic A. J. Liebling, one of the early graduates of Columbia University's journalism school, derided his education there. In a chapter in his autobiography *The Wayward Pressman* called "How to Learn Nothing," he wrote of his alma mater: "It had all the intellectual status of a training school for future employees of the A&P."

Joseph Pulitzer, the publisher who endowed the school at Columbia, wrote a long essay to rebut critics of the school and to reassure the trustees of Columbia. His essay still stands as the most fully articulated statement of why journalism should be taught at all.

For most of this century, journalists have operated under a special assumption: they were generalists who could absorb any new material quickly. It did not matter if they were untrained in science, economics, law, or Russian, so long as they could grasp quickly the essence of a story. This journalistic conceit has been often challenged. It was dealt one of its severest jolts by the President's Commission on Civil Disorders, which cogently argued that more black journalists were needed to report on issues relating to race. Since that report was published, specialists have flourished on American newspapers, but the number of black reporters has grown only at a modest rate.

189

SELECTION FROM THE
COLLEGE OF JOURNALISM

JOSEPH PULITZER

North America Review, May 1904

———
———
———

"What is a journalist?" asked Joseph Pulitzer, the owner of the *New York World,* a bastion of progressive liberalism. He answered: "A journalist is the lookout on the bridge of the ship of state." It was his hope that a school of journalism would raise the standards of reporters, and he wrote this essay to persuade doubters. Pulitzer spent much of his career trying to upgrade journalism. He first offered Columbia University money to start a school of journalism in 1892. The trustees rejected his offer. He renewed his offer, which was accepted in 1903, although the school did not open its doors until 1912. (In the meantime, five other journalism programs had begun, including one at the University of Missouri in 1908, now generally recognized as the first journalism school.)

Writing at the start of the century, Pulitzer predicted: "Before the century closes, schools of journalism will be generally accepted as a feature of specialized higher education like schools of law or of medicine." His prediction has not come to pass. In 1987, more than 100,000 students were enrolled in journalism schools, but the majority of these specialized in advertising or public relations, and certainly not all of the graduates actually entered journalism. Most people entering journalism do in fact have some formal training in journalism. However, many of the most highly regarded organizations of journalists, especially those located in the Northeast, continue to treat specialized journalism training with skepticism.

SELECTION FROM THE COLLEGE OF JOURNALISM

The man who writes, the man who month in and month out, week in and week out, day in and day out, furnishes the material which is to shape the thoughts of our people, is essentially the man who more than any other determines the character of the people and the kind of government this people shall possess.
—PRESIDENT THEODORE ROOSEVELT

The editor of the *North American Review* has asked me to reply to an article recently printed in its pages criticizing the College of Journalism which it has been my pleasure to found and permanently to endow in Columbia University. In complying with his request I have enlarged the scope of the reply to include all other criticisms and misgivings, many honest, some shallow, some based on misunderstanding, but most representing only prejudice and ignorance. If my comment upon these criticisms shall seem to be diffuse and perhaps repetitious, my apology is that—alas!—I am compelled to write by voice, not by pen, and to revise the proofs by ear, not by eye—a somewhat difficult task.

Some of my critics have called my scheme "visionary." If it be so I can at least plead that it is a vision I have cherished long, thought upon deeply, and followed persistently. Twelve years ago I submitted the idea to President Low of Columbia, when it was declined. I have ever since continued to perfect and organize the scheme in my mind, until it is now accepted. In examining the criticisms and misgivings I have endeavored to do so without prejudice, anxious only to find the truth. I admit that the difficulties are many, but after weighing them all impartially I am more firmly convinced than ever of the ultimate success of the idea. Before the century closes schools of journalism will be generally accepted as a feature of specialized higher education, like schools of law or of medicine.

And now for our critics and objectors:

MUST A JOURNALIST BE "BORN?"

They object, the critics and cavillers, that a "newspaper man" must depend solely upon natural aptitude, or, in the common phrase, that he must be "born, not made."

Perhaps the critics can name some great editor, born full-winged like Mercury, the messenger of the gods? I know of none. The only position that occurs to me which a man in our Republic can successfully fill by the simple fact of birth is that of an idiot. Is there any other position for which a man does not demand and receive training—training at home, training in schools and colleges, training by master craftsmen, or training through bitter experience—through the burns that make the child dread the fire, through blunders costly to the aspirant?

This last is the process by which the profession of journalism at present obtains its recruits. It works by natural selection and the survival of the fittest, and its failures are strewn along the wayside.

The "born editor" who has succeeded greatly without special preparation is simply a man with unusual ability and aptitude for his chosen profession, with great power of concentration and sustained effort. He is one who loves his work and puts his whole heart and mind into it. He is in the strictest sense an educated man, but he has merely substituted self-education for education by others, making up for any deficiencies in his training by the unreserved sacrifice of strength, energy, and pleasure. Even in his case might it not be an advantage to have a system of instruction that would give him the same results at a saving of much time and labor?

Education begins in the cradle, at home, with a mother's teaching, and is continued by other influences through life. A college is one of those influences—useful, but with no magical power. A fool trailing an alphabet of degrees after his name is still a fool, and a genius, if necessary, will make his own college, although with a painful waste of effort which might be better reserved for productive work. I seem to remember that Lincoln, whose academy was a borrowed book read by the light of a pine-knot on the hearth, studied Euclid in Congress when nearly forty. But would it not have been better if that work had been done at fourteen?

All intelligence requires development. The highest profits by it; the lowest is helpless without it. Shakespeare's best play, *Hamlet,* was not his first, but his nineteenth, written after growth and maturity—after the hard work, the experience, the exercise of faculties and the accumulation of knowledge gained by writing eighteen plays. As Shakespeare was a "born" genius why did he not write *Hamlet* first?

John Stuart Mill had natural talents, but they were strained to the last possible limit of accomplishment by a course of early training that was not only thorough but inhuman. His father was his college—a great college, better than any in England. Like Mill, Herbert Spencer, Buckle, Huxley, Tyndall, and Lewes were without college education, but their mental discipline was most severe. Cobden was undoubtedly a genius born, but if we compare his original style—turgid, clumsy—with the masterly clearness and force of his trained maturity, can we doubt that his brain was developed by the hardest work, just as Sandow's muscles were developed?

Of course in every field natural aptitude is the key to success. When the experiment was tried of turning Whistler into a disciplined soldier, even West Point had to lay down its arms. Your sawmill may have all the modern improvements, but it will not make a pine board out of a basswood log. No college can create a good lawyer without a legal mind to work on, nor make a successful doctor of a young man whom nature designed to sell tape. Talleyrand took holy orders, but they did not turn him into a holy man.

The great general, even more than the great editor, is supposed to be born, not made. The picturesque historian tells us that he "fell like a thunderbolt upon the enemy," and we imagine a miracle-working magician. But the truth is, that the brilliant general is simply a man who has learned how to apply skillfully the natural laws of force, and who has the nerve to act on his knowledge. Hannibal, the greatest of all in my opinion, is called a typical example of native military genius. But can we forget that he was the son and pupil of Hamilcar, the ablest soldier of his generation, born in the camp, never outside the military atmosphere, sworn in earliest boyhood to war and hatred of Rome, and endowed by his father with all the military knowledge that the experience of antiquity could give? He was educated. In his father he had a military college to himself. Can we think of Napoleon without remembering that he had the best military education of his time at the college of Brienne, and that he was always an eager student of the great campaigns of history? Frederick the Great lost his head in his first battle. It took him years to learn his trade and finally to surpass his instructors. There is not a cadet at any military school who is not expected as a necessary part of his professional preparation to study every important battle on record—to learn how it was fought, what mistakes were committed on each side, and how it was won.

Every issue of a newspaper represents a battle—a battle for excellence. When the editor reads it and compares it with its rivals he knows that he has scored a victory or suffered a defeat. Might not the study of the most notable of these battles of the press be as useful to the student of journalism as is the study of military battles to the student of war?

WHAT SHOULD NOT BE TAUGHT

What is a College of Journalism? It is an institution to train journalists. What is a journalist? Not any business manager or publisher, or even proprietor. A journalist is the lookout on the bridge of the ship of state. He notes the passing sail, the little things of interest that dot the horizon in fine weather. He reports the drifting castaway whom the ship can save. He peers through fog and storm to give warning of dangers ahead. He is not thinking of his wages, or of the profits of his owners. He is there to watch over the safety and the welfare of the people who trust him.

Few men in the business office of a newspaper know anything about the principles of journalism. The proprietor himself is not necessarily a journalist. He may be, if he is capable of understanding public questions, of weighing public interests, of carrying out public tasks; if he is in touch with public feeling, realizes public duties, is in sympathy with the public welfare, and is capable of presenting his ideas to the people, either by his own pen or by the pens of others. But it is quite conceivable that some proprietors are deficient in these points.

My hope is that this College of Journalism will raise the standard of the editorial profession. But to do this it must mark the distinction between real journalists and men who do a kind of newspaper work that requires neither culture nor conviction, but merely business training. I wish to begin a movement that will raise journalism to the rank of a learned profession, growing in the respect of the community as other professions far less important to the public interests have grown.

There is an obvious difference between a business and a profession. An editor, an editorial writer, or a correspondent is not in business. Nor is even a capable reporter. These men are already in a profession, though they may not admit it, or even realize it, as many of them unhappily do not. Ill or well, they represent authorship, and authorship is a profession.

The man in the counting-room of a newspaper is in the newspaper business. He concentrates his brain (quite legitimately) upon the commercial aspects of things, upon the margin of profit, upon the reduction of expenses, upon buying white paper and selling it printed—and that is business. But a man who has the advantage, honor, and pleasure of addressing the public every day as a writer or thinker is a professional man. So, of course, is he who directs these writers and reporters, who tells them what to say and how to say it, who shows them how to think—who inspires them, though he may never write a line himself, and decides what the principles of the paper shall be. For example, the greatest editor in the whole history of European journalism, John Delane, never wrote any articles of his own, although for thirty-six years he was the head, the heart, the brain of the London *Times*. But he directed every writer, he furnished the thought, the policy, the initiative; he bore the responsibility, and he corrected both manuscript and proofs.

In this relation perhaps it may be interesting to note that Delane studied law and was admitted to the bar before he became its editor at the age of twenty-four. But it was without any intention of practicing. His father, who was a lawyer for the *Times,* destined him for its service from his boyhood, and he joined its staff as a reporter soon after passing his legal examinations. Delane, with his editorial revision, elimination, and substitution, was like some of the great old painters, who seem to have much of their work, measured by mere bulk, done for them by pupils. Rubens, or Van Dyck, or Raphael furnished the idea, the design, the composition, in an original drawing; the pupils did the drudgery of execution. Then the artist added the finishing touches that lifted the picture to the rank of masterpiece. Only in that way could the enormous output ascribed to those masters have been produced. So it was with Delane, and so it is with every editor who knows how to make the most of his powers.

That a newspaper, however great as a public institution and a public teacher, must also be a business is not to be denied, but there is nothing exceptional in this. Elements of business, of economy, of income and outgo, are in the government of the city, the State, the nation, in art, in every school, in every college, in every university, indeed, in every church. But a bishop, even though he receives pay for his work, is not regarded as a businessman; nor is a great artist, though he charge the highest possible price for his paintings and die as rich as Meissonier or Rubens. Many distinguished lawyers, such as Mr. Tilden—one of the greatest—were shrewd businessmen, able probably to outwit the majority of publishers, yet they were rightly considered members of a learned profession.

George Washington had extraordinary business capacity. By intelligent economy, method, sound judgment, and the closest attention to details he accumulated the greatest American fortune of his time. Yet when he was called to serve the country in the field he did it without a salary. At Mount Vernon he was a businessman; in history he is a soldier, a statesman, and the father of his country.

To sum up, the banker or broker, the baker or the candlestickmaker is in business—in trade. But the artist, the statesman, the thinker, the writer—all who are in touch with the public taste and mind, whose thoughts reach beyond their own livelihood to some common interest—are in professions.

DANGERS OF PLUTOCRACY AND DEMAGOGY

Our improvement is in proportion to our purpose.
—*MARCUS AURELIUS*

Nothing less than the highest ideals, the most scrupulous anxiety to do right, the most accurate knowledge of the problems it has to meet, and a sincere sense of its moral responsibility will save journalism from subservience to business interests, seeking selfish ends, antagonistic to the public welfare. For instance, Jay Gould once owned the principal Democratic newspaper of America. He had obtained it from Col. "Tom" Scott in a trade for the Texas Pacific Railroad, and I was fortunate enough to be able to relieve him of his unprofitable burden. C. P. Huntington bought a New York newspaper and turned it into a Democratic organ, he himself, like Gould, being an ardent Republican. He hoped in this way to influence Mr. Cleveland's administration and the Democrats in Congress against making the Pacific railroads pay their debts of about $120,000,000 to the Government. Incidentally he testified under oath that his journalistic experiment cost him over a million dollars, although his newspaper was so obscure that its utterances were hardly more than soliloquies. Mr. Huntington did somehow succeed in delaying for a number of years the enforcement of the Treasury's claims. More dangerous, however, than the plutocratic control of newspapers for sordid private ends is their control by demagogues for ambitious, selfish ends. The people know, with unerring instinct, when a newspaper is devoted to private rather than to public interests; and their refusal to buy it limits its capacity for harm. But when a demagogic agitator appeals to "the masses" against "the classes" and poses as the ardent friend of the people against their "oppressors," assailing law and order and property as a means of gaining followers among the discontented and unthinking, the newspaper becomes a dangerous power for evil. Especially is this true when money is freely used to mislead the people.

Commercialism has a legitimate place in a newspaper, namely, in the business office. The more successful a newspaper is commercially, the better for its moral side. The more prosperous it is, the more independent it can afford to be, the higher salaries it can pay to editors and reporters, the less subject it will be to temptation, the better it can stand losses for the sake of principle and conviction. But commercialism, which is proper and necessary in the business office, becomes a degradation and a danger when it invades the editorial rooms. Once let the public come to regard the press as exclusively a commercial business and there is an end of its moral power. Influence cannot exist without public confidence. And that confidence must have a human basis. It must rest in the end on the character of the journalist. The editor, the real "journalist" of the future, must be a man of such known integrity that he will be above the suspicion of writing or editing against his convictions. He must be known as one who would resign rather than sacrifice his principles to any business interest. It would be well if the editor of every newspaper were also its proprietor, but every editor can be at least the proprietor of himself. If he cannot keep the paper from degrading itself, he can refuse to be a party to the degradation.

By far the larger part of the American press is honest, although partisan. It means to do right; it would like to know how. To strengthen its resolution and give to its wisdom the indispensable basis of knowledge and independence is the object of training in journalism.

THE MARCH OF PROGRESS

I know but two ways by which society can be governed:
the one is by Public Opinion, the other by the Sword.
                                        —MACAULAY

We are embarked, whether we like it or not, upon a revolution in thought and life. Progress is sweeping forward with accelerating force, outstripping in decades the advance of former centuries and millenniums. All professions, all occupations but one, are keeping step with that majestic march. Its inspiration has fired all ranks of the marching army, or must we except the standard-bearers? The self-constituted leaders and enlighteners of the people—what are they doing? Standing still, lost in self-admiration, while the hosts march by? Are they even doing as well as that? Is it not a fact that the editors of seventy years ago were, as a rule, better informed in law, politics, government, and history than those of to-day? The statesmen and lawyers and political students who used to do editorial work for ambition or intellectual pleasure have ceased to frequent the newspaper offices. There is no trade so humble that it is not developing a standard of competence based on thorough training. For the more intellectual professions—law, medicine, art, architecture, music, engineering in all its varied branches—the years of preparation are stretching over ever-lengthening periods.

Is the most exacting profession of all—the one that requires the widest and the deepest knowledge and the firmest foundations of character—to be left entirely to the chances of self-education? Is the man who is everybody's critic and teacher the only one who does not need to be taught himself? . . .

PUBLIC SERVICE THE SUPREME END

What are great gifts but the correlative of great work?
We are not born for ourselves but for our kind, for our
neighbors, for our country.
                                        —CARDINAL NEWMAN

It has been said by some that my object in founding the College of Journalism was to help young men who wish to make this their vocation. Others have commended it as an effort to raise journalism to its real rank as one of the learned professions. This is true. But while it is a great pleasure to feel that a large number of young men will be helped to a better start in life by means of this college, this is not my primary object. Neither is the elevation of the profession which I love so much and regard so highly. In all my planning the chief end I had in view was the welfare of the Republic. It will be the object of the college to make better journalists, who will make better newspapers, which will better serve the public. It will impart knowledge—not for its own sake, but to be used for the public service. It will try to develop character, but even that will be only a means to the one supreme end—the public good. We are facing that hitherto-unheard-of portent—an innumerable, world-wide, educated, and self-conscious democracy. The little revolutions of the past have been effected by a few leaders working upon an ignorant populace, conscious only of vague feelings of discontent. Now the masses read. They know their grievances and their power. They discuss in New York the position of labor in Berlin and in Sydney. Capital, too, is developing a world-wide class feeling. It likewise has learned the power of cooperation.

What will be the state of society and of politics in this Republic seventy years hence, when some of the children now in school will be still living? Shall we preserve the government of the Constitution, the equality of all citizens before the law and the purity of justice—or shall we have the government of either money or the mob?

The answers to these questions will depend largely upon the kind of instruction the people of that day draw from their newspapers—the textbooks, the orators, the preachers of the masses.

I have said so much of the need for improvement in journalism that to avoid misconception I must put on record my appreciation of the really admirable work so many newspapermen are doing already. The competent editorial writer, for instance—how much sound information he furnishes every day! How generally just his judgments are, and how prompt his decisions! Unknown to the people he serves, he is in close sympathy with their feelings and aspirations, and, when left to himself and unhampered by party prejudices, he generally interprets their thought as they would wish to express it themselves.

It is not too much to say that the press is the only great organized force which is actively and as a body upholding the standard of civic righteousness. There are many political reformers among the clergy, but the pulpit as an institution is concerned with the Kingdom of Heaven, not with the Republic of America. There are many public-spirited lawyers, but the bar as a profession works for its retainers, and no law-defying trust ever came to grief from a dearth of legal talent to serve it. Physicians work for their patients and architects for their patrons. The press alone makes the public interest its own. "What is everybody's business is nobody's business"— except the journalist's; it is his by adoption. But for his care almost every reform would fall stillborn. He holds officials to their duty. He exposes secret schemes of plunder. He promotes every hopeful plan of progress. Without him public opinion would be shapeless and dumb. He brings all classes, all professions together, and teaches them to act in concert on the basis of their common citizenship.

The Greeks thought that no republic could be successfully governed if it were too large for all the citizens to come together in one place. The Athenian democracy could all meet in the popular assembly. There public opinion was made, and accordingly as the people listened to a Pericles or to a Cleon the state flourished or declined. The orator that reaches the American democracy is the newspaper. It alone makes it possible to keep the political blood in healthful circulation in the veins of a continental republic. We have—it is unfortunately true—a few newspapers which advocate dangerous fallacies and falsehoods, appealing to ignorance, to partisanship, to passion, to popular prejudice, to poverty, to hatred of the rich, to socialism, sowing the seeds of discontent—eventually sure, if unchecked, to produce lawlessness and bloodshed. Virtue, said Montesquieu, is the principle of a republic, and therefore a republic, which in its purity is the most desirable of all forms of government, is the hardest of all to preserve. For there is nothing more subject to decay than virtue.

Our Republic and its press will rise or fall together. An able, disinterested, public-spirited press, with trained intelligence to know the right and courage to do it, can preserve that public virtue without which popular government is a sham and a mockery. A cynical, mercenary, demagogic press will produce in time a people as base as itself. The power to mould the future of the Republic will be in the hands of journalists of future generations. This is why I urge my colleagues to aid the important experiment which I have ventured to endow. Upon their generous aid and cooperation the ultimate success of the project must depend.

THE ROLE OF THE MASS MEDIA
IN REPORTING OF NEWS
ABOUT MINORITIES

COMMISSION ON CIVIL DISORDERS

1968

———

———

———

The decade of the 1960s was a period of tumult and confusion. One device employed to make sense out of disparate events—and to deflect political criticism as well—was the national commission. There was the Warren Commission to investigate the death of President John F. Kennedy, there was a commission to investigate pornography, and there was a commission to investigate violence.

One of the most impressive of these commissions was appointed by President Lyndon Johnson to investigate the causes of the ghetto riots in 1967. The National Advisory Commission on Civil Disorders was popularly known as the Kerner Commission after its chairman, Otto Kerner, the Governor of Illinois, whose later career was a checkered one: he was appointed a Federal judge and then he served time in the Federal penitentiary for tax-related crimes.

On the first page of its report, the Kerner Commission presented its stark conclusion: "Our nation is moving towards two societies, one black, one white—separate and unequal." In its chapter on the news coverage of the riots, the commission credited the media with generally trying to give a balanced, factual account of the disorders. But, it concluded, the media were guilty of exaggerating the mood and scale of disturbances. Too often, the commission said, journalists were reporting solely "from the standpoint of a white man's world."

The underlying message of this chapter goes against the grain of what so many journalists hold sacred: the notion that reporters leave their beliefs at home and can cover any story.

A key recommendation was that the media seek out, hire, and promote black journalists to counteract the all-white perspective. Up to the mid-1960s, the report said, "the journalistic profession has been shockingly backward" in its hiring practices. Two decades after this rather modest recommendation, adequate representation of blacks in newsrooms remains elusive. Although reliable statistics are frustratingly hard to come by, currently between 6 and 7 percent of journalists are from minorities, a proportion far from representative of the minority population within the society at large. In the mid-1980s, nearly 60 percent of the daily papers employed no minority members at all. Few minority journalists are in management positions either in newspapers or in television.

The American Society of Newspaper Editors, an organization of editors from leading newspapers, has set a goal of having minority newsroom employment reach levels equal to the proportion of minorities within the general population. The deadline for this parity is the year 2000. But at the present pace of hiring, parity will not be achieved until a century later.

THE ROLE OF THE MASS MEDIA
IN REPORTING OF NEWS
ABOUT MINORITIES

INTRODUCTION

The President's charge to the Commission asked specifically: "What effect do the mass media have on the riots."

The question is far reaching, and a sure answer is beyond the range of presently available scientific techniques. Our conclusions and recommendations are based upon subjective as well as objective factors; interviews as well as statistics; isolated examples as well as general trends.

Freedom of the press is not the issue. A free press is indispensable to the preservation of the other freedoms this Nation cherishes. The recommendations in this chapter have thus been developed under the strong conviction that only a press unhindered by government can contribute to freedom. . . .

The Commission also determined, very early, that the answer to the President's question did not lie solely in the performance of the press and broadcasters in reporting the riots proper. Our analysis had to consider also the overall treatment by the media of the Negro ghettos, community relations, racial attitudes, urban and rural poverty—day by day and month by month, year in and year out.

On this basis, we have reached three conclusions:

First, that despite instances of sensationalism, inaccuracies, and distortions, newspapers, radio, and television, on the whole, made a real effort to give a balanced, factual account of the 1967 disorders.

Second, that despite this effort, the portrayal of the violence that occurred last summer failed to reflect accurately its scale and character. The overall effect was, we believe, an exaggeration of both mood and event.

Third, and ultimately most important, we believe that the media have thus far failed to report adequately on the causes and consequences of civil disorders and the underlying problems of race relations.

With these comments as a perspective, we discuss first the coverage of last summer's disturbances. We will then summarize our concerns with overall coverage of race relations.

COVERAGE OF THE 1967 DISTURBANCES

We have found a significant imbalance between what actually happened in our cities and what the newspaper, radio, and television coverage of the riots told us happened. The Commission, in studying last summer's disturbances, visited many of the cities and interviewed participants and observers. We found that the disorders, as serious as they were, were less destructive, less widespread, and less of a black-white confrontation than most people believed.

Lacking other sources of information, we formed our original impressions and beliefs from what we saw on television, heard on the radio, and read in newspapers and magazines. We are deeply concerned that millions of other Americans, who must rely on the mass media, likewise formed incorrect impressions and judgments about what went on in many American cities last summer.

As we started to probe the reasons for this imbalance between reality and impression, we first believed that the media had sensationalized the disturbances, consistently overplaying violence and giving disproportionate amounts of time to emotional events and militant leaders. To test this theory, we commissioned a systematic, quantitative analysis, covering the content of newspaper and television reporting in 15 cities where disorders occurred. The results of this analysis do not support our early belief. Of 955 television sequences of riot and racial news examined, 837 could be classified for predominant atomsphere as either "emotional," "calm," or "normal." Of these, 494 were classified as calm, 262 as emotional, and 81 as normal. Only a small proportion of all scenes analyzed showed actual mob action, people looting, sniping, setting fires, or being injured, or killed. Moderate Negro leaders were shown more frequently than militant leaders on television news broadcasts.

Of 3,779 newspaper articles analyzed, more focused on legislation which should be sought and planning which should be done to control ongoing riots and prevent future riots than on any other topic. The findings of this analysis are explained in detail later in this chapter. They make it clear that the imbalance between actual events and the portrayal of those events in the press and on the air cannot be attributed solely to sensationalism in reporting and presentation.

We have, however, identified several factors which, it seems to us, did work to create incorrect and exaggerated impressions about the scope and intensity of the disorders.

First, despite the overall statistical picture, there were instances of gross flaws in presenting news of the 1967 riots. Some newspapers printed scare headlines unsupported by the mild stories that followed. All media reported rumors that had no basis in fact. Some newsmen staged riot events for the cameras. Examples are included in the next section.

Second, the press obtained much factual information about the scale of the disorders—property damage, personal injury, and deaths—from local officials who often were inexperienced in dealing with civil disorders and not always able to sort out fact from rumor in the confusion. At the height of the Detroit riot, some news reports of property damage put the figure in excess of $500 million. Subsequent investigation shows it to be $40 to $45 million. The initial estimates were not the independent judgment of reporters or editors. They came from beleaguered government officials. But the news media gave currency to these errors. Reporters uncritically accepted, and editors uncritically published, the inflated figures, leaving an indelible impression of damage up to more than 10 times greater than actually occurred.

Third, the coverage of the disorders—particularly on television—tended to define the events as black-white confrontations. In fact, almost all of the deaths, injuries, and property damage occurred in all-Negro neighborhoods, and thus the disorders were not "race riots" as that term is generally understood.

Closely linked to these problems is the phenomenon of cumulative effect. As the summer of 1967 progressed, we think Americans often began to associate more or less neutral sights and sounds (like a squad car with flashing red lights, a burning building, a suspect in police custody) with racial disorders, so that the appearance of any particular item, itself hardly inflammatory, set off a whole sequence of association with riot events. Moreover, the summer's news was not seen and heard in isolation. Events of these past few years—the Watts riot, other disorders, and the growing momentum of the civil rights movement—conditioned the responses of readers and viewers and heightened their reactions. What the public saw and read last summer thus produced emotional reactions and left vivid impressions not wholly attributable to the material itself.

Fear and apprehension of racial unrest and violence are deeply rooted in American society. They color and intensify reactions to news of racial trouble and threats of racial conflict. Those who report and disseminate news must be conscious of the background of anxieties and apprehension against which their stories are projected. This does not mean that the media should manage the news or tell less than the truth. Indeed, we believe that it would be imprudent and even dangerous to downplay coverage in the hope that censored reporting of inflammatory incidents somehow will diminish violence. Once a disturbance occurs, the word will spread independently of newspapers and television. To attempt to ignore these events or portray them as something other than what they are can only diminish confidence in the media and increase the effectiveness of those who monger rumors and the fears of those who listen.

But to be complete, the coverage must be representative. We suggest that the main failure of the media last summer was that the totality of its coverage was not as representative as it should have been to be accurate. We believe that to live up to their own professed standards, the media simply must exercise a higher degree of care and a greater level of sophistication than they have yet shown in this area—higher, perhaps, than the level ordinarily acceptable with other stories.

This is not "just another story." It should not be treated like one. Admittedly, some of what disturbs us about riot coverage last summer stems from circumstances beyond media control. But many of the inaccuracies of fact, tone, and mood were due to the failure of reporters and editors to ask tough enough questions about official reports and to apply the most rigorous standards possible in evaluating and presenting the news. Reporters and editors must be sure that descriptions and pictures of violence, and emotional or inflammatory sequences or articles, even though "true" in isolation, are really representative and do not convey an impression at odds with the overall reality of events. The media too often did not achieve this level of sophisticated, skeptical, careful news judgment during last summer's riots.

THE MEDIA AND RACE RELATIONS

Our second and fundamental criticism is that the news media have failed to analyze and report adequately on racial problems in the United States and, as a related matter, to meet the Negro's legitimate expectations in journalism. By and large, news organizations have failed to communicate to both their black and white audiences a sense of the problems America faces and the sources of potential solutions. The media report and write from the standpoint of a white man's world. The ills of the ghetto, the difficulties of life there, the Negro's burning sense of grievance, are seldom conveyed. Slights and indignities are part of the Negro's daily life, and many of them come from what he now calls the "white press"—a press that repeatedly, if unconsciously, reflects the biases, the paternalism, the indifference of white America. This may be understandable, but it is not excusable in an institution that has the mission to inform and educate the whole of our society.

Our criticisms, important as they are, do not lead us to conclude that the media are a cause of riots, any more than they are the cause of other phenomena which they report. It is true that newspaper and television reporting helped shape people's attitudes toward riots. In some cities, people who watched television reports and read newspaper accounts of riots in other cities later rioted themselves. But the causal chain weakens when we recall that in other cities, people in very much the same circumstances watched the same programs and read the same newspaper stories but did not riot themselves.

The news media are not the sole source of information and certainly not the only influence on public attitudes. People obtained their information and formed their opinions about the 1967 disorders from the multiplicity of sources that condition the public's thinking on all events. Personal experience, conversations with others, the local and long distance telephone are all important as sources of information and ideas and contribute to the totality of attitudes about riots.

No doubt, in some cases, the knowledge or the sight on a television screen of what had gone on elsewhere lowered inhibitions, kindled outrage or awakened desires for excitement or loot—or simply passed the word. Many ghetto residents we interviewed thought so themselves. By the same token, the news reports of riots must have conditioned the response of officials and police to disturbances in their own cities. The reaction of the authorities in Detroit was almost certainly affected in some part by what they saw or read of Newark a week earlier. The Commission believes that none of these private or official reactions was decisive in determining the course of the disorders. Even if they had been more significant than we think, however, we cannot envision a system of governmental restraints that could successfully eliminate these effects. And an effort to formulate and impose such restraints would be inconsistent with fundamental traditions in our society.

These failings of the media must be corrected and the improvement must come from within the media. A society that values and relies on a free press as intensely as ours is entitled to demand in return responsibility from the press and conscientious attention by the press to its own deficiencies. The Commission has seen evidence that many of those who supervise, edit, and report for the news media are becoming increasingly aware of and concerned about their performance in this field. With that concern, and with more experience, will come more sophisticated and responsible coverage. But much more must be done, and it must be done soon.

The Commission has a number of recommendations designed to stimulate and accelerate efforts toward self-improvement. And we propose a privately organized, privately funded Institute of Urban Communications as a means for drawing these recommendations together and promoting their implementation.

NEWS COVERAGE OF CIVIL DISORDERS—
SUMMER 1967
THE METHOD OF ANALYSIS

As noted, the Commission has been surveying both the reporting of disorders last summer and the broader field of race relations coverage. With respect to the reporting of disorders, we were trying to get a sense of content, accuracy, tone, and bias. We sought to find out how people reacted to it and how reporters conducted themselves while carrying out their assignments. The Commission used a number of techniques to probe these matters and to provide cross-checks on data and impressions.

To obtain an objective source of data, the Commission arranged for a systematic, quantitative analysis of the content of newspapers, local television, and network coverage in 15 cities for a period from 3 days before to 3 days after the disorder in each city. The cities were chosen to provide a cross-section in terms of the location and scale of the disorders and the dates of their occurrence.

Within each city, for the period specified, the study was comprehensive. Every daily newspaper and all network and local television news films were analyzed, and scripts and logs were examined. In all, 955 network and local television sequences and 3,779 newspaper articles dealing with riot and race relations news were analyzed. Each separate analysis was coded and the cards were cross-tabulated by computer to provide results and comparisons for use by the Commission. The material was measured to determine the amount of space devoted to news of riot activity; the nature of the display given compared with other news coverage; and the types of stories, articles, and television programming presented. We sought specific statistical information on such matters as the amount of space or time devoted to different kinds of riot stories, the types and identities of persons most often depicted or interviewed, the frequency with which race relations problems were mentioned in riot stories or identified as the cause of riot activity.

The survey was designed to be objective and statistical. Within its terms of reference, the Commission was looking for broad characterizations of media tone and content.

The Commission is aware of the inherent limitations of content analysis techniques. They cannot measure the emotional impact of a particular story or television sequence. By themselves, they provide no basis for conclusions as to the accuracy of what was reported. Particular examples of good or bad journalistic conduct, which may be important in themselves, are submerged in a statistical average. The Commission therefore sought through staff interviews and personal contact with members of the press and the public to obtain direct evidence of the effects of riot coverage and the performance of the media during last summer's disturbances.

CONCLUSIONS ABOUT CONTENT
Television

1. Content analysis of television film footage shows that the tone of the coverage studied was more "calm" and "factual" than "emotional" and "rumor-laden." Researchers viewed every one of the 955 television sequences and found that twice as many "calm" sequences as "emotional" ones were shown. The amount and location of coverage were relatively limited, considering the magnitude of the events. The analysis reveals a dominant, positive emphasis on control of the riot and on activities in the aftermath of the riot (53.8 percent of all scenes broadcast), rather than on scenes of actual mob action, or people looting, sniping, setting fires, or being injured or killed (4.8 percent of scenes shown). According to participants in our Poughkeepsie conference, coverage frequently was of the post-riot or interview variety because newsmen arrived at the scene after the actual violence had subsided. Overall, both network and local television coverage was cautious and restrained.

2. Television newscasts during the periods of actual disorder in 1967 tended to emphasize law enforcement activities, thereby overshadowing underlying grievances and tensions. This conclusion is based on the relatively high frequency with which television showed and described law enforcement agents, police, National Guardsmen, and army troops performing control functions.

Television coverage tended to give the impression that the riots were confrontations between Negroes and whites rather than responses by Negroes to underlying slum problems. The control agents were predominantly white. The ratio of white male adults to Negro male adults shown on television is high (1:2) considering that the riots took place in predominantly Negro neighborhoods. And some interviews with whites involved landlords or proprietors who lost property or suffered business losses because of the disturbances and thus held strongly antagonistic attitudes.

The content analysis shows that by far the most frequent "actor" appearances on television were Negro male adults, white male adults, law enforcement agents, and public officials. We cannot tell from a content analysis whether there was any preconceived editorial policy of portraying the riots as racial confrontations requiring the intervention of enforcement agents. But the content analysis does present a visual three-way alignment of Negroes, white bystanders, and public officials or enforcement agents. This alignment tended to create an impression that the riots were predominantly racial confrontations involving clashes between black and white citizens.

3. About one-third of all riot-related sequences for network and local television appeared on the first day following the outbreak of rioting, regardless of the course of development of the riot itself. After the first day there was, except in Detroit, a very sharp decline in the amount of television time devoted to the disturbance. In Detroit, where the riot started slowly and did not flare out of control until the evening of July 24, 48 hours after it started, the number of riot-related sequences shown increased until July 26 and then showed the same sharp dropoff as noted after the first day of rioting in the other cities. These findings tend to controvert the impression that the riot intensifies television coverage, thus in turn intensifying the riot. The content analysis indicates that whether or not the riot was getting worse, television coverage of the riot decreased sharply after the first day.

4. The Commission made a special effort to analyze television coverage of Negro leaders. To do this, Negro leaders were divided into three categories: (a) celebrities or public figures, who did not claim any organizational following (e.g., social scientist Dr. Kenneth B. Clark, comedian Dick Gregory); (b) "moderate" Negro leaders, who claim a political or organizational following; and (c) "militant" Negro leaders who claim a political or organizational following. During the riot periods surveyed, Negro leaders appeared infrequently on network news broadcasts and were about equally divided among celebrity or public figures, moderate leaders, and militant leaders. On local television, Negro leaders appeared more often. Of the three categories, "moderate" Negro leaders were shown on local stations more than twice as often as Negro leaders identified primarily as celebrities or public figures and three times more frequently than militant leaders.

Newspapers

1. Like television coverage, newspaper coverage of civil disturbances in the summer of 1967 was more calm, factual, and restrained than outwardly emotional or inflammatory. During the period of the riot there were many stories dealing exclusively with non-riot racial news. Considering the

magnitude of the events, the amount of coverage was limited. Most stories were played down or put on inside pages. Researchers found that almost all the articles analyzed (3,045 of 3,770) tended to focus on one of 16 identifiable subjects. Of this group, 502 articles (16.5 percent) focused primarily on legislation which should be sought and planning which could be done to control ongoing riots and prevent future riots. The second largest category consisted of 471 articles (15.5 percent) focusing on containment or control of riot action. Newspaper coverage of the disorders reflects efforts at caution and restraint.

2. Newspapers tended to characterize and portray last summer's riots in national terms rather than as local phenomena and problems, especially when rioting was taking place in the newspaper's own city. During the actual disorders, the newspapers in each city studied tended to print many stories dealing with disorders or racial troubles in other cities. About 40 percent of the riot or racial stories in each local newspaper during the period of rioting in that city came from the wire services. Furthermore, most newspaper editors appear to have given more headline attention to riots occurring elsewhere than to those at home during the time of trouble in their own cities.

ACCURACY OF THE COVERAGE

We have tested the accuracy of coverage by means of interviews with local media representatives, city and police officials, and residents of the ghettos. To provide a broad base, we used three separate sources for interview data: The Commission's field survey teams, special field teams, and the findings of a special research study.

As is to be expected, almost everyone had his own version of "the truth," but it is noteworthy that some editors and reporters themselves, in retrospect, have expressed concern about the accuracy of their own coverage. For example, one newspaper editor said at the Commission's Poughkeepsie conference:

> We used things in our leads and headlines during the riot I wish we could have back now, because they were wrong and they were bad mistakes . . .
> We used the words "sniper kings" and "nests of snipers." We found out when we were able to get our people into those areas and get them out from under the cars that these sniper kings and these nests of snipers were the constituted authorities shooting at each other, most of them. There was just one

confirmed sniper in the entire eight-day riot and he was . . .
drunk and he had a pistol, and he was firing from a window.

Television industry representatives at the conference stressed their
concern about "live" coverage of disorders and said they try, whenever
possible, to view and edit taped or filmed sequences before broadcasting
them. Conference participants admitted that live television coverage via
helicopter of the 1965 Watts riot had been inflammatory, and network news
executives expressed doubts that television would ever again present live
coverage of a civil disorder.

Most errors involved mistakes of fact, exaggeration of events, overplaying of particular stories, or prominently displayed speculation about unfounded rumors of potential trouble. This is not only a local problem; because of the wire services and networks, it is a national one. An experienced riot reporter told the Commission that initial wire service reports
of a disturbance tend to be inflated. The reason, he said, is that they are
written by local bureau men who in most cases have not seen a civil disorder before. When out-of-town reporters with knowledge in the field or
the wire services' own riot specialists arrive on the scene, the situation is
put into a more accurate context.

Some examples of exaggeration and mistakes about facts are cataloged
here. These examples are by no means exhaustive. They represent only
a few of the incidents discovered by the Commission and, no doubt, are
but a small part of the total number of such inaccuracies. But the Commission believes that they are representative of the kinds of errors likely
to occur when, in addition to the confusion inherent in civil disorder situations, reporters are rushed and harried or editors are superficial and careless. We present these as examples of mistakes that we hope will be avoided
in the future.

In particular, we believe newsmen should be wary of how they play
rumors of impending trouble. Whether a rumor is reliable and significant
enough to deserve coverage is an editorial decision. But the failure of many
headlined rumors to be borne out last summer suggests that these editorial
decisions often are not as carefully made as the sensitivity of the subject
requires.

- In Detroit, a radio station broadcast a rumor, based on a telephone tip, that Negroes planned to invade suburbia one night
  later; if plans existed, they never materialized.
- In Cincinnati, several outlets ran a story about white youths arrested for possessing a bazooka; only a few reports mentioned
  that the weapon was inoperable.

■ In Tampa, a newspaper repeatedly indulged in speculation about impending trouble. When the state attorney ruled the fatal shooting of a Negro youth justifiable homicide, the paper's news columns reported: "There were fears today that the ruling would stir new race problems for Tampa tonight." The day before, the paper quoted one "top lawman" as telling reporters "he now fears that Negro residents in the Central Avenue Project and in the West Tampa trouble spots feel they are in competition and are trying to see which can cause the most unrest—which area can become the center of attraction."

■ A West Coast newspaper put out an edition headlined: "Rioting Erupts in Washington, D.C. / Negroes Hurl Bottles, Rocks at Police Near White House." The story did not support the headline. It reported what was actually the fact: that a number of teenage Negroes broke store windows and threw bottles and stones at police and firemen near downtown Washington, a mile or more from the White House. On the other hand, the same paper did not report unfounded local rumors of sniping when other news media did.

Television presents a different problem with respect to accuracy. In contrast to what some of its critics have charged, television sometimes may have leaned over too far backward in seeking balance and restraint. By stressing interviews, many with whites in predominantly Negro neighborhoods, and by emphasizing control scenes rather than riotous action, television news broadcasts may have given a distorted picture of what the disorders were all about.

The media—especially television—also have failed to present and analyze to a sufficient extent the basic reasons for the disorders. There have, after the disorders, been some brilliant exceptions. As the content analysis findings suggest, however, coverage during the riot period itself gives far more emphasis to control of rioters and black-white confrontation than to the underlying causes of the disturbances.

GHETTO REACTIONS TO THE MEDIA COVERAGE

The Commission was particularly interested in public reaction to media coverage; specifically, what people in the ghetto look at and read and how it affects them. The Commission has drawn upon reports from special teams of researchers who visited various cities where outbreaks occurred last summer. Members of these teams interviewed ghetto dwellers and middle-class Negroes on their responses to news media. In addition, we have used information from a statistical study of the mass media in the Negro ghetto in Pittsburgh.

These interviews and surveys, though by no means a complete study of the subject, lead to four broad conclusions about ghetto and, to a lesser degree, middle-class Negro reactions to the media.

Most Negroes distrust what they refer to as the "white press." As one interviewer reported:

> The average black person couldn't give less of a damn about what the media say. The intelligent black person is resentful at what he considers to be a totally false portrayal of what goes on in the ghetto. Most black people see the newspapers as mouthpieces of the "power structure."

These comments are echoed in most interview reports the Commission has read. Distrust and dislike of the media among ghetto Negroes encompass all the media, though in general, the newspapers are mistrusted more than the television. This is not because television is thought to be more sensitive or responsive to Negro needs and aspirations but because ghetto residents believe that television at least lets them see the actual events for themselves. Even so, many Negroes, particularly teenagers, told researchers that they noted a pronounced discrepancy between what they saw in the riots and what television broadcast.

Persons interviewed offered three chief reasons for their attitude. First, they believe, as suggested in the quotation above, that the media are instruments of the white power structure. They think that these white interests guide the entire white community, from the journalists' friends and neighbors to city officials, police officers, and department store owners. Publishers and editors, if not white reporters, they feel, support and defend these interests with enthusiasm and dedication.

Second, many people in the ghettos apparently believe that newsmen rely on the police for most of their information about what is happening during a disorder and tend to report much more of what the officials are doing and saying than what Negro citizens or leaders in the city are doing and saying. Editors and reporters at the Poughkeepsie Conference acknowledged that the police and city officials are their main—and sometimes their only—source of information. It was also noted that most reporters who cover civil disturbances tend to arrive with the police and stay close to them—often for safety and often because they learn where the action is at the same time as the authorities—and thus buttress the ghetto impression that police and press work together and toward the same ends (an impression that may come as a surprise to many within the ranks of police and press).

Third, Negro residents in several cities surveyed cited as specific examples of media unfairness what they considered the failure of the media:

- To report the many examples of Negroes helping law enforcement officers and assisting in the treatment of the wounded during disorders.
- To report adequately about false arrests.
- To report instances of excessive force by the National Guard.
- To explore and interpret the background conditions leading to disturbances.
- To expose, except in Detroit, what they regarded as instances of police brutality.
- To report on white vigilante groups which allegedly came into some disorder areas and molested innocent Negro residents.

Some of these problems are insoluble. But more firsthand reporting in the diffuse and fragmented riot area should temper easy reliance on police information and announcements. There is a special need for news media to cover "positive" news stories in the ghetto before and after riots with concern and enthusiasm.

A multitude of news and information sources other than the established news media are relied upon in the ghetto. One of our studies found that 79 percent of a total of 567 ghetto residents interviewed in seven cities first heard about the outbreak in their own city by word of mouth. Telephone and word of mouth exchanges on the streets, in churches, stores, pool halls, and bars, provide more information—and rumors—about events of direct concern to ghetto residents than the more conventional news media.

Among the established media, television and radio are far more popular in the ghetto than newspapers. Radios there, apparently, are ordinarily listened to less for news than for music and other programs. One survey showed that an overwhelmingly large number of Negro children and teenagers (like their white counterparts) listen to the radio for music alone, interspersed by disc jockey chatter. In other age groups, the response of most people about what they listen to on the radio was "anything," leading to the conclusion that radio in the ghetto is basically a background accompaniment.

But the fact that radio is such a constant background accompaniment can make it an important influence on people's attitudes, and perhaps on their actions once trouble develops. This is true for several reasons. News presented on local "rock" stations seldom constitutes much more than terse headline items which may startle or frighten but seldom inform. Radio disc jockeys and those who preside over the popular "talk shows" keep a steady patter of information going over the air. When a city is beset by civil strife, this patter can both inform transistor radio-carrying young people where the action is, and terrify their elders and much of the white community. "Burn, baby, burn," the slogan of the Watts riot, was inadvertently originated by a radio disc jockey.

Thus, radio can be an instrument of trouble and tension in a community threatened or inundated with civil disorder. It can also do much to minimize fear by putting fast-paced events into proper perspective. We have found commendable instances, for example, in Detroit, Milwaukee, and New Brunswick, of radio stations and personalities using their air time and influence to try to calm potential rioters. In the next section, we recommend procedures for meetings and consultations for advance planning among those who will cover civil disorders. It is important that radio personnel, and especially disc jockeys and talk show hosts, be included in such preplanning.

Television is the formal news source most relied upon in the ghetto. According to one report, more than 75 percent of the sample turned to television for national and international news, and a larger percentage of the sample (86 percent) regularly watched television from 5 to 7 p.m., the dinner hours when the evening news programs are broadcast.

The significance of broadcasting in news dissemination is seen in Census Bureau estimates that in June 1967, 87.7 percent of nonwhite households and 94.8 percent of white households had television sets.

When ghetto residents do turn to newspapers, most read tabloids, if available, far more frequently than standard size newspapers and rely on the tabloids primarily for light features, racing charts, comic strips, fashion news, and display advertising.

CONDUCT OF PRESS REPRESENTATIVES

Most newsmen appear to be aware and concerned that their very physical presence can exacerbate a small disturbance, but some have conducted themselves with a startling lack of common sense. News organizations, particularly television networks, have taken substantial steps to minimize the effect of the physical presence of their employees at a news event. Networks have issued internal instructions calling for use of unmarked cars and small cameras and tape recorders, and most stations instruct their cameramen to film without artificial light whenever possible. Still, some newsmen have done things "for the sake of the story" that could have contributed to tension.

Reports have come to the Commission's attention of individual newsmen staging events, coaxing youths to throw rocks and interrupt traffic, and otherwise acting irresponsibly at the incipient stages of a disturbance. Such acts are the responsibility of the news organization as well as of its individual reporter.

Two examples occurred in Newark. Television cameramen, according to officials, crowded into and in front of police headquarters, interfering with law enforcement operations and "making a general nuisance of themselves." In a separate incident, a New York newspaper photographer covering the Newark riot repeatedly urged and finally convinced a Negro boy to throw a rock for the camera. Crowding may occasionally be unavoidable; staging of events is not.

We believe every effort should be made to eliminate this sort of conduct. This requires the implementation of thoughtful, stringent staff guidelines for reporters and editors. Such guidelines, carefully formulated, widely disseminated, and strictly enforced, underlie the self-policing activities of some news organizations already, but they must be universally adopted if they are to be effective in curbing journalistic irresponsibility.

The Commission has studied the internal guidelines in use last summer at the Associated Press, United Press International, the *Washington Post,* and the Columbia Broadcasting System. Many other news organizations, large and small, have similar guidelines. In general, the guidelines urge extreme care to ensure that reporting is thorough and balanced and that words and statistics used are appropriate and accurate. The AP guidelines call for broad investigation into the immediate and underlying causes of an incident. The CBS guidelines demand as much caution as possible to avoid the danger of camera equipment and lights exacerbating the disturbance.

Internal guidelines can, and all those studied do, go beyond problems of physical presence at a disturbance to the substantive aspects of searching out, reporting, and writing the story. But the content of the guidelines is probably less important than the fact that the subject has been thoughtfully considered and hammered out within the organization, and an approach developed that is designed to meet the organization's particular needs and solve its particular problems.

We recommend that every news organization that does not now have some form of guidelines—or suspects that those it has are not working effectively—designate top editors to (a) meet with its reporters who have covered or might be assigned to riots, (b) discuss in detail the problems and procedures which exist or are expected and (c) formulate and disseminate directives based on the discussions. Regardless of the specific provisions, the vital step is for every news-gathering organization to adopt and implement at least some minimal form of internal control.

A RECOMMENDATION TO IMPROVE RIOT COVERAGE
A NEED FOR BETTER COMMUNICATION

A recurrent problem in the coverage of last summer's disorders was friction and lack of cooperation between police officers and working reporters. Many experienced and capable journalists complained that policemen and their commanding officers were at best apathetic and at worst overtly hostile toward reporters attempting to cover a disturbance. Policemen, on the other hand, charged that many reporters seemed to forget that the task of the police is to restore order.

After considering available evidence on the subject, the Commission is convinced that these conditions reflect an absence of advance communication and planning among the people involved. We do not suggest that familiarity with the other's problems will beget total amity and cooperation. The interests of the media and the police are sometimes necessarily at variance. But we do believe that communication is a vital step toward removing the obstacles produced by ignorance, confusion, and misunderstanding of what each group is actually trying to do.

MUTUAL ORIENTATION

What is needed first is a series of discussions, perhaps a combination of informal gatherings and seminar-type workshops. They should encompass all ranks of the police, all levels of media employees, and a cross-section of city officials. At first these would be get-acquainted sessions—to air complaints and discuss common problems. Working reporters should get to know the police who would be likely to draw duty in a disorder. Police and city officials should use the sessions for frank and candid briefings on the problems the city might face and official plans for dealing with disturbances.

Later sessions might consider procedures to facilitate the physical movement of personnel and speed the flow of accurate and complete news. Such arrangements might involve nothing more than a procedure for designating specific locations at which police officers would be available to escort a reporter into a dangerous area. In addition, policemen and reporters working together might devise better methods of identification, communication, and training.

Such procedures are infinitely variable and depend on the initiative, needs, and desires of those involved. If there is no existing institution or procedure for convening such meetings, we urge the mayor or city manager to do so in every city where experience suggests the possibility of future trouble. To allay any apprehension that discussions with officials might lead to restraints on the freedom to seek out and report the news, participants in these meetings should stipulate beforehand that freedom of access to all areas for reporters will be preserved.

DESIGNATION OF INFORMATION OFFICERS

It is desirable to designate and prepare a number of police officers to act as media information officers. There should be enough of these so that, in the event of a disturbance, a reporter will not have to seek far to find a policeman ready and able to give him information and answer questions. Officers should be of high enough rank within the police department to have ready access to information.

CREATION OF AN INFORMATION CENTER

A nerve center for reliable police and official government information should be planned and ready for activation when a disturbance reaches a prede-termined point of intensity. Such a center might be located at police head-quarters or city hall. It should be directed by an experienced, high-ranking information specialist with close ties to police officials. It is imperative, of course, that all officials keep a steady flow of accurate information coming into the center. Ideally, rooms would be set aside for taping and filming interviews with public officials. Local television stations might cut costs and relieve congestion by pooling some equipment at this central facility. An information center should not be thought of as replacing other news sources inside and outside the disturbance area. If anything, our studies suggest that reporters are already too closely tied to police and officials as news sources in a disorder. An information center should not be permitted to intensify this dependence. Properly conceived, however, a center can sup-plement on-the-spot reporting and supply news about official action.

OUT-OF-TOWN REPORTERS

Much of the difficulty last summer apparently revolved around relations between local law enforcement officials and out-of-town reporters. These reporters are likely to be less sensitive about preserving the "image" of the local community.

Still, local officials serve their city badly when they ignore or impede national media representatives instead of informing them about the city, and cooperating with their attempts to cover the story. City and police officials should designate liaison officers and distribute names and telephone numbers of police and other relevant officials, the place they can be found if trouble develops, and other information likely to be useful.

National and other news organizations, in turn, could help matters by selecting a responsible home office official to act as liaison in these cases and to be accessible by phone to local officials who encounter difficulty with on-the-spot representatives of an organization.

GENERAL GUIDELINES AND CODES

In some cases, if all parties involved were willing, planning sessions might lead to the consideration of more formal undertakings. These might include: (a) agreements on specific procedures to expedite the physical movement of men and equipment around disorder areas and back and forth through police lines; (b) general guidelines on the behavior of both media and police personnel; and (c) arrangements for a brief moratorium on reporting news of an incipient disturbance. The Commission stresses once again its belief that though each of these possibilities merits consideration, none should be formulated or imposed by unilateral government action. Any procedure finally adopted should be negotiated between police and media representatives and should assure both sides the flexibility needed to do their respective jobs. Acceptance of such arrangements should be frankly based on grounds of self-interest, for negotiated methods of procedure can often yield substantial benefits to each side—and to the public which both serve.

At the request of the Commission, the Community Relations Service of the Department of Justice surveyed recent experiences with formal codes. Most of the codes studied: (a) set forth in general terms common sense standards of good journalistic conduct, and (b) established procedures for a brief moratorium (seldom more than 30 minutes to an hour) on reporting an incipient disturbance.

In its survey, the Community Relations Service described and analyzed experiences with codes in 11 major cities where they are currently in force. Members of the CRS staff conducted interviews with key citizens (newsmen, city officials, and community leaders) in each of the 11 cities, seeking comments on the effectiveness and practicality of the codes and guidelines used. CRS's major findings and conclusions are:

- All codes and guidelines now in operation are basically voluntary arrangements usually put forward by local authorities and accepted by the news media after consultation. Nowhere has an arrangement or agreement been effected that binds the news media without their assent.
- No one interviewed in this survey considered the code or guidelines in effect in his city as useless or harmful. CRS thought that, where they were in effect, the codes had a constructive impact

on the local news media. Observers in some cities, however, thought the increased sense of responsibility manifested by press and television was due more to experience with riot coverage than to the existence of the codes.

■ The more controversial and often least understood aspect of guidelines has been provision for a brief voluntary moratorium on the reporting of news. Some kind of moratorium is specified in the codes of six cities surveyed (Chicago, Omaha, Buffalo, Indianapolis, Kansas City, and Toledo), and the moratorium was invoked last summer in Chicago and Indianapolis. In each case, an effort to prevent quite minor racial incidents from escalating into more serious trouble was successful, and many thought the moratorium contributed.

■ The confusion about a moratorium, and the resulting aversion to it, is unfortunate. The specific period of delay is seldom more than 30 minutes. In practice, under today's conditions of reporting and broadcasting, this often will mean little if any delay before the full story gets into the paper or on the air. The time can be used to repair and edit the story and to verify and assess the reports of trouble. The only loss is the banner headline or the broadcast news bulletin that is released prematurely to avoid being beaten by "the competition." It is just such reflexive responses that can lead to sensationalism and inaccuracy. In cities where a moratorium is part of the code, CRS interviewers detected no discontent over its presence.

■ The most frequent complaint about shortcomings in existing codes is that many of them do not reach the underpinnings of crisis situations. Ghetto spokesmen, in particular, said that the emphasis in the codes on conduct during the crisis itself tended to lead the media to neglect reporting the underlying causes of racial tension.

At the Poughkeepsie conference with media representatives, there was considerable criticism of the Chicago code on grounds that the moratorium is open-ended. Once put into effect it is supposed to be maintained until "the situation is under control." There were doubts about how effective this code had been in practice. The voluntary news blackout in Detroit for part of the first day of the riot—apparently at the request of officials and civil rights groups—was cited as evidence that suppression of news of violence does not necessarily defuse a riot situation.

On the basis of the CRS survey and other evidence, the Commission concludes that codes are seldom harmful, often useful, but no panacea. To be of any use, they must address themselves to the substance of the problems that plague relations between the press and officialdom during a disorder, but they are only one of several methods of improving those relations. Ultimately, no matter how sensitive and comprehensive a code or set of guidelines may be, efficient, accurate reporting must depend on the intelligence, judgment, and training of newsmen, police, and city officials together.

REPORTING RACIAL PROBLEMS
IN THE UNITED STATES
A FAILURE TO COMMUNICATE

The Commission's major concern with the news media is not in riot reporting as such, but in the failure to report adequately on race relations and ghetto problems and to bring more Negroes into journalism. Concern about this was expressed by a number of participants in our Poughkeepsie conference. Disorders are only one aspect of the dilemmas and difficulties of race relations in America. In defining, explaining, and reporting this broader, more complex, and ultimately far more fundamental subject, the communications media, ironically, have failed to communicate.

They have not communicated to the majority of their audience—which is white—a sense of the degradation, misery, and hopelessness of living in the ghetto. They have not communicated to whites a feeling for the difficulties and frustrations of being a Negro in the United States. They have not shown understanding or appreciation of—and thus have not communicated—a sense of Negro culture, thought, or history.

Equally important, most newspaper articles and most television programming ignore the fact that an appreciable part of their audience is black. The world that television and newspapers offer to their black audience is almost totally white, in both appearance and attitude. As we have said, our evidence shows that the so-called "white press" is at best mistrusted and at worst held in contempt by many black Americans. Far too often, the press acts and talks about Negroes as if Negroes do not read the newspapers or watch television, give birth, marry, die, and go to PTA meetings. Some newspapers and stations are beginning to make efforts to fill this void, but they have still a long way to go.

The absence of Negro faces and activities from the media has an effect on white audiences as well as black. If what the white American reads in the newspapers or sees on television conditions his expectation of what is ordinary and normal in the larger society, he will neither understand nor accept the black American. By failing to portray the Negro as a matter of routine and in the context of the total society, the news media have, we believe, contributed to the black-white schism in this country.

When the white press does refer to Negroes and Negro problems it frequently does so as if Negroes were not a part of the audience. This is perhaps understandable in a system where whites edit and, to a large extent, write news. But such attitudes, in an area as sensitive and inflammatory as this, feed Negro alienation and intensify white prejudices.

We suggest that a top editor or news director monitor his news production for a period of several weeks, taking note of how certain stories and language will affect black readers or viewers. A Negro staff member could do this easily. Then the staff should be informed about the problems involved.

The problems of race relations coverage go beyond incidents of white bias. Many editors and news directors, plagued by shortages of staff and lack of reliable contacts and sources of information in the city, have failed to recognize the significance of the urban story and to develop resources to cover it adequately.

We believe that most news organizations do not have direct access to diversified news sources in the ghetto. Seldom do they have a total sense of what is going on there. Some of the blame rests on Negro leaders who do not trust the media and will not deal candidly with representatives of the white press. But the real failure rests with the news organizations themselves. They—like other elements of the white community—have ignored the ghettos for decades. Now they seek instant acceptance and cooperation.

The development of good contacts, reliable information, and understanding requires more effort and time than an occasional visit by a team of reporters to do a feature on a newly discovered ghetto problem. It requires reporters permanently assigned to this beat. They must be adequately trained and supported to dig out and tell the story of a major social upheaval—among the most complicated, portentous, and explosive our society has known. We believe, also, that the Negro press—manned largely by people who live and work in the ghetto—could be a particularly useful source of information and guidance about activities in the black community. Reporters and editors from Negro newspapers and radio stations should be included in any conference between media and police-city representatives, and we suggest that large news organizations would do well to establish better lines of communication to their counterparts in the Negro press.

In short, the news media must find ways of exploring the problems of the Negro and the ghetto more deeply and more meaningfully. To editors who say "we have run thousands of inches on the ghetto which nobody reads" and to television executives who bemoan scores of underwatched documentaries, we say: find more ways of telling this story, for it is a story you, as journalists, must tell—honestly, realistically, and imaginatively. It is the responsibility of the news media to tell the story of race relations in America, and with notable exceptions, the media have not yet turned to the task with the wisdom, sensitivity, and expertise it demands.

NEGROES IN JOURNALISM

The journalistic profession has been shockingly backward in seeking out, hiring, training, and promoting Negroes. Fewer than 5 percent of the people employed by the news business in editorial jobs in the United States today are Negroes. Fewer than 1 percent of editors and supervisors are Negroes, and most of them work for Negro-owned organizations. The lines of various news organizations to the militant blacks are, by admission of the newsmen themselves, almost nonexistent. The plaint is, "we can't find qualified Negroes." But this rings hollow from an industry where, only yesterday, jobs were scarce and promotion unthinkable for a man whose skin was black. Even today, there are virtually no Negroes in positions of editorial or executive responsibility and there is only one Negro newsman with a nationally syndicated column.

News organizations must employ enough Negroes in positions of significant responsibility to establish an effective link to Negro actions and ideas and to meet legitimate employment expectations. Tokenism   the hiring of one Negro reporter, or even two or three—is no longer enough. Negro reporters are essential, but so are Negro editors, writers, and commentators. Newspaper and television policies are, generally speaking, not set by reporters. Editorial decisions about which stories to cover and which to use are made by editors. Yet, very few Negroes in this country are involved in making these decisions, because very few, if any, supervisory editorial jobs are held by Negroes. We urge the news media to do everything possible to train and promote their Negro reporters to positions where those who are qualified can contribute to and have an effect on policy decisions.

It is not enough, though, as many editors have pointed out to the Commission, to search for Negro journalists. Journalism is not very popular as a career for aspiring young Negroes. The starting pay is comparatively low and it is a business which has, until recently, discouraged and rejected them. The recruitment of Negro reporters must extend beyond established journalists, or those who have already formed ambitions along these lines. It must become a commitment to seek out young Negro men and women, inspire them to become—and then train them as—journalists. Training programs should be started at high schools and intensified at colleges. Summer vacation and part-time editorial jobs, coupled with offers of permanent employment, can awaken career plans.

We believe that the news media themselves, their audiences and the country will profit from these undertakings. For if the media are to comprehend and then to project the Negro community, they must have the help of Negroes. If the media are to report with understanding, wisdom, and sympathy on the problems of the cities and the problems of the black man—for the two are increasingly intertwined—they must employ, promote, and listen to Negro journalists.

THE NEGRO IN THE MEDIA

Finally, the news media must publish newspapers and produce programs that recognize the existence and activities of the Negro, both as a Negro and as part of the community. It would be a contribution of inestimable importance to race relations in the United States simply to treat ordinary news about Negroes as news of other groups is now treated.

Specifically, newspapers should integrate Negroes and Negro activities into all parts of the paper, from the news, society, and club pages to the comic strips. Television should develop programing which integrates Negroes into all aspects of televised presentations. Television is such a visible medium that some constructive steps are easy and obvious. While some of these steps are being taken, they are still largely neglected. For example, Negro reporters and performers should appear more frequently—and at prime time—in news broadcasts, on weather shows, in documentaries, and in advertisements. Some effort already has been made to use Negroes in television commercials. Any initial surprise at seeing a Negro selling a sponsor's product will eventually fade into routine acceptance, an attitude that white society must ultimately develop toward all Negroes.

In addition to news-related programming, we think that Negroes should appear more frequently in dramatic and comedy series. Moreover, networks and local stations should present plays and other programs whose subjects are rooted in the ghetto and its problems.

INSTITUTE OF URBAN COMMUNICATIONS

The Commission is aware that in this area, as in all other aspects of race relations, the problems are great and it is much easier to state them than to solve them. Various pressures—competitive, financial, advertising—may impede progress toward more balanced, in-depth coverage and toward the hiring and training of more Negro personnel. Most newspapers and local television and radio stations do not have the resources or the time to keep abreast of all the technical advances, academic theories, and government programs affecting the cities and the lives of their black inhabitants.

During the course of this study, the Commission members and the staff have had many conversations with publishers, editors, broadcasters, and reporters throughout the country. The consensus appears to be that most of them would like to do much more but simply do not have the resources for independent efforts in either training or coverage.

The Commission believes that some of these problems could be resolved if there were a central organization to develop, gather, and distribute talent, resources, and information and to keep the work of the press in this field under review. For this reason, the Commission proposes the establishment of an Institute of Urban Communications on a private, nonprofit basis. The Institute would have neither governmental ties nor governmental authority. Its board would consist in substantial part of professional journalists and, for the rest, of distinguished public figures. The staff would be made up of journalists and students of the profession. Funding would be sought initially from private foundations. Ultimately, it may be hoped, financial support would be forthcoming from within the profession.

The Institute would be charged, in the first instance, with general responsibility for carrying out the media recommendations of the Commission, though as it developed a momentum and life of its own it would also gain its own view of the problems and possibilities. Initial tasks would include:

1. *Training and Education for Journalists in the Field of Urban Affairs.* The Institute should organize and sponsor, on its own and in cooperation with universities and other institutions, a comprehensive range of courses, seminars, and workshops designed to give reporters, editors, and publishers the background they need to cover the urban scene. Offerings would vary in duration and intensity from weekend conferences to grants for year-long individual study on the order of the Nieman fellowships.

All levels and all kinds of news outlets should be served. A most important activity might be to assist disc jockeys and commentators on stations that address themselves especially to the Negro community. Particularly important would be sessions of a month or more for seasoned reporters and editors, comparable to middle management seminars or midcareer training in other callings. The press must have all of the intellectual resources and background to give adequate coverage to the city and the ghetto. It should be the first duty of the Institute to see that this is provided.

2. *Recruitment, Training, and Placement of Negro Journalists.* The scarcity of Negroes in responsible news jobs intensifies the difficulties of communicating the reality of the contemporary American city to white newspaper and television audiences. The special viewpoint of the Negro who has lived through these problems and bears their marks upon him is, as we have seen, notably absent from what is, on the whole, a white press. But full integration of Negroes into the journalistic profession is imperative in its own right. It is unacceptable that the press, itself the special beneficiary of fundamental constitutional protections, should lag so far behind other fields in giving effect to the fundamental human right to equality of opportunity.

To help correct this situation, the Institute will have to undertake far-ranging activities. Providing educational opportunities for would-be Negro journalists is not enough. There will have to be changes in career outlooks for Negro students and their counselors back to the secondary school level. And changes in these attitudes will come slowly unless there is a change in the reality of employment and advancement opportunities for Negroes in journalism. This requires an aggressive placement program, seeking out newspapers, television and radio stations that discriminate, whether consciously or unconsciously, and mobilizing the pressures, public, private, and legal, necessary to break the pattern. The Institute might also provide assistance to Negro newspapers, which now recruit and train many young journalists.

3. *Police-Press Relations.* The Commission has stressed the failures in this area, and has laid out a set of remedial measures for action at the local level. But if reliance is placed exclusively on local initiative we can predict that in many places—often those that need it most—our recommended steps will not be taken. Pressure from the Federal Government for action along the lines proposed would be suspect, probably, by both press and local officials. But the Institute could undertake the task of stimulating community action in line with the Commission's recommendations without arousing local hostility and suspicion. Moreover, the Institute could serve as a clearinghouse for exchange of experience in this field.

4. *Review of Media Performance on Riots and Racial Issues.* The Institute should review press and television coverage of riot and racial news and publicly award praise and blame. The Commission recognizes that government restraints or guidelines in this field are both unworkable and incompatible with our Constitution and traditions. Internal guidelines or voluntary advance arrangements may be useful, but they tend to be rather

general and the standards they prescribe are neither self-applying nor self-enforcing. We believe it would be healthy for reporters and editors who work in this sensitive field to know that others will be viewing their work and will hold them publicly accountable for lapses from accepted standards of good journalism. The Institute should publicize its findings by means of regular and special reports. It might also set a series of awards for especially meritorious work of individuals or news organizations in race relations reporting.

5. *An Urban Affairs Service.* Whatever may be done to improve the quality of reporting on urban affairs, there always will be a great many outlets that are too small to support the specialized investigation, reporting, and interpreting needed in this field. To fill this gap, the Institute could organize a comprehensive urban news service, available at a modest fee to any news organization that wanted it. The Institute would have its own specially trained reporters, and it would also cull the national press for news and feature stories of broader interest that could be reprinted or broadcast by subscribers.

6. *Continuing Research.* Our own investigations have shown us that academic work on the impact of the media on race relations, its role in shaping attitudes, and the effects of the choices it makes on people's behavior, is in a rudimentary stage. The Commission's content analysis is the first study of its type of contemporary riot coverage, and it is extremely limited in scope. A whole range of questions needs intensive, scholarly exploration, and indeed the development of new modes of research and analysis. The Institute should undertake many of these important projects under its own auspices and could stimulate others in the academic community to further research.

Along with the country as a whole, the press has too long basked in a white world, looking out of it, if at all, with white men's eyes and a white perspective. That is no longer good enough. The painful process of readjustment that is required of the American news media must begin now. They must make a reality of integration—in both their product and personnel. They must insist on the highest standards of accuracy—not only reporting single events with care and skepticism, but placing each event into meaningful perspective. They must report the travail of our cities with compassion and in depth.

In all this, the Commission asks for fair and courageous journalism—commitment and coverage that are worthy of one of the crucial domestic stories in America's history.

5

NEWS AND REALITY

N ewspapers, Frederick Lewis Allen wrote in his 1922 essay, "are the eyes through which largely we see the life of our time, and the news that they print is in great measure the raw material of our ideas. Nothing is more important than that through these eyes we shall see, not a distorted picture, but the reality."

This theme, while rarely stated so clearly, runs throughout many of these essays. By the middle 1960s, though, a growing dissatisfaction with the standard twentieth-century form of journalism emerged. Many journalists rebelled at the thought that they were mere stenographers devoid of opinions and feelings. A "new journalism" emerged. In an introduction to *The Best American Essays, 1987,* Gay Talese, one of the most talented of the "new journalists," reminisced: "Since my earliest days in journalism, I was far less interested in the exact words that came out of people's mouths than in the essence of their meaning."

It is this literary journalism that so troubled John Hersey, who in his essay insists on two rules: "The writer of fiction must invent. The journalist must not invent."

NEWSPAPERS AND THE TRUTH

FREDERICK LEWIS ALLEN

Atlantic Monthly, January 1922

———
———
———

The issues that troubled Frederick Lewis Allen in 1922—inaccuracies in news reports, the fallibility of eyewitness testimony, bias in selection of the news, the timidity of journalists in dealing with entrenched interests—are similar to the issues that troubled his contemporaries. But in contrast to, say, Upton Sinclair, Allen wrote with restrained anger about the limitations of the press and the factors that rendered objective reporting so difficult. Allen was less concerned with the political content of stories than he was with the larger reality reporters portrayed.

When this article appeared, Allen held the title of Secretary of the Harvard Corporation, which meant he was in charge of publicity at the college. But he spent most of his career on magazines—the *Atlantic Monthly,* the *Century* and *Harper's,* where he served as editor-in-chief for more than two decades. (Of *Harper's* he once said: "It is all very well to be serious, but there is no excuse for being solemn.") Allen was also a popular historian and was the author of *Only Yesterday,* a best-selling history of the 1920s which sold an astonishing 750,000 copies.

In this article, Allen emphasized the need for reporting that was unencumbered by personal opinions. In the introduction to a recent biography about Allen, Russell Lynes, his long-time colleague at *Harper's,* recalled: "He would have been appalled at what is called 'the new journalism' in which fact is embellished and beclouded and often falsified by fantasy."

NEWSPAPERS AND THE TRUTH

I

It is a significant fact that public interest in newspaper ethics and the conduct of the press was never so widespread in this country as it is to-day. Before the war, people who discussed the subject concerned themselves primarily with the question whether the newspapers degraded public morals by their exploitation of divorce scandals and their general preoccupation with men's misdeeds, and the question whether large advertisers, and especially department stores, could bring about the suppression or distortion of news affecting their financial interests. The war, however, with its censorship, its development of the art of propaganda, and the improvement which it brought about in methods of swaying masses of men by controlling or doctoring the news, has made us realize that the problem of newspaper conduct is larger and more fundamental than we had supposed it to be. We now see that it is immensely important that the press shall give us the facts straight; and not merely the facts relating to department stores and other large business concerns, but the entire mass of facts about the world in which we live—political, economic, religious, scientific, social, and industrial.

It is beginning to be understood that, as Mr. Walter Lippmann ably argued in his recent book on *Liberty and the News,* access to accurate accounts of what is going on about us is one of the indispensable conditions of freedom. We talk a great deal about the right of the individual to express his opinions, and somewhat less about the advantage to the community, or the nation, or the world, of determining its collective action after the freest discussion; but we are just beginning to see that it is still more vital that the individual shall be able to form his opinion upon the facts. If these facts are withheld from him or misrepresented to him, his opinion is as valueless as that of a judge who has heard incomplete or false evidence in a case. Though the individual may be at liberty to shout his ideas from the housetops, he is still a slave to illusion; and all the more completely a slave than if he were in bonds, because he fancies that he walks freely in the light.

There never was such an age of newspaper-reading as the present. Most of us read—or at least glance at—one, two, or more newspapers a day. They are the eyes through which largely we see the life of our time, and the news that they print is in great measure the raw material of our

ideas. Nothing is more important than that through these eyes we shall
see, not a distorted picture, but the reality. It is often contended in England, where the Northcliffe press wields far more power than any existing
group of American newspapers, and it is occasionallly contended in this
country by those who take a gloomy view of affairs, that the public is at
the mercy of the lords of the press, who feed it such garbled news as will
best serve their own selfish purposes. Other critics, such as Professor
James Melvin Lee, the author of an illuminating history of American journalism, assure us that the ethics of the newspaper profession are higher
to-day than those of any other. It would seem worth while to consider the
whole matter afresh, and decide for ourselves what the public interest requires of the press in the interest of truth, and how far these requirements
are being met.

The public interest requires that all unsigned news on the news pages—
all news, in other words, which does not bear its own tag, to warn the
reader that he is seeing the facts through the spectacles of somebody's
personal opinion—shall be presented as accurately and impartially as is
humanly possible. On the editorial page every newspaper proprietor or
editor has a right to state his views as forcibly as he wishes; and I for one
do not believe, as some people do, that it is necessary for editorials to be
individually signed, provided the names of the proprietor and editor are
regularly printed somewhere in the paper; for editorials are usually, to
some extent, the work of a group rather than of an individual; and in any
case, the fact that they appear on the editorial page is fair warning that
they are to be regarded as comment rather than as sheer fact.

Papers also have an unquestionable right to commission correspondents
to include in their dispatches their personal view of events, provided these
dispatches are signed. The imperative thing is that what the press presents
as fact shall be fact, given correctly and without bias.

Bias is all the more completely the enemy of truth on account of the
slovenly way in which most of us are accustomed to read the papers. For
every report that we read through thoroughly and weigh for ourselves,
checking the generalizations and summaries in headline and leading paragraph by the details which follow, there are ten that we only glance at.
Usually we carry away nothing but the dim impression that Mr. X has done
something disastrous, or that Governor Y has made another fine speech;
we retain the bias, and little else. If you doubt that you yourself skim the
paper in this way, try handing it to somebody else after you have finished,
and making him examine you on the contents of an important article. You
will probably soon realize how vaguely most of your news-reading is done,
and understand how easily the twist of a phrase in headline or leading para-

graph, by giving a biased impression, may cause thousands of readers to form opinions based, not on the facts, but on somebody else's view of the facts.

This cardinal rule of newspaper ethics — that what is presented as sheer fact should be accurate and without bias—is easy to state. It is harder to live up to than anybody can imagine who has not faced the newspaper man's problem for himself.

In the first place, it is hard for a reporter, just as for any other person, to give an absolutely accurate account of any event, even when he has seen it with his own eyes. The fallibility of even first-hand evidence from eye-witnesses is well known; no one can read a book like the late Professor Munsterberg's *On the Witness Stand* without appreciating what the reporter is up against. Furthermore, it is also exceedingly hard to write an account of any event without coloring it with one's own opinions. Though the reporter has every intention of stating only the clear facts, he may give them bias simply through his choice of language.

Suppose one senator denounces another in a speech. Shall the reporter write, "Senator A—sternly rebuked Senator B—," or shall he use the words "vigorously attacked," or "sharply attacked," or "fiercely attacked"? If he decides upon "sternly rebuked," he seems to favor Senator A—, who uttered the rebuke; if he says "fiercely attacked," he gives no favorable impression, and the reader tends instinctively to side with the senator who was attacked. Shall he, in describing an automobile accident, say, "The truck was going at a terrific rate," or content himself with, "The truck was said to have been going thirty miles an hour," and leave the reader to decide whether this was a "terrific" rate for a truck to be going at in that place at that time?

Or suppose he must give an account of something really difficult to record objectively—the applause, let us say, which greeted the closing sentence of President Harding's inaugural address. Was it enthusiastic or perfunctory; was it general, or half-hearted and scattered? The truth here is a matter of judgment. One man thinks the applause large, because he knows beforehand how hard it is to hear a public speech out of doors without distractions, and therefore expects something less impressive than actually occurs. Another man, who comes to the inaugural expecting an ovation, is disappointed. Then again the reporter's political sympathies, his personal opinion of Mr. Harding, and his own enthusiasm or lack of enthusiasm for the address are almost sure to influence his judgment of the facts.

If he were the crack reporter of an opposition paper, he might, with every intention of giving the exact truth, write something like this, which appeared in the *New York Times* on the morning of March 5, 1921:

Mr Harding has a good voice, and the amplifier in the roof of the kiosk carried his voice as far as the House and Senate office-buildings. Considering that the average inaugural address is audible only to those who stand within fifteen feet of the President, this was an enormous improvement, and enabled the crowd to manifest its feelings, when it had any, with something like spontaneity.

The address was only thirty-seven minutes long, and Mr. Harding delivered its final pledge with a devout solemnity which did not fail to have its effect on the crowd.

There was a roar of applause as he concluded and turned to receive the congratulations of those near by, Vice President Coolidge being the first to shake hands with him.

Another reporter of Democratic sympathies might regard the applause as Mr. Louis Seibold did in his dispatch to the *New York World.* After noting earlier in his account that "Five times his [President Harding's] reading was interrupted by applause, but at no time was there a demonstration in which all of the people gathered in front of him united," he quoted the President's peroration and then wrote:

The applause that approved this sentiment was rather more general than had followed any other statement made by the new President. Before it had died away, and while the Marine Band was rendering the national anthem, the crowd began to melt away. Mr. Harding acknowledged the congratulations that were showered upon him by the members of his Cabinet and the leaders of the two Houses.

If, on the other hand, the reporter were favorably inclined toward Mr. Harding and impressed with the speech, he might see its reception as did the correspondent of the *New York Herald,* who quoted President Hardings's final sentence and then continued:

There was a palpable moment of absolute silence. The President remained as if transfixed. The small group standing with him in the white-covered stand seemed stayed from speech or action by the deep and moving solemnity of the voluntary promise. Then a wave of applause started up from the fringe of the crowd nearest the portico, rolled backward and to the right and left, carried through the massed thousands and became a solid roar. The President waved a hand in happy acknowledgement and turned to meet the eager compliments of his friends.

Readers of the *Herald* on that March 5 must have thought the address an immense success; readers of the *Times* and *World* undoubtedly gained quite a different opinion; and yet each correspondent may have described the event conscientiously as it appeared to him. In such cases it is almost impossible not to let personal feeling color one's report.

II

News may also be colored in the process of selection as well as in that of presentation. Let me take an example such as frequently occurs in my own experience. It is my duty to give to the press the news of a great university. I do not happen to be a newspaper reporter, but my problem is essentially the same as the reporter's. When the university's enrollment figures for the year are made up, the Freshman Class shows a gain in numbers. If, in my announcement to the press, I compare the 1921 figures with those of 1920, or with those of any other year since the war, the gain looks very large. On the other hand, if I compare them with those of 1911, when the Freshman Class happened to be unusually big, the gain looks less impressive. If I mention the fact that part of the gain is caused by a difference in the method of classifying undergraduates, which automatically adds to the Freshman Class a number of men who were formerly listed elsewhere, it looks still less significant. There are thus three or four ways of making the statement. Even though I am honestly anxious to give an accurate impression, it is hard to decide just what facts to select for presentation. And there is, of course, always a temptation to make the gain look more imposing than it actually is.

Or let us suppose that a reporter is sent to cover a dinner. Shall he devote his leading paragraph to the size and enthusiasm of the gathering, or to the consternation caused by the single untoward event of the evening—a violent and inappropriate statement made by one of the speakers? This again is a question of selection. Sometimes it is a toss-up in the reporter's mind between the two treatments of the event; and yet the opinion which thousands of readers form of the organization which held the dinner may depend on this apparently unimportant decision.

An added element of difficulty is caused by the speed with which newspapers have to work, and the circumstance that much of the color of a story is necessarily given it in the newspaper office by men who lack a first-hand acquaintance with the facts. There is no opportunity to wait a few hours for a chance to check facts; they are usually worthless unless given to the public instantly. City reporters telephone much of their news

to the office, where their statements are taken down hurriedly in a telephone booth, and then thrown into shape by a member of the office staff.
Always the headlines are written by the office staff; they have to be, because the reporter cannot tell what size and style of headline is needed,
and because the writing of headlines requires a special training. The man
who concocts them must read each news-story rapidly and write his "head"
promptly. He cannot waste time upon niceties of emphasis; the all-impor-
tant thing for him is that the head shall have exactly the right number of
letters to fill its space, and that it shall be original and dramatic enough to
catch the reader's attention. Like the reporter, he finds that bias insists
on creeping into his presentation of the gist of the news.

Most newspaper inaccuracy is not, however, the result so much of the
inherent difficulty of properly collecting and presenting the facts, as of the
ignorance, carelessness, and thoughtless indifference to truth of a considerable proportion of newspaper men.

By the very nature of newspaper organization, the man sent out on
assignments usually know too little about the matter in hand. One day a
man is instructed to get a story on the immigration problem; the next day,
he had to write a breezy interview of a bootlegging case; the next day, he
may have to report the visit of Dr. Einstein to a university. He has not
the time, even if he had the inclination, to make a preliminary study of the
immigration problem, the liquor laws, and the theory of relativity. Newspapers try to develop special abilities in their reporters and, so far as possible, to keep men assigned to the subjects which they know about; but
the field of news is so immense that much of it has to be covered by
inexpert men. Besides, many reporters have only a limited education; they
know so little that they have no idea how their ignorance handicaps them.
And they generally tend to be careless. Their immediate object is usually
to get the most newsy and sensational story they can. If they are being
paid at space-rates, a breezy story which pleases the jaded eye of the city
editor will be printed and will put money in their pocket. If they are salaried
reporters, such a story will at least give them prestige with the critics at
the city desk. No reporter wants to get the reputation of returning empty-
handed, or with a dull story. The temptation is to make a bluff at knowing
the subject, and slap the story together anyhow.

Here, for instance, are the headlines and the first two paragraphs of an
item which appeared lately in a Boston paper:

DISCOVERS NEW NEBULAR
MASS
Prof. Sliphe of Harvard Finds It Going
at Record Speed

Prof. V. M. Sliphe of Harvard, stationed at the Flagstaff, Ariz., observatory, peered through his telescope a few nights ago, according to a dispatch received at the Cambridge observatory, and much to his surprise saw a faint, cloud-like, self-luminous mass of attenuated matter situated far outside the solar system, traveling at the rate of 2000 kilometres per second. This rate of speed is twice as great as the fastest nebula yet discovered and 100 times greater than the average speed of the lowly star. In fact, it is the greatest velocity known to astronomy.

The telescope at Flagstaff is situated on San Francisco peak at an altitude of 13,000 feet. Harvard astronomers are manifesting much interest in the matter because of its supposed great distance from the stars ordinarily seen in the heavens and because of the tremendous speed at which it is traveling.

Now, the facts of the case were that the discoverer's name was not Sliphe, but Slipher; that he was not connected with Harvard, but with the Lowell Observatory; that he did not discover the nebula, which had been known for a long time, but only ascertained its speed; that the telescope at Flagstaff is not at an altitude of thirteen thousand feet, but of about seven thousand; and that it is not situated on San Francisco Peak, but merely in the neighborhood. It would be difficult for ignorance and carelessness to bring about more errors in the space of two paragraphs. What happened was that the Lowell Observatory reported its discovery to the Harvard Observatory, which made a brief announcement to the press; and the news-writer took this announcement, and tried, as he would put it, "to make a good story out of it."

"Make a good story." That is the cause of infinite newspaper inaccuracy. It is to the interest of each reporter and editor to make a small piece of news look like a big one. College officials soon become resigned to the fact that, to the press, any teacher at a college, no matter of how low a rank, is a "professor." An assistant in applied physiology at the Harvard Medical School, a man on one of the lowest rungs of the academic ladder, was arrested not long ago for having a still in his house; and the headline on the front page of a New York paper, the next morning, referred to him as a "noted Harvard professor." Ignorance of the significance of academic titles may have been partly responsible; but, pretty surely, the desire to make the story look as big as possible was a contributory cause.

The same desire often leads reporters at a public meeting to lay disproportionate emphasis on a sensational remark made by a speaker. The remark may have little real significance, and the reporters may misquote it because they happen to be half asleep when it is made, or are not even in the room and get it second-hand afterward from some neighbor of uncertain memory; but, if the remark seems striking enough to make a big story, that fact may outweigh in their minds every other consideration.

Akin to the temptation to make a small story look big is the temptation to make an otherwise dignified story look breezy. A Boston newspaper recently printed an interview with a Harvard physician on the importance of using the feet properly in standing and walking, as shown in the physical examinations of Harvard freshmen. It was an interesting interview, carefully prepared by an intelligent and well-equipped reporter. But the editor to whom the interview was submitted decided that it was too heavy: it needed to be brightened up. So he headed it—

WHY BE SAD? FEET ARE THE
SOURCE OF ALL JOY
Harvard Expert Tells How to Drive
Clouds Away in Six Short Weeks

And the illustration—a photograph of the physician—the editor surrounded with a border of "Joys" and "Glooms," after the fashion of the comic cartoons. In thus misrepresenting the nature of the interview, he succeeded in making ridiculous the man who had taken the trouble to give it; but to this particular editor nothing mattered except that he made it look like the sort of low-comedy stuff to which his mind was attuned.

The newspaper that goes in for entertainment at all costs is bound to distort the news, because it leaves out much that is important but not entertaining, and puts in much that is entertaining but not important. If General Dawes, at a Congressional hearing, speaks his mind vigorously about critics of the A.E.F., that is important news. If, in doing so, he uses highly picturesque profanity, that makes for entertainment. To put in the profanity and leave out the argument might make the story more brisk, but it would be misrepresenting General Dawes and the significance of what he said.

Writing recently of the treatment of Parliamentary news by the Northcliffe press, Mr. A. G. Gardiner, formerly editor of the London *Daily News,* said, "Parliament was treated as a music-hall turn. If it was funny, it was reported; if it was serious, it was ignored. . . . The Midlothian Campaign of Gladstone, which used to fill pages of the newspapers, would to-day be dismissed in an ill-reported half-column summary, devoted, not to the argument, but to the amusing asides and the irrelevant interruptions." The same thing might be said of the Washington correspondence of all too many

American newspapers. What makes so-called yellow journalism really dangerous is not so much its appetite for scandal as its continual distortion of the news in the interest of undiluted entertainment.

III

Sometimes, it must be admitted, misrepresentation is brought about, not by the inherent difficulty of stating the facts without prejudice, not by ignorance, carelessness, or the desire to entertain, but by deliberate intention. The newspaper profession is made up of all sorts of people, some of whom eagerly seize opportunities to present the news so as to favor their friends and put in an unfavorable light their enemies—personal, political, and economic. It is this practice which that extraordinry diatribe, *The Brass Check,* by Mr. Upton Sinclair, is devoted to exposing. Mr. Sinclair cites case after case in which the press has falsified the news, and comes to the conclusion that the newspapers are in a plot to twist the news to their own ends, and thus to serve the purposes of capital.

It is a pretty safe plan to take with several grains of salt most allegations regarding the existence of widespread conspiracies. We have been fed to repletion lately with supposed conspiracies of radicals, Bolsheviki, Jews, and so forth, and we are happily beginning to acquire some common sense. To my mind the evidence of misrepresentation collected by Mr. Sinclair and by other critics of the press proves, not that there is any conspiracy among newspaper men to withhold the truth from the public, but merely that newspaper owners, editors, and reporters are fallible; actuated too often by self-interest; too often ready to take the "practical" view of things and to see on which side their bread is buttered; too often inclined to fight by illegitimate means what they dislike; and too often subject to those surges of mob-feeling that lead men to pillory those whom they detest.

Take, for example, that part of Mr. Sinclair's book in which he tells of his own unfortunate experiences with the press. It shows with what glee newspaper men—like other ordinary mortals—will sometimes join the pack to hunt those whom they dislike. Mr. Sinclair is unpopular with the press. When he founds Helicon Hall, a cooperative "home colony"; when he gets into difficulties with the Delaware authorities for playing Sunday tennis; when he disputes the amount of his bill for shredded wheat at a San Francisco hotel, the newspapers are after him like a gang of small boys after a stray dog.

Other examples of the same sort of hoodlumism on the part of newspapers come readily to mind. Recently the press howled similarly about

the heels of Mr. Bouck White. When the inhabitants of the village where
he was staying saw fit to tar-and-feather him because of charges his young
French wife had made against him, the press joined in the fun, and in
lengthy reports, satirically written, applied their own kind of tar-and-feath-
ers. They did not like him or his economic views, and they leaped at the
chance to make him an object of ridicule and scorn. Plots on the part of
the capitalist press? Not a bit of it. Average men on the rampage, using
the weapon of misrepresentation because it is nearest at hand.

⌐ ˌ There is no question that newspapers often give biased reports of strikes
and other industrial conflicts. But, again, the charge of a conspiracy is too
farfetched. The reason these things happen is that the press is a human
institution, and that much capital is required to run a newspaper. Owners
of papers mostly have large financial interests and positive views on political, economic, and other matters. Many of them are excessively timid
about offending financially influential people, which usually means conservative people. Newspaper owners are not all equally conscientious about
the fairness of their news. Editors and reporters find out that what pays
is to write the sort of news stories which pleases the man at the top. In
rare cases, of course, there may be actual corruption; but more often what
puts bias into the news is merely the permeation of the staff by a sense
of expediency. They put their jobs first and the truth second.⌐

Often, oddly enough, the motives that lead to such misrepresentation
of the news are praiseworthy. A newspaper proprietor believes that the
unions are a menace. He believes that every good citizen ought to understand and oppose their methods. He wants to stir up the public. He thinks
of himself as crusading against radicalism. He would be ashamed to print
in his paper a word of news which would seem to favor the unions. He
does not go so far as to pass the word down that the news must be distorted, for he does not believe in distortion. He simply wants to keep his
paper clean of pro-union propaganda, as he fancies it. An item in the paper
meets his eye; to him it seems radical; he explodes, and soon the staff is
on its guard against another explosion. And then, perhaps, actual misrepresentation takes place. It is so easy! If even honest reporters, trying their
best, find it difficult to exclude prejudice from their reports, how simple it
is, when you don't try too hard, to make a strikers' meeting look like a
failure when it really was a success, or to make Mr. William Z. Foster
look redder than he is, or to pick out just the proper incidents to show
how local public opinion looks upon the issues of the strike! How easy to
make Senator A——'s denunciation of Senator B—— appear the well-
justified act of a man sorely tried and at least giving vent to righteous
indignation! And all because the men on the staff of the paper are weak,
like other human beings, and because the owner fails to realize that the

triumph of any cause, no matter how excellent, should be to him secondary to the duty of telling the truth.

There is much less outright intimidation or domination of the newspapers by advertisers than is often supposed. Many a newspaper has defied department stores successfully. Domination of the press by the department stores are probably common thirty years ago; to-day it is comparatively infrequent. And the whole process of corrupting the news, where corruption to-day exists, is less often the deliberate work of men bent on falsehood than a process of drifting before the winds of circumstance, timidity, and self-interest.

The newspaper profession is steadily advancing, not only in the effectiveness of its news-gathering machinery, but also in its standing in the community and in its ethical standards. Early in the last century there was so little recognition of the rights of the press that Henry Clay, making a political speech in Kentucky, ordered off the field a reporter who had the impertinence to report him without first getting special permission. It was not until some time after the beginning of the Civil War that the Government at Washington made satisfactory arrangements for issuing its news to all newspaper men simultaneously, instead of giving it haphazardly to the first comer. Now the President and the members of his Cabinet confer with the press representatives once or twice a day; and, as a matter of course, reporters are given front seats at almost every kind of public occasion.

Two generations ago the leading New York editors called each other blackguards and scoundrels in their editorial columns—a practice which to-day would be considered disreputable. Some twenty years ago Mr. Henry Watterson declared that journalism was "without any code of ethics or system of self-restraint and self-respect." The standard of newspaper conduct and of impartiality has risen conspicuously since then. The papers of one political party cannot dismiss the deeds of their opponents with such brief notice as they could once. In the recent presidential campaign, a Republican paper in Boston gave more space than any of the Democratic papers to an appeal for Mr. Cox issued by a group of men in New York, while a Democratic paper in the same city ran a straw ballot and printed the results day by day on its front page, although they favored Mr. Harding. Despite all that I have said about the frequent tendency among newspaper owners to side with large financial interests, it must in fairness be acknowledged that most papers give front-page space to Mr. Gompers quite as readily as to Judge Gary. Editors now observe with the utmost care release dates on material furnished them in advance, and most newspapermen can be trusted with confidential information or with facts not yet ripe for publication.

Assiduous as Mr. Sinclair may be in picking out for display the black spots in the record of the Associated Press, I believe this great news-disseminating service to be about as thoroughly imbued with the spirit of impartiality as any organization of its size and extent could well be. Its reports from Washington are models of fairness as between Republicans and Democrats. When I wrote of the difficulty of preparing an unbiased report, perhaps I should have added, "But it can be done—witness the A.P. service from Washington." The conduct of the Associated Press in political campaigns is equally scrupulous. If sometimes, in some places, its correspondents reflect the economic prejudices of the owners of its member papers, no one should judge it for such transgressions without taking into account the tremendous influence that it wields elsewhere on behalf of accuracy.

IV

Yet, if the press is to carry successfully the increasing responsibility which results from the public's increasing reliance upon it, it must not be content with its present record of improvement. How can improvement be hastened?

I believe that the newspapers ought, first of all, to make a more deliberate effort to secure men of education and discrimination for reporters. Schools of journalism are valuable to this end, both on account of the preparation they give and of the added prestige they lend to the profession. One of the things which deter many men of ability and character from entering newspaper work is the prospect of low pay and difficult hours. A man on a morning paper has to be on his job when his friends are enjoying their hours of recreation and sleep. I once met an experienced newspaper man who breakfasted when his family took their dinner, at 7 P.M.; who worked all night, had his playtime in the early morning, dined while his family breakfasted, and then went to bed for the day: not a schedule that many people would look forward to as their lot in middle life! Most newspaper men do not get a Sunday holiday: their day of rest may come at any time in the week. Again, most newspaper offices are ugly, crowded, and grimy—far less agreeable places to work in than business offices. The exceptions to this rule—such, for example, as the offices of the *New York Times* and the *Christian Science Monitor*—are conspicuous. All these circumstances tend to make journalism an unattractive calling.

In some cities reporters' unions are said to have proved useful in securing better conditions of work; but I cannot believe that this is the right solution of the problem. The reporter should be regarded and should regard himself, not as a laborer, but as a professional man. Whatever news-paper proprietors can do to enhance the dignity and prestige of his occu-pation, whether by increasing his pay, compensating him for his difficult hours by giving him more holidays, — as Lord Northcliffe is already said to have done—or making his workingplace more attractive, will bear divi-dends in the form of more intelligent and responsible work by a generally better type of reporter.

A deliberate attempt ought also to be made by the more conscientious newspaper publishers and editors, acting presumably through their various professional associations, to formulate in more definite terms a code of newspaper ethics. It would be useful if they would discuss and ventilate such ethical problems as that of the propriety of printing dispatches actually prepared in the newspaper office but purporting to come from a distance. Associations of publishers or editors might also advantageously offer prizes for accuracy in the treatment of critical events, the awards to be made after thorough investigation by an impartial jury. The Pulitzer prizes, now awarded annually, are cases in point; but these do not reward accuracy so much as reportorial brilliance and editorial initiative, which usually are fi-nancially profitable in any case. The important thing is to stimulate news-papers to present the unbiased truth.

Most of the suggestions usually made for the improvement of news-paper ethics seem to me to miss the mark. One idea constantly brought forward is that of the endowed newspaper, which would not depend on advertising for its revenue. The endowed paper might possibly be more accurate than its competitors; but again it might not, and it would all too surely be less interesting. To remove the necessity of making profits is to remove incentives to originality, as well as temptations. Municipal news-papers are often advocated, and Mr. Bryan would like to see an Official Bulletin, which would issue news of the Federal Government. But gov-ernment control of any sort would bring about inevitably the sort of political bias least to be desired; and an Official Bulletin would almost certainly be-come an instrument of political propaganda by the party in power.

Another more fruitful suggestion is that of creating independent news-agencies at important centers, such as Washington, to send out unprejud-iced reports and thus to serve as a check upon the established press as-sociations and the regular Washington correspondents. Such agencies would, I fear, only irritate newspaper men if they attempted direct competition with the press associations. They might serve a useful purpose, however, if they confined themselves to indirect competition, serving, not newspa-pers, but magazines, business houses, and the like, somewhat as several statistical agencies now furnish data on business conditions to banks and other subscribers. The trained Washington correspondents of various pe-

riodicals now do excellent service in giving the public a view of the workings of the government rather different from that gained through the eyes
of the press. And a privately controlled Washington news-agency, furnishing carefully prepared news from week to week, would be of use to individuals whose local newspapers have an inadequate Washington service,
and yet who want to keep close track of government affairs, and also would
tend to have a tonic effect upon the news-gathering organization of the
press. It would challenge, not any single press association or single newspaper, but the whole profession. Nothing stimulates one to tell an accurate
story so much as the knowledge that one's hearer has an independent means
of getting his information, and will pick one up if one goes far wrong.

Yet even such agencies would have only a limited allure. They might
be helpful in Washington or other critical points, but for the present we
must remain dependent on the newspaper for our principal knowledge of
what is going on all over the country and the world. And improvement of
the newspaper profession must come about principally from within.

Criticism by the outside public there must be, however, — constant,
watchful, and constructive, — accompanied by an increasing public appreciation of the dignity of journalism. In some quarters the obsolescent notion
still prevails that reporters are impudent interlopers and busybodies. Thick-
skinned reporters grow callous to such an attitude, but the thick-skinned
are not always the most sensitive to accuracy. Ignorant and insolent as
newspaper men sometimes are, their profession alone should be enough
to command courteous treatment. It is useless to expect a high standard
from men, unless the attitude of the community toward them contributes
to their self-respect.

Meanwhile, it would be a good thing if all of us who read the newspapers—and that means pretty nearly everybody—knew enough about
newspaper organization and methods to be better judges of the credibility
of the news. I should like to see lectures on "How to Read the Newspapers" given in colleges and schools and elsewhere. It is as essential for
the citizen of this day to be able to read the morning paper with a discriminating eye—to be able to distinguish the A.P. dispatch from the special correspondent's forecast of conditions, and the fact story from the rumor story, and to be able to take into account the probable bias of the
paper and make allowance for it—as it is for a lawyer to learn to assess
the value of evidence. Only as we are able to estimate the relative amount
of credence to be given to conflicting reports, and to judge for ourselves
the reliability of the sources of the news, do we come somewhere near
seeing that true picture of the world about us which we must see if we
are to play our part in it intelligently and independently.

THE LEGEND ON
THE LICENSE

JOHN HERSEY

Yale Review, Autumn 1980

Long before a phrase was invented for it, new journalism was being practiced. In 1721, it was the style used by Daniel Defoe in his *Journal of the Plague Year.* In the 1960s, the phrase "new journalism" evoked a number of different styles: it was saturation reporting, advocacy journalism, participatory journalism, underground journalism, or the nonfiction novel. Its practitioners sought to make reporting as interesting and as artistic as fiction. They relied on the narrative form, and they used extensive dialogue and evocative adjectives and verbs. They took the freedom to express their points of view, and they often were given the space to do so. Many writers injected novelistic techniques into their daily writing. Only a few could pull it off. Those who did not pull it off wrote highly opinionated, impressionistic, and inaccurate articles similar to those that so bothered the critics of the early twentieth century.

Some new journalists have credited John Hersey, particularly in his book *Hiroshima,* with being a founder of new journalism. Hersey, who is difficult to categorize by narrow definitions of literary genre, began as a wartime correspondent for *Life* and *Time* and has alternated between fiction and stylish journalism. He has described himself as a "novelist of contemporary history," but in this essay he most vigorously disavows any patrimony linking him to the birth of new journalism. Here, he clearly demarcates what for him separates journalism from fiction. The one sacred rule of journalism, he writes, is "The writer must not invent. The legend on the license must read: NONE OF THIS WAS MADE UP."

THE LEGEND ON
THE LICENSE

The imminent death of the novel is announced from time to time, but the very repetitiousness of the bulletins testifies to stubborn vital signs. I bring other news from the hospital. Journalism is on a sickbed and is in a very bad way.

The trouble did not begin but came out into the open with the appallingly harmful phrase Truman Capote used in 1965 to categorize *In Cold Blood.* It was, he said, a "nonfiction novel." The blurring of fiction and journalism sanctioned by that phrase is now widely practiced and widely condoned. This has not been particularly good for fiction; it may be mortal to journalism.

In fiction that *is* fiction, no holds need be barred. Novelists may introduce or disguise real people and real events as they choose. Tolstoy disguised all but the generals. Dreiser's *An American Tragedy* was suggested by an actual crime, but he did not feel the need to call his creation "a true-life novel." Malraux, who had an enormous influence on some of the novelists of my generation (e.g., Ralph Ellison), often depicted originals— among others, Chiang Kai-shek in all the splendid irony of his left-wing youth. E. L. Doctorow has had harmless fun with Morgan, Ford, and others. And so on.

The only caution in all this is the one so acutely perceived by Flannery O'Conner (in *Mystery and Manners*): "It's always wrong of course to say that you can't do this or you can't do that in fiction. You can do anything you can get away with, but nobody has ever gotten away with much." In other words, there are tests. A test, for one thing, of quality; of art. Or, to put it more brutally for authors, a test of gifts. But the point is that always, in fiction, there is a saving notice on the license: THIS WAS MADE UP.

As to journalism, we may as well grant right away that there is no such thing as absolute objectivity. It is impossible to present in words "*the* truth" or "the whole story." The minute a writer offers nine hundred ninety-nine out of one thousand facts, the worm of bias has begun to wriggle. The vision of each witness is particular. Tolstoy pointed out that immediately after a battle there are as many remembered versions of it as there have been participants.

Still and all, I will assert that there is one sacred rule of journalism. The writer must not invent. The legend on the license must read: NONE OF THIS WAS MADE UP. The ethics of journalism, if we can be allowed such a boon, must be based on the simple truth that every journalist knows the difference between the distortion that comes from subtracting observed data and the distortion that comes from adding invented data.

The threat to journalism's life by the denial of this difference can be realized if we look at it from the reader's point of view. The reader assumes the subtraction as a given of journalism and instinctively hunts for the bias; the moment the reader suspects additions, the earth begins to skid underfoot, for the idea that there is no way of knowing what is real and what is not real is terrifying. Even more terrifying is the notion that lies are truths. Or at least these things used to be terrifying; the dulling of the terror that has come about through repeated exposure tells us how far this whole thing has gone.

Let me now drive my own stakes in the ground. I have always believed that the *devices* of fiction could serve journalism well and might even help it to aspire now and then to the level of art. But I have tried to honor the distinction between the two forms. To claim that a work is both fiction and journalism, or to assert, as Doctorow recently did, that "there is no longer any such thing as fiction or nonfiction; there is only narrative—these are, in my view, serious crimes against the public. In a backward look in *The New Journalism* Tom Wolfe, citing a piece of mine from 1944, remarked, "Here we start getting into the ancestry of the New Journalism." The word "ancestry" makes me feel a bit like the Peking Man, and in laying claim to authority in this field I prefer to think of myself as nothing more remote than a grandfather.

Now. After reading three recent publications—Tom Wolfe's *The Right Stuff,* an entertaining book, Wolfe's best so far; Norman Mailer's *The Executioner's Song,* a powerful work that unquestionably enhances Mailer's claim to the kind of literary top billing he has always so tiresomely whined after; and Truman Capote's "Handcarved Coffins," a gobbet of commercial trash by this once brilliant writer in his new collection, *Music for Chameleons*—I am one worried grandpa. These three hybrids clinch it. The time has come to redraw the line between journalism and fiction.

I

"Handcarved Coffins," which Capote calls both "nonfiction" and "a short novel," belongs here, in the company of the Wolfe and Mailer books, only because of Capote's place in the line of parentage of the hybrid form; it can be dealt with briefly. The story must represent to its author a nostalgic yearning for the remembered powers of *In Cold Blood,* the fine, shapely, hard-fibered novel (as novel) that appears to have been the model Norman Mailer wanted to knock off its pedestal, but couldn't quite, with *The Executioner's Song.* Vivid as *In Cold Blood* was as a novel, it had serious flaws on the nonfiction side, arising from the fact that its actions and dialogue had been reconstructed long after the described events, yet were presented in the book with all assurance as being exactly what had happened; the dialogue, rebuilt from a great distance, stood within the authenticating marks of direct quotation. Besides suffering from troubles like these, which are intrinsic to a genre that claims to be both fiction and not, "Handcarved Coffins" groans under others far more grievous.

For one thing, the tale does something that journalism simply must not do: It strains credulity well beyond the breaking point. There is a much-too-muchness about it, which convinces one that the fictionist has decidedly had the upper hand over the journalist. The story is told in interview form, through a series of dialogues between Capote and a number of characters, the most prominent being a detective from a certain State Bureau of Investigation, who is trying to solve a succession of ghastly murders that have been announced beforehand to the victims, in all cases but one, by the arrival in their hands of beautiful miniature coffins, carved from "light balsam wood" and containing candid photographs of the doomed persons. The murderer has dispatched two of his victims, an elderly pair, by insinuating into their parked car, to await their return to it, nine rattlesnakes that have been "injected with amphetamine." Perhaps we can swallow that one. But try this: A recipient of one of the little coffins, driving along a lonely road in "an eccentric vehicle of his own invention" with no top and no windshield, is cleanly decapitated by "a strong steel wire sharpened thin as a razor" and stretched across the road between a tree and a telephone pole at exactly the right height to catch him just under the chin; the wire "slice[s] off his head as easily as a girl picking petals off a daisy." And so on, murder after murder, until we have been taken far beyond the last shore of belief. (We will come back in due course to this crucial matter of belief.)

An even worse fault of this creaky tale is that it is told as if in a game of blindman's buff. It is the reader who is blindfolded. He has no idea where he is. The story takes place in an invisible place: a nameless town in an unspecified state. The characters are *there,* but they are unseeable as real people. Their names have been changed. Capote says he "had to omit a few identifying things" (*The New York Times,* January 7, 1979)—which implies his having substituted other made-up ones. (The principal suspect "had long simian-like arms; the hands dangled at his knees, and the fingers were long, capable, oddly aristocratic.") Altogether, the ace among rules of reliable reporting—that the facts should be "hard"—is here repeatedly and fatally broken.

II

Tom Wolfe's *The Right Stuff* is a vivid book, a tainted book. It gives an account of the Mercury phase of the United States space program, and its thesis is that test pilots of rocket aircraft, genuinely, and the seven Mercury astronauts, more ambiguously, shared an ineffable quality compounded of spiffy courage, arrogant recklessness, dry-palmed sass, and super-jock male potency (on earth they indiscriminately balled "juicy little girls," and in the sky they whipped around in Pynchonesque flying phalluses), to all of which Wolfe gives the catchy tag "the right stuff." Wolfe's style-machine has never run more smoothly than in this book. The writing is at times wonderfully funny. Some of the passages on flying are classy. A quick and easy read.

Then why tainted? Because Wolfe is the paradigm of the would-be journalist who cannot resist the itch to improve on the material he digs up. The tricks of fiction he uses dissolve now and then into its very essence: fabrication. The notice on the license reads: THIS WAS NOT MADE UP (EXCEPT FOR THE PARTS THAT WERE MADE UP)

The source of the taint is the pair of pieces Wolfe wrote in 1965 for the *Herald-Tribune* Sunday magazine about *The New Yorker*. We must recall them at some length, because in them one finds in a gross form the fundamental defect that has persisted ever since in Wolfe's writing, and that is to be found in the work of many of the "new journalists," and also indeed in that of many "nonfiction novelists"   namely, the notion that mere facts don't matter.

In the introduction to *The New Journalism* Wolfe tried to laugh off his *New Yorker* pieces. He called them "some lighthearted fun . . . A very droll *sportif* performance, you understand." They were nothing of the kind. They made up a vicious, slashing lampoon. Begging the question whether *The New Yorker* may at some point have deserved a serious critique, there seems to be no way to explain the stunningly irresponsible street cruelty of Wolfe's exercise except by guessing that he could not bear to face it that "his" New Journalism would have to be measured sooner or later against the meticulously accurate and vivid reporting of such *New Yorker* writers as the wonderful Joseph Mitchell or, let's say, Lillian Ross and Truman Capote; who in turn were writing in an honorable tradition, not New at all, reaching back to George Orwell, Henry Mayhew, James Boswell. . . .

Wolfe called his first piece "Tiny Mummies! The True Story of the Ruler of 43rd Street's Land of the Walking Dead." This "true" story was a collage of shameless inventions. Not satisfied with making up lots of little decorative details, such as imaginary colors and types of paper used at *The New Yorker* for memos and manuscripts, Wolfe reached farther into the territory of fiction to devise blunt weapons with which to assault William Shawn, the magazine's editor. He dreamed up a Shawn memorandum which was supposed to have warned the staff against talking to him; he gave a description of the magazine's editorial process which, according to an analysis of Wolfe's pieces by Renata Adler and Gerald Jonas, was erroneous "in every particular, large and small"; and he gave a picture of Shawn's role that "was not a little untrue, not half true, but totally, stupefyingly false."

Shawn's "retiring" nature, Wolfe asserted, could be accounted for by "what the records show, actually, in the Cook County (Chicago) Criminal Court"—that Leopold's and Loeb's original intended victim in their famous murder had been "a small and therefore manageable teen-age boy from the Harvard School," whose first name was William ("the court records do not give the last name"), and that the two had decided not to kill William Shawn "only because they had a personal grudge against him and somebody might remember that." Shawn's trauma is totally a Wolfe fantasy. The court records *do* give the last name of the intended victim, and the first as well. It was not a teen-aged William Shawn. It was a nine-and-a-half-year-old boy named John O. Levinson, who testified at the trial.

The coda of the second piece, the climax of the whole charade, is a perfect example of a Wolfe fantasy flying out of control. Wolfe has been building a (false) picture of Shawn slavishly attached to the formulas of the founder of the magazine, Harold Ross. In this scene we see Shawn sitting alone at home, on the very evening when down at the St. Regis the staff is celebrating the magazine's fortieth anniversary. According to Wolfe, Shawn is listening to "that wonderful light zinc plumbing sound" of Bix Beiderbecke's recording of "I Can't Get Started": "(those other trumpet players, like Harry James, they never played the real 'I Can't Get Started')." At the end of the recording "Bix hits that incredible high one he died on, popping a vessel in his temporal fossa, bleeding into his squash, drowning on the bandstand. . . . *That* was the music of Harold Ross's lifetime. . . . Here, on that phonograph, those days are *preserved*. . . ."

Adler and Jonas:

The facts are, of course, that *"That"* was not "the music of Harold Ross's lifetime." Or anybody else's. The facts are that "Bix" did not die playing, nor did his death have anything to do with his "temporal fossa." He died in bed, of pneumonia. Nor did Beiderbecke make a recording of "the real 'I Can't Get Started.' " In fact, he never played it—with or without "that incredible high one." It would have been difficult for him to play it. "I Can't Get Started with You" was written in 1935, four years after Beiderbecke's death.

When Wolfe wrote his advertisements for himself in *The New Journalism,* nine years later, he still couldn't suppress his snickers at the reaction to his *New Yorker* caper, and to the subsequent new wave of nonfiction, on the part of "countless journalists and literary intellectuals," who, he said, were screaming, *"The bastards are making it up!* (I'm telling you, Ump, that's a spitball he's throwing. . . .)." But his laughter had an edge of nerves; altogether too many folks in the stands had seen and called attention to his applying a little greasy stuff to the pellet.

In the seven years since then, two things have happened: Wolfe has grown quite a bit more careful (and hard-working), and the public has become increasingly inured, or maybe the word is numb, to the blurring of fiction and journalism. *The Right Stuff* has been accepted as fairly accurate by people in the know. I talked with a number of journalists who had covered the space program, and while one complained of "outright lies" in the book, all the others seemed to think that Wolfe had "made an effort to be as accurate as he could be," that he had "done his homework," that he had made mistakes, but those had been errors of judgment and value that any conventional journalist might have made. Most of them thought he had been too kind to Scott Carpenter and too hard on John Glenn. The official National Aeronautics and Space Administration view was also favorable. Christopher Kraft, in charge of the Johnson Space Center in Houston, declined to talk about the book, but his public relations chief, John MacLeish, said after consultation with others that despite a number of technical errors there was "a high degree of accuracy" in the book. The two astronauts I talked with, John Glenn and Deke Slayton, said, respectively, that Wolfe was "accurate on the details of my flight" and "mostly pretty accurate."

Taint, then? Well, alas, yes. Some questions remain. Enough to add up. Enough so that, in the end, one cannot help wondering whether even these interested parties, in their numbed acceptance of the premise that there is no difference between fiction and nonfiction, between real life and a skillfully drawn mirror image of a dream of it, haven't been to some extent taken in. I give you the example of the way in which Senator Glenn, in speaking to me, paid tribute to the hypnotic ambiguity of Wolfe's prose. Glenn is pictured in the book as an insufferable prig, a prude, a killjoy, yet he said to me, "I came out pretty good in the book, so I can't complain." NASA seemed to think it had come out pretty well, too. Did it?

Wolfe's fiction-aping journalism, he wrote in 1973, "enjoys an advantage [over fiction] so obvious, so built in, one almost forgets what a power it has: the simple fact that the reader knows *all this actually happened* . . . The writer is one step closer to the absolute involvement of the reader that Henry James and James Joyce dreamed of and never achieved. . . ." Whew. That *is* a big advantage. But let's focus for a moment on much smaller things, such as that little word "all."

In defining the New Journalism, Wolfe wrote that a journalist need use just four devices of fiction to bring this amazing power to the page: scene-by-scene construction, dialogue, point of view, and what he called "status details." But the resources of fiction are by no means so barren as all that. One essential requisite and delight of fiction, for example, is the absolute particularity it can give to every individual, every character. Wolfe has apparently ruled this out; he is a generalizer. Let him find a vivid or funny trait in more than one member of a class, then without exception the whole class has it. Thirty-six military pilots show up at the Pentagon to apply for the space program; without exception they wear "Robert Hall clothes that cost about a fourth as much as their watches." "They had many names, these rockets, Atlas, Navajo, Little Joe, Jupiter, but they all blew up." All test pilots talked something he calls Army Creole. All seven astronauts went in for Flying and Drinking, Drinking and Driving, Driving and Balling. All Russian space vehicles were launched "by the Soviet's mighty and mysterious Integral"—though, as Wolfe knows, Integral was not a person or a state organ but a space ship in Evgeny Zamyatin's novel, *We*. "Every wife . . ." "Every young fighter jock . . ." "Everyone . . ." "Invariably . . ." "All these people . . ." "All . . . (*All this actually happened* . . .")

Another big advantage over other writers that Wolfe apparently feels he has is that since he is using fictional modes, he is, even though dealing with nonfictional matter, freed from the boring job of checking verifiable details. If something turns out to have been dead wrong—well, that was just the free play of fancy. Some of the many details Wolfe should have checked but obviously did not are: The kind of car John Glenn drove. Whether Slayton, pictured as an active partisan at the meeting Wolfe calls the Konokai Seance, was even present. What operant conditioning means. The Latin name for the chimpanzee. What jodhpurs are. What cilia means. When the compass was invented . . .

But there are disadvantages in the method, too, at least for the reader. One is the frequent juxtaposition of passages that are wholly made up with others that are only partly made up or, beyond the use of one of the four devices, not made up at all. Side by side, for example, are a long parody of an airline pilot's voice reassuring the passengers on the last leg of a flight from Phoenix to New York when the landing gear won't lock, and an account of how the test pilot Chuck Yaeger gets drunk, breaks two ribs falling off a horse on a moonlight gallop, doesn't tell the base doctor, and two days later goes up in an X-1 and buffets through the sound barrier, hurting so badly his right arm is useless. (Right stuff.) Both passages are funny, wildly hyperbolic, interchangeable in voice and tone. It is not hard to tell which of these is mostly made up (or is it wholly made up?). But what becomes not so easy, after many such oscillations, is to perceive exactly where the line between reporting and invention in any "real-life" episode actually lies.

This difficulty is immensely reinforced by the way Wolfe uses his third fictional device: point of view. At will, he enters the consciousness of his characters. We have the stream (or in Wolfe's case one has to say river) of consciousness of wives of astronauts, waiting out re-entry. We find ourselves in each astronaut's mind as he barrels across the sky. For an awful moment we become Lyndon Johnson. We may be dismayed to find ourselves suddenly trapped in a chimpanzee's head. Finally (James and Joyce certainly never gave us *this* pleasure) we are right there in God's mind, out of patience with John Glenn and barking at him, "Try the automatic, you ninny." Beyond the dicey issue of freely inventive recreation of thoughts and dialogue, long after their transaction, a further trouble is that Wolfe never makes the slightest attempt, which any novelist would make as a matter of course, to vary the voice to fit each character. What we hear throughout, ringing in every mind, is the excited shout of Tom Wolfe. Each astronaut in turn *becomes* Tom Wolfe. Without even a little jiggle of lexical sex-change each astronaut's wife becomes Tom Wolfe. Right Stuffers who are alleged to speak nothing but Army Creole are garlanded with elegant tidbits like *esprit, joie de combat, mas allá!* The chimp talks pure Wolfe. God help us, God becomes Tom Wolfe and with His sweet ear chooses the Wolfeish "ninny."

"Class has always been Tom Wolfe's subject," John Gregory Dunne has written (*The New York Review of Books,* November 8, 1979). Dunne sees Wolfe as exposing the unmentionable in a purportedly egalitarian soceity: the existence of class. Wolfe is always on the side of the outsider, the underdog. Low Rent is good. He declares himself a literary lumpenprole, one of "the Low Rent rabble at the door," one of "the Kentucky Colonels of Journalism and Literature." Placing such great emphasis on status seems to have affected Wolfe's decibel range. Whispering, as any outsider knows, is genteel. Understatement is upper class. A consequence of such understandings is the central disaster of this gifted writer's voice: He never abandons a resolute tone of screaming. The test of every sentence is: Will its sound waves shatter a wine glass at twenty feet? It is not surprising that he writes so beautifully about the rupture of the sound barrier.

While he has largely cooled his typographical excesses in this book (there are only three exclamation points, and no italicized words at all, on the first page), the aural and psychological overamplification is still very much there. The voice of every character, even that of a quiet woman like Glenn's wife, is Jovian. One can say that the charm in Wolfe is his enthusiasm. On nearly every page, though, this attractive quality sends him floating off the ground. When he is establishing the driving part of Flying and Drinking, Drinking and Driving, Driving and Balling, in which "all" astronauts indulged, his excitement over their recklessness at the wheel leads him to write, doubtless in a *sportif* spirit: "More fighter pilots died in automobiles than airplanes." No time period. According to Navy statistics which Wolfe himself cites, there was a 23 percent probability that a Navy career pilot would die in an aircraft accident. Did one in four die on the road? In 1952 sixty-two Army Air Force pilots died in crashes in thirty-six weeks of flying at Edward Air Force Base, 1.7 per week. Did two a week die in cars? The point is not that this little example of possibly humorous overkill announces in itself the death of journalism. The point is that this one happened to be readily catchable. How many others are not? Are they on every page? How can we know? How can we ever know?

And so we come through many cumulative small doubts back to the issues of "accuracy." Let us grant that among Wolfe's works, this book is relatively "accurate" (perhaps because relatively much of it is based on written records, notably the NASA official history, *The New Ocean: A History of Project Mercury*). But "relatively 'accurate'" may not be good enough, when we look for the whole meaning of the work.

By now we are thoroughly skeptical, and, remembering John Glenn's having read the abuse he took at Wolfe's hand as praise, we begin to see abysses of ambiguity, of ambivalence, in the book. Wolfe loves what he loathes. The individual words mock and slash and ridicule; the sentences into which they are combined somehow ogle and stroke and admire. As Eric Korn put it (*Times Literary Supplement*, November 30, 1979), "If there's one thing more unlovable than the man of letters showing his contempt for physical valor, it's the man of letters fawning on physical valor. Wolfe contrives to do both at once." Glenn and NASA are both right and awfully wrong to think they come out "pretty good."

Looking back, we see that this double-think has been there, off and on, all through Wolfe's work. His class struggle seems to be in his own heart. The New Journalism was a product of the sixties, and like much of what hit the kids in that decade, Wolfe's struggle seems to have been a generational one. To adopt his voice: Young and new are good, old and old are bad; but O I love you Mummy and Daddy, you bitch and bastard. This lumpenprole affects beautifully tailored white suits and his prose often gives off a donnish perfume—*prima facie, beruf,* pick your language. If Tom Wolfe is at all interested in class, it is in a new elite of those few "outsiders" who, at any given moment, are "in." The quasi-fictional methods allowed Wolfe to be both out and in.

Precisely this ambiguity makes for real zippy entertainment—the dazzle of the magic show. Great fun. But. It leaves us with serious doubts about a mode of Journalism that straddles in its ambiguities the natural and obligatory substance of such a book: the horrendous issues of the space program, its cost, philosophy, technological priorities, and impact on national jingoism and machismo in a cold-war atmosphere which, as we saw in the winter of 1979–1980, could so easily be brought to dangerous warmth.

I believe that the double-think flaw is intrinsic to Wolfe's method. One who gets the habit of having it both ways in form slips into the habit of having it both ways in attitude and substance. The legend on the license really does matter.

As to deeper and subtler forms of social harm that this journalism also may cause, more later.

III

The case of Norman Mailer is much more complicated, because Mailer is so richly talented and so grossly perverse.

Readers know by now that the first half of *The Executioner's Song* is based on the horrifying story of two wanton murders in Utah by a bright, sick, witty, cowboyish paroled recidivist named Gary Gilmore, who, having been condemned to death for the crimes, staunchly insisted on being executed. The second half tells how the strong smell of money given off by this death-row drama drifted east with the weather systems and attracted New York's media vultures, the swiftest among them being one Lawrence Schiller, who had already picked the bones clean from other carrion: Jack Ruby, Marina Oswald, Susan Atkins, for examples. (Schiller had also— though Mailer finds it convenient to omit this from 1,056 pages which seem to leave absolutely nothing else out—arranged for Mailer to make bucks cleaning the dear flesh from the skeleton of poor Marilyn Monroe; and was, of course, to arrange the same for Mailer with Gilmore's remains.)

Besides nursing Gilmore along, making sure to keep the condemned man's death-resolve firm (else contracts might fly away), Schiller dug up a mass of background material, including the element that was eventually to attract the romantic fictionist in Mailer—the love story between Gilmore and a sad, dumb, compliant doxy named Nicole Baker, who had been married at thirteen, had been twice a mother and twice divorced by nineteen, had long been in and out of mental hospitals, and would do anything for her man, whoever he might happen to be, including "rubbing pee-pees" (for "Uncle Lee," at five), turning tricks (not exactly for a pimp, just for a nice guy who had some horny friends), ratting (to attractive cops), attempting suicide (at Gary's request through the mail), and spilling all the details of Gary's limp erections and requests to shave pubic hair and experiments in threesome (to Larry Schiller). Schiller's pumping out of this pathetic Nicole is a shocking tale of commercial sadism from which Mailer, who later used every jism-dripping morsel of the material, manages to remain somehow serenely detached. One of the conveniences of having a book be both fiction and journalism is that when the journalist's money-grubbing dirty tricks begin to stink, the novelist can soar away on wings of art, far above it all.

Mailer does want it both ways. Had he, like Orwell with *Down and Out in Paris and London,* for instance, or like Solzhenitsyn in his first three books, simply called his work a novel and let it go at that, we could perhaps have lived with the immediacy of the reality underlying the fiction—remembering that some reality underlies every fiction. But no. This had to be labeled "A True-Life Novel." (Mailer has played this doppelgänger game before, of course. *Armies of the Night* was subtitled "The Novel as History, History as a Novel.") "I called [*The Executioner's Song*] a novel because it reads like one," Mailer has said in an interview (*New York Times,* October 26, 1979). And it does. He is right. A powerful and moving novel. But also: "This story does its best to be a factual account . . . and the story is as accurate as one can make it." The book jacket praises the work as fiction and also calls it "a model of complete, precise, and accurate reporting." The legend on this license reads: THIS WAS MADE UP AND IT WAS SIMULTANEOUSLY NOT MADE UP.

It simply cannot have been both. What it cannot be, if we look closely, is "precise and accurate reporting." Asserting that it is can only mean sending journalism into the intensive-care unit.

There is a false syllogism at work here, having to do with a Wolfeish "all this actually happened." A: Gary Gilmore did kill, was condemned, did insist on being executed. B: Mailer has written an immensely detailed and artful novel about the Gary Gilmore case, in which he uses mostly real names. Therefore C: This must be reporting. Mailer puts it somewhat differently, though of course not diffidently. "God," he says (*New York Times,* January 27, 1980), "was at least as good a novelist as I am."

The novel is presented in terse, highly charged paragraphs, like tiny chapters, which allow Mailer both to keep the point of view rapidly shifting among a very large cast of vivid characters—Mormons, families in their cobwebs, druggies and deadbeats, a whirligig mother of a murderer, straight victims and their heart-breaking survivors, Nicole and her procession of men, jailbirds, jailers, civil libertarians, lawyers, television and movie con men, and, of course, the fascinating psychopath at the heart of the yarn, as well as many others; and also to build a grim, gripping suspense. Since we know the outcome from the very beginning, this latter is a brilliant feat. It is a deeply disturbing story, told by a bewitching minstrel of the dark side of the soul. But let us not say that it is accurate reporting.

Mailer reveals his method of work in three ways: by indirection through what we can infer from his picture of Schiller's researches; through his own direct account of his sources and routines in an afterword; and by what he has said about the book after its publication.

He freely admits that he has tinkered with dialogue. And here we go: Is a reporter entitled (was Capote, writing *In Cold Blood,* were Woodward and Bernstein, in *All the President's Men,* were Woodward and Armstrong, in *The Brethren,* entitled) to reconstruct extensive exchanges of direct speech from passages of action that had taken place long before the research—and claim that the published result is "precise and accurate"? Mailer evidently relied for bits of his dialogue on interviews of his own, many months after the events; but most of his raw material was at least secondhand, given to him by Schiller, who had extracted it, also mostly after the events, from the principals—so that the filtration leading to direct quotation is through three and (when the informant is repeating something another person has told him) even four sensibilities, to say nothing of a fallible memory or two or three. And then, on top of all that, for art's sake, Mailer has tinkered.

A more serious question is raised by what Mailer appears to have done with Gilmore's letters to Nicole. These are the stuff of old-fashioned melodrama—purloined letters. That is to say, a cub reporter for the *Deseret News* named Tamera Smith sweet-talked her way into Nicole's trust; Nicole asked Tamera to take the letters for safekeeping; Tamera promptly photocopies them without telling Nicole; and on Nicole's request returned the originals but not the copies. After Gilmore and Nicole had jointly attempted suicide, Tamera wrote a story partly based on the letters. Alerted by the story, the prosecutor's office then picked up the originals. And later "the carrion bird," as Mailer from his artistic distance calls Schiller, having clamped a money-lock on Gilmore's lawyers, bullied them into demanding the letters from the prosecutor under laws of discovery; and so got his hands (and eventually Mailer's) on them. Gilmore, the copyright owner, of course never gave his permission for the use of the letters. He never had a chance. He got four bullets in the heart.

The journalistic shadow on these letters, however, hasn't to do with this sordid history. The question is, rather, just how far Mailer moved them away from "precise and accurate" replication. What Mailer says about his editing of them in his afterword is wonderfully careful. He is frank to say he altered the interviews with Gilmore that Gary's lawyers taped, just as one would alter one's own remarks on a transcript: "The aim was not to improve his diction so much as to treat him decently." But watch the prestidigitator's hand very closely here:

> With Gilmore's letters, however, it seemed fair to show him at a level higher than his average. One wanted to demonstrate the impact of his mind on Nicole, and that might be best achieved by allowing his brain to have its impact on us. Besides, he wrote well at times. His good letters are virtually intact. . . .

It is true that Gilmore had a weird and interesting mind, and there is no way of knowing exactly where and how much Mailer meddled. One clue is in "voice." Granting that one's spoken and written voices may differ markedly, there seems such a gulf between Gilmore's articulation on the tapes and in his letters that we can't help wondering exactly whose brain it is, in the latter, that is having its impact on us.

First, from the tapes (altered for decent treatment):

> I seen that she wasn't on the list until just, you know, yesterday. . . .
>
> I guess perhaps they didn't quite take me literal. . . .
>
> They act like they're really doing something by giving you a big meal, but it ain't like the menu in the paper. You don't get it good, you know.

And then this Mailerish voice in . . . the letters:

> I'm so used to bullshit and hostility, deceit and pettiness, evil and hatred. Those things are my natural habitat. They have shaped me. I look at the world through eyes that suspect, doubt, fear, hate, cheat, mock, are selfish and vain. All things unac-

ceptable, I see them as natural. . . . There are dead cockroaches in the corners. . . . I can hear the tumbrel wheels creak.

What will I meet when I die? The Oldness? Vengeful ghosts? A dark gulf? Will my spirit be flung about the universe faster than thought? Will I be judged and sentenced, as so many churches would have us believe? Will I be called to and clutched at by lost spirits? Will there be nothing? . . . Just an end?

Mailer may conceivably be able to produce photocopies of many letters like these with elevated language in Gilmore's longhand, but any reader who is the least bit interested in journalism will have grown suspicious long before reading them in print. For an interesting reason.

Almost without exception, reviewers of *The Executioner's Song* called attention to what they saw as the simple and direct language Mailer uses in the novel. "A meticulously limited vocabulary," Joan Didion wrote, "and a voice as flat as the horizon" (*New York Times,* October 7, 1979). Only one reviewer I have come across (Diane Johnson in *New York Review of Books,* December 6, 1979) seemed even to notice what I quickly came to think of as Mailer's tag lines—touches of prose, nearly always final lines in the chapterettes, buffed to such hummingbird-feather iridescence as almost to hurt the eye with the lights of their beauty and intensity. Pure Mailer. From a journalistic standpoint, the significant thing about these tag lines is that each Mailerism is presented as if *within the point of view of a character* This is not reporting; it is projection. And the cumulative force of the projections pushes the book right out of the country of journalism. To feel this cumulation, we must look at quite a few examples:

NICOLE (*on a visit to Gary in prison*): It was as if they stood on a ledge and sorrow was as light as all the air below the fall.

She felt modest in the middle of her own sorrow, as if some quiet person in heaven was crying with her too.

(*On her druggy sister April*): She was in touch with the heavy strings on the fiddle. (*And*): Most of the time she had a toothache in her expression.

BRENDA: Gary sat there like he was grinding bones in his mind.

SPENCE MCGRATH (*Gary's employer, watching Gary eat a brown-bag lunch*): [He] ate the food in all the presence of his own thoughts.

BESSIE GILMORE (*Gary's mother*): She thought it had to be the way a tomb would smell if a strong man was buried in it.

Pain was a boring conversationalist who never stopped, just found new topics.

The picture would flicker over her eyes like a moth in a closet.

"Oh Gary," whispered the child that never ceased to live in the remains of her operations and twisted joints.

MIKAL (*Gary's brother*): It was like a bigger dude squeezing your machismo to see if it leaked.

LARRY SCHILLER: The memory burned into the skin right under the beard. At times like that, fat felt comfortable—one more layer of asbestos against the flames.

[Nicole was] like a waif in a house whose windows were wet with fog.

VERN DAMICO: Stranger's eyes were gleaming, like his hooves were flashing in the air.

EARL DORIUS (*Assistant Attorney General*): That hand moved around the clock like anxiety circulating in one's chest.

DENNIS BOAZ (*Gary's first lawyer*): The mind could undulate like a jellyfish.

RIKKI BAKER: [Gary] got upset about it the way people can brood about bad weather.

NOALL WOOTTON (*prosecutor, reaction to Gary's changes of mind during the trial*): It was like dealing with a crazy pony who was off on a gallop at every wind.

JOHN WOODS (*psychiatrist*): wished for some absolute dazzler of a lawyer who could handle the jury like a basketball and take them up and down the court.

JERRY SCOTT (*state patrolman, taking Gary to prison after his sentencing*): Night had come, and the ridge of the mountain came down to the Interstate like a big dark animal laying out its paw.

Some scenes, if you rub them carefully between thumb and finger, turn out to have a palpable nap of invention on them—not whole cloth, but finished goods with miraculously tidy hems. For instance, some time after the excecution, there is a scene in a drinking place near Provo called The Stirrup.

As Mailer tells it, three of the marksmen who had delivered bullets to Gilmore's chest were drinking and playing liars' dice in the bar one late afternoon. A waitress named Willa Brant sat down with them. One of the men pulled out of his pocket a bit of the webbing that had strapped Gilmore's arm to the death chair and one of the slugs that, the guy said, had killed him, for her to touch. After a while a young married woman whom Willa knew slightly, named Rene Wales, came in and got talking with the executioners about the CBs in their pickups. "Before you knew it" Mrs. Wales went out with one of them to check out his radio. Forty-five minutes passed. Then the Mailer tag line: "Rene came in with the fellow, and both had a look on their faces like they'd been sopping up some of the gravy."

Now, the trouble with this as reporting is that it is told from the point of view of Willa Brant. But she is *not*, it turns out, one of the roughly 150 persons Mailer lists in his afterword as having been interviewed by Schiller, himself, or both. In telling of the scene she is said to be a friend of Toni Gurney, whose name we do find on the list. So Schiller or Mailer got the episode from someone who was not there, and *we* get it at third or fourth hand. But the anecdote is told in considerable fine detail. It bears all the marks of having been so promising to begin with, in this game of pass-the-whisper, that the fictionist in Mailer simply couldn't resist touching up the whisper he heard. He writes in his afterword: "The names . . . of certain characters have been changed to protect their privacy"—and also, quite possibly, to ward off lawsuits. Of course we never know which names have been changed, so we can't tell whether Mrs. Wales's has been; we can only hope for her sake it has been. So the trouble with many scenes in the book, is that we can never know where Mailer the reporter leaves off and Mailer the novelist takes over.

In fiction, the writer's voice matters; in reporting, the writer's authority matters. We read fiction to fortify our psyches, and in the pleasure that that fortification may give us, temperament holds sway. We read journalism—or most of us still do, anyway—to try to learn about the external world in which our psyches have to struggle along, and the quality we most need in our informant is some measure of trustworthiness. *The Executioner's Song* may satisfy us as fiction—it does me—precisely because the author's voice is so pungent, so active, so eloquent, so very alive. But there is deep trouble when we come to the journalistic pretensions of this novel, precisely because the temperament of the reporter is so intrusive, so vaunting, and, considering the specific story being told, so hard to trust.

When we read a novel of Mailer's, the wild shenanigans of his private life are none of our business, really; the art is there to speak for itself, and so is the strong voice of the weaver behind the arras. With good fiction, those are enough. But when we are told that a tale with the massive

social implications of *The Executioner's Song* is "a model of complete, precise, and accurate reporting," we are entitled to know a bit more about
the mind and temperament that have shaped our instruction. The facts
about Mailer's life—and he himself has been the trumpeting source of most
of our knowledge of them—raise some questions about the trustworthiness of the authority behind this book.

Like Hemingway before him, Norman Mailer has made himself at home
in a fantasy of pugilism, and has challenged all champs and all pretenders
in all weights to fifteen rounds in the ring of letters; he has scattered his
macho boasts and seed among a block of wives, mistresses, and bare ac-
quaintances; near dawn after a night of carousal and quarrels he made a
pretty fair attempt on the life of one of these ladies with a cheap knife; he
has romanticized marijuana, "the smoke of the assassins," and rewrote one
novel "bombed and sapped and charged and stoned with lush, with pot,
with benny, saggy, Miltown, coffee, and two packs a day"; in a rage while
directing a pseudo-movie he tried to bite an earlobe off an actor with the
right name for the scene, Rip Torn; considering a mayoral run in New York
he advocated jousting in Central Park as a therapy for muggers.

Can we trust a reporter with such a bizarre history of brutality, inse-
curity, mischief, and voguishness when he gives us, thinly, just three implied reasons (do they seem to be *justifications?*) for Gary Gilmore's crimes:
(1) the desperation of a young lover afraid of losing his beloved; (2) the
damage done him by psychiatrists in, for instance, having transiently administered to him, long before the murders, a drug called Prolixin; and (3)
a vague possibility, only glancingly hinted at, of a strain of infantilism in
the killer?

Or can we trust this reporter when he devotes so much energy and
space to rendering the sex and violence in the story—making of it not
Romeo and Juliet but a mongrel, out of *Tristan and Isolde* by *Bonnie and
Clyde*—and skimps the intricate, fascinating, and socially consequential
questions of law and philosophy that hovered over the first execution in
the country in many years?

Or when, in his eagerness to give us a dope-smoky, drive-in, stick-shift,
gang-bang Western romance, he does not do anything like justice to the
vision of the kindly people of the town of Provo, firmly (and perhaps, in
the context of this drama, disastrously) fixed and drenched in Mormon
ideas of the correctional effects of love and decency; or to their views of
proper sexual conventions, and of the regions beyond death?

Am I saying that we can accept what Mailer says as a novelist and
cannot accept what he says as a journalist? Baffled by the impossibility of
knowing when he is which, I am. When we read a novel, we are asked to

suspend disbelief, and as soon as we close the book we can be expected in normal circumstances to bring the suspension to an end along with the story, for in fiction, as Auden wrote is the case in poetry (in *The Dyer's Hand*), "all facts and beliefs cease to be true or false and become interesting possibilities." But when we read an ambitious journalistic work, we are asked to believe, and to carry belief away with the book. This is a crucial difference.

Why does Mailer claim so much? He has repeatedly said over the years that he would rather be known as a novelist than as a journalist. In a *Paris Review* interview some years ago, which he liked well enough to include in *Cannibals and Christians,* he said:

> If what you write is a reflection of your own consciousness, then even journalism can become interesting. One wouldn't want to spend one's life at it and I wouldn't want ever to be caught justifying journalism as a major activity (it's obviously less interesting to write than a novel), but it's better, I think, to see journalism as a venture of one's ability to keep in shape than to see it as an essential betrayal of the chalice of your literary art. Temples are for women.

Disregard that last line. That was just Norman being a bad boy. But since the publication of *The Executioner's Song,* he had insisted over and over, that, yes, the book is both fiction and journalism. Asked how that could be, he said on one occasion (*New York Times,* October 26, 1979): "A writer has certain inalienable rights, and one is the right to create confusion."

At the risk of taking Mailer seriously at a moment when we can see his tongue poking his cheek out, I would flatly assert that for a reporter that right is distinctly and preeminently alienable. If there is any one "right" a journalist never had to begin with, it is purely that one. This perversity of Mailer's brings us straight home: The widespread acceptance of *The Executioner's Song* as a "true-life story" is an ominous sign of journalism's ill-health these days.

IV

Good writers care about what words mean. Francis Steegmuller said not long ago (*New York Times,* March 26, 1980) that when Auden died his *Oxford English Dictionary* was "all but clawed to pieces." The better the writer, it seems, the more frequent the appeals to the lexicographer. Yet some very good writers have lately seemed to want to ignore what the dictionaries say about matters essential to their craft: That "fiction" means something; which something is excluded from "nonfiction." Both the *OED* and *Webster's* point to original, central, and rather copious meanings of "fiction": fashioning, imitating, or inventing. Both dictionaries, in elaborating the active, current definition of the word, lay stress on a fundamental antithesis. *OED*: "invention as opposed to fact." *Webster*: "that which is invented, feigned, or imagined . . . —opposed to *fact* or *reality*" (emphasis *Webster's*).

Our grasp on *reality,* our relationship with the real world, is what is at stake here. We have to grope our way through that world from day to day. To make sense of our lives, we need to know what is going on around us. This need plunges us at once into complicated philosophical issues, having to do with trees falling in distant forests. Can we always rely on what others tell us about what is "really" going on? A suspicion that we cannot has led to the great fallacy, as I see it, of the New Journalism, and indirectly to the blurring in recent years of fiction and nonfiction.

That fallacy can be crudely stated as follows: Since perfect objectivity in reporting what the eyes have seen and the ears have heard is impossible, there is no choice but to go all the way over to absolute subjectivity. The trouble with this is that it soon makes the reporter the center of interest rather than the real world he is supposed to be picturing or interpreting. A filter of temperament discolors the visible universe. The report becomes a performance. What is, or may be, going on in "reality" recedes into a backdrop for the actor-writer; it dissolves out of focus and becomes, in the end, fuzzy, vague, unrecognizable, and false.

The serious writer of fiction hopes to achieve a poetic truth, a human truth, which transcends any apparent or illusory "reality." And in good novels, the temperament of the author as expressed through the complex mix of elements that writers call "voice," subtly becomes part of the impression of human truth that the reader gets. The fictionist may at times use real people or real events, sometimes deliberately remaking and transforming them, in order to flesh out imitation or make invention seem like reality. This sleight of hand works beautifully if the novelist is gifted, artful, and inventive; it is a disaster (and an open invitation to libel suits) when the writing is bad, when the invention is weak or nonexistent—in short, when fiction is not fiction.

Two kinds of grave social harm, beyond those already suggested, come from works like Capote's and Wolfe's and Mailer's.

The first is that their great success, whether in kudos or cash or both, attracts imitators. The blurring of the crafts becomes respectable, fashionable, profitable, enviable. The infection spreads. If the great Mailer can do it, so can any tyro, and the only certainty is that the tyro will fuzz things up worse than Mailer does. Headlines tell us that Capote has sold "Hand-carved Coffins" to the movies for "nearly $500,000." The blurring has long since made its way into investigative journalism, which, of all forms of reporting, bears the heaviest weight of social responsibility. In *The Brethren,* the Woodward and Armstrong book on the Supreme Court which recently spent some time at the top of the bestseller list, the processes of filtration we have seen in the Mailer novel are similarly at work. Clerks vouch for Justices' subjective states, moods, thoughts, and exact words—mostly recaptured in distant retrospect. Chief Justice Burger refused all contact with the authors, yet: "Burger vowed to himself that he would grasp the reins of power immediately. . . ."

The second harm, related to the first, is far more serious. It is that these blurrings lead to, or at the very least help soften the way for, or confirm the reasonableness of, public lying. The message of Jules Feiffer's *Little Murders* is that tiny symbolic killings, done with the tongue, lead to big actual ones, done with guns. Habitual acceptance of little fibs leads to the swallowing whole of world-shaking lies. In the Dodge Aspen commercial, we are told we are watching two people in a following car through a hidden camera; what we watch (and overhear, as a hidden camera in a leading van could not possibly overhear) is a carefully rehearsed advertising routine. We write that off; it's just a formula; we're used to all that stuff. But have we also gotten used to writing off big lies? Did we write off—I am afraid the vast majority of Americans *did* write off—being told in official announcements that bombs were being dropped on North Vietnam, when in fact they were being dropped on Cambodia?

It would be preposterous, of course, to hold Mailer's and Wolfe's recent inventions responsible, retroactively, for lies told a decade ago. But the point is that the two phenomena—the blurring of fiction and journalism, as Mailer and Wolfe and many others have practiced it (for quite a bit more than a decade), and public lying, as Kissinger and Nixon and many others have practiced it (and some still do)—the two have had something like a symbiotic relationship with each other. Each has nourished and needed the other. Each in its way has contributed to the befogging of the public vision, to subtle failures of discrimination, and to the collapse of important sorts of trust.

But how could the blurring possibly be corrected at this late date? Hasn't the process gone too far? Isn't all this much too complicated? Aren't the shadings too subtle?

Not at all. It is very simple. To redraw the line we need merely think clearly about the legends on the licenses. All we need do is insist upon two rules:

The writer of fiction must invent. The journalist must not invent.

INDEX